Love and Kindness
in Islamic and Christian Scriptures

Bartolomeo Pirone
Mohammad Sahaf Kashani

**Top Ten Award
International Network**

Vancouver, BC CANADA

Copyright © 2025 by Top Ten Award International Network

All rights reserved. No part of this publication may be reproduced, distributed or transmitted in any form or by any means, including photocopying, recording, or other electronic or mechanical methods, without the prior written permission of the publisher, except in the case of brief quotations embodied in critical reviews and certain other noncommercial uses permitted by copyright law. For permission requests, write to the publisher, addressed "Attention: Permissions Coordinator," at the address below.

Published by: Top Ten Award International Network
Vancouver, BC **CANADA**
Email: Info@toptenaward.net
www.toptenaward.net

Ordering Information:
Quantity sales. Special discounts are available on quantity purchases by universities, schools, corporations, associations, and others. For details, contact the "Sales Department" at the above mentioned email address.

Love and Kindness, B.Pirone & Mohammad Sahaf Kashani

ISBN 978-1-77899-023-6   Paperback

Love and Kindness
in Islamic and Christian Scriptures

◆ Bartolomeo Pirone ◆
◆ Mohammad Sahaf Kashani ◆

Love and Kindness in Islamic and Christian Scriptures

- **Authors:** Mohammad Sahaf Kashani, Bartolomeo Pirone
- **Publisher:**
- **Publication Year:**
- **Number of printed copies:**
- **Layout Designer:** Seyed Mohsen Hosseini

Contents

Preface /6

6 | Preface by Professor Bartolomeo Pirone

9 | Preface by Hujjat al-Islam Professor Mohammad Sahaf Kashani

Introduction /14

Love and Kindness in Islam Scriptures /27

29 | Significance and Etiquettes of Love

39 | Love and Kindness towards Others

42 | Love towards Believers

56 | Love for Followers of Other Religions

58 | Love for One's Spouse

63 | Love for Children

69 | Love and Kindness towards Parents

73 | Love and Kindness towards Relatives

74 | Love and Compassion toward Teachers and Students

78 | Showing Love and Kindness to Friends

83 | Love and Kindness towards Servants and Subordinates

85 | Love and Kindness between Merchants and Customers

86 | Love and Kindness towards Charitable and Benevolent Individuals

87 | Love and Kindness towards Fellow Travelers

88 | Love and Kindness towards Neighbors

90 | Love and Kindness towards Guests

94 | Love and Kindness towards the Elderly

95 | Showing Love and Kindness to the Poor

99 | Love and Kindness towards Orphaned Children

102 | Love and Kindness towards the Sick

104 | Love and Kindness towards Tragedy-Stricken Individuals

Contents

- 106 | Kindness of Rulers towards Citizens
- 112 | Love and Kindness towards Enemies
- 118 | Love and Kindness towards Prisoners of War
- 120 | Factors Contributing to and Obstacles in Attracting Others' Affection
- 136 | Obstacles to Attraction of Love
- 142 | Instances of Blameworthy Love

Love and Kindness in Christian Scriptures / 147

- 154 | Love towards People
- 157 | Love for Those of Other Faiths in Christian Scriptures
- 159 | Love of Spouse
- 162 | Love of Children
- 163 | Love and Kindness towards Parents
- 164 | Love for Relatives
- 165 | Love and Kindness towards Teachers and Students
- 167 | Love and Kindness towards Friends
- 169 | Love and Kindness towards Charitable Individuals
- 170 | Love and Kindness to Neighbors
- 172 | Love and Kindness towards Guests
- 174 | Kindness towards the Poor and Indigent
- 175 | Showing Love and Kindness to Orphans
- 176 | Showing Love and Kindness to Patients
- 176 | Reciprocal Kindness between Rulers and Citizens
- 177 | Kindness to Enemies and Opponents
- 179 | Kindness to Prisoners of War
- 180 | Factors Contributing to and Obstacles in Attracting Others' Affection
- 182 | Blameworthy Love and Kindness
- 184 | References

Preface

Preface by Professor Bartolomeo Pirone
Divine Gifts in One's Daily Life

I have been fortunate to have visited Iran several times in recent years. During my visits, I had the opportunity to meet numerous individuals from different cities and villages, forming strong and frequent connections with them.

My first visit to Iran dates back to 2000 when my daughter resided in Tehran. She was employed at Iran's Italian radio, and her dissertation focused on Salman al-Farsi, the first Iranian to convert to Islam.

Studying Salman al-Farsi deepened my appreciation for Persian culture, as I delved into various works about this remarkable figure. He displayed extraordinary faith, shifting from Zoroastrianism to Christianity before ultimately embracing Islam. This spiritual journey brought peace and fulfillment to his soul, fulfilling his quests and hopes.

Love and Kindness in Islamic and Christian Scriptures

The character of Salman al-Farsi resembled prominent figures in Christianity, marking a turning point for those seeking a journey towards God, those desiring to live with Him. Perhaps similar characters exist not just in Iran, Jordan, or Australia, but potentially everywhere worldwide.

Salman al-Farsi's character, along with those of other truth seekers, is a fundamental and symbolic reference point for me. With this reference, I can better understand the nature and origin of what we perceive today as aspects of interfaith dialogues.

Interfaith dialogues never imply losing one's cultural and faith identity. Instead, they demonstrate our commitment to showcasing the value of our spirit and intelligence.

Fortunate as I was, in subsequent journeys to Iran, I explored its extraordinary and captivating cities, along with its fascinating mosques. These experiences provided me with a deeper understanding of the true essence of faith and religiosity among Iranian Shias. Additionally, I had the opportunity to visit several Iranian universities and institutes alongside my colleagues from the University of Naples, leaving cherished memories in my heart.

One of the most remarkable opportunities came when my friend, Mr. Jafar Hossein Nejad, the director of Shia-Catholic Dialogues and president of the International Institute for Shia and Global Peace, invited me to the International Conference of Imam Rida and Interreligious Dialogues in winter 2019 in Mashhad. The headquarters of this institute is located in the city of Qom, and I have the honor and privilege of serving as a member of its academic committee. Through this institute, I had the chance to meet Professor Mohammad Sahaf Kashani, an intellectual and scholar of Christian theology, actively engaged in interfaith dialogues for peace and coexistence.

Today, the theme of dialogue for peace and coexistence holds considerable importance. Conflicts among nations have eroded the essence of life, causing harm and marginalization of vulnerable classes of society. Professor Kashani's studies primarily draw from people's religious traditions, which serve as authentic sources to unveil each individual's dignity in relation to the one God who created the world for peace and coexistence. God desires peace for all of us, as He is singular and the God of life and peace.

To achieve and uphold this value, it is crucial to possess the foundational tools. With the spirit of dialogue, as emphasized by the International Institute for Shia and Global Peace, we can scrutinize and highlight all sections of Shiite and Catholic sacred texts that focus on life and peace.

Before embarking on writing this book, we asked whether the two words, "peace" and "life," can coexist. The answer was obvious, as these two elements are inseparable. Those who live for peace indeed live in peace.

Love and Kindness in Islamic and Christian Scriptures

In this book, Professor Kashani, with remarkable clarity and precision and drawing upon two revealed texts, elucidates that kindness and love, when combined, can foster a peaceful life for everyone. The selected passages show the essence of love and kindness themselves and the contexts in which they are applied. Thus, on one hand, it addresses a philosophical question, while on the other hand, it delves into a phenomenological problem by asserting that God's essence is mercy and love. Professor Kashani uses sacred texts to illustrate that love is equally present in both texts. In essence, there is a unity in kindness and love that is accessible to everyone, without exception, although each plays its distinct role in our religious beliefs as well.

This book aims to advocate for a valid and responsible interreligious dialogue. As previously noted, the themes of love and kindness, rooted in the concepts of life and peace, ultimately lead to God. Subsequently, the book will explore the impacts that love and kindness should have on those around us and those with whom we share our lives.

What is the foundation of love and kindness? How are they revealed to humanity through God's words as conveyed by the prophets? What significance do they hold in our lives, and to what extent should they contribute to the construction of human society?

These are the questions to which this book provides answers. To repeat, this research is not an end in itself; rather, it pursues a broader methodological approach.

It is important to note that this study employs interreligious dialogues as a key method to demonstrate numerous spiritual energies and fundamental values of life based on scriptures.

This book argues that love and kindness merely await rediscovery and implementation in the daily lives of each individual. This idea is deeply rooted in religion, faith, and morality. Love and kindness serve as the keys to attaining the divine kingdom, in addition to peace in our life on Earth.

◆ **Bartolomeo Pirone** ◆

Love and Kindness in Islamic and Christian Scriptures

● Preface by Hujjat al-Islam Professor Mohammad Sahaf Kashani

Since about 2004, when I started studying religions, I wished to have an opportunity to have firsthand experiences of various religions, in addition what I had learned through books. I feel lucky to have had many chances to coexist with people of diverse faiths. During my travels, I have lived among people of different religions.

During my travels to different countries, I spent time staying in monasteries and temples of various religions. This allowed me to engage in real and meaningful dialogues with priests, monks, and clergy members of other faiths. These connections greatly enriched my understanding of other religions.

One of the most memorable visits of this kind was in November 2015 when a group of my friends and I traveled to Italy at the invitation of San Lorenzo monastery in Rome. We explored numerous beautiful churches and ancient monasteries throughout the city.

During this visit, one notable event was a joint assembly at the Pontifical Lateran University on mercy and kindness in Islam and Christianity, where Professor Bartolomeo Pirone was also present. During the assembly, Professor Pirone presented a book he had written on "Bism Allah al-Rahman al-Rahim" (In the Name of God the All-Compassionate the All-Merciful), and we had fruitful dialogues on the issue.

Our exchanges continued in winter 2019, where I met Professor Bartolomeo Pirone in the Conference on Imam Rida and Interreligious Dialogues in Mashhad, Iran. Our third encounter occurred in numerous interreligious meetings held in Qom by the International Institute for Shia and Global Peace.

I was fascinated by Professor Pirone's deep dedication and interest in studying Islam, particularly his comparisons between Islam and Christianity, reflected in his extensive writings on the subject. As a prolific Catholic author, he has conducted compelling research on Islamic as well as comparative Islamic-Christian studies at the Pontifical Institute for Arabic and Islamic Studies. He has authored numerous books on Islamic studies and comparative Islamic-Christian studies.

His admirable character, inquisitive nature, and dedication to doing research on comparative Islamic-Christian studies, along with his strong sense of responsibility towards fostering peace and friendship among religions, as well as his humble moral demeanor, aroused my profound respect for him.

During those meetings, I shared with Professor Pirone a concern that had been on my mind for quite some time. I expressed my worry that gatherings and discussions focusing on interfaith dialogues between Muslim and Christian scholars often revolved around formalities and scholarly comments, rarely leading to substantial, profound, and investigative dialogues. As a result, along with a group of researchers, we took the initiative to conduct extensive research on comparative Islamic-Christian ethics and spirituality separately, aiming to address this shortfall to some extent.

In this regard, we organized a specialized conference in Qom centered on comparing ethics and spirituality in Islam and Christianity. I shared a portion of our research with Professor Pirone, and he received it warmly.

It occurred to me that there was a gap here. I thought it might be a good idea to publish a book co-authored by a Muslim and a Christian researcher, where each would explain aspects of their respective religion. This would provide a reliable resource for both Muslim and Christian readers alike.

During our shared meetings, we proposed the collaborative writing of a book on kindness and love in the sacred texts of Islam and Christianity. Professor Pirone enthusiastically supported the idea. The International Institute for Shia and Global Peace facilitated a memorandum of understanding, which I and Professor Pirone signed to outline the creation of a book on this topic. Each of us would contribute perspectives from our respective religions, and the book would be published with both authors' names. To accelerate the writing process, my research assistants compiled verses related to love and kindness from the Bible, which we provided to Professor Pirone for confirmation, revision, or supplementation.

Love and Kindness in Islamic and Christian Scriptures

We chose the topic of love and kindness as our first priority because in today's world, humanity suffers from widespread violence. Much of this violence stems from misguided extremist interpretations of sacred religious texts by individuals who claim to adhere to Islam or Christianity, despite the shared message of all divine religions: that religion is rooted in love.

Christianity emphasizes love as a central tenet of faith. The Gospel portrays God as love (1 John 4:8), and Jesus instructs followers to extend love not only to friends but also to enemies (Luke 6:32-35).

Similarly, Islam teaches that God is merciful, as stated in the Quran (Quran 6:12): "He has made mercy incumbent upon Himself." In essence, all teachings of Islam boil down to love and kindness.

According to Islamic sources, "Is religion but love?" Furthermore, the Quran commands followers to extend love even to their enemies and non-Muslims (Quran 41:34).

On the other hand, God commands Prophet Muhammad, peace be upon him and his household, in the Quran to invite Christians and Jews to find common ground: "Say, 'O People of the Book! Come to a common word between us and you'" (Quran 3:64). Thus, a shared message of Islam and Christianity is love and kindness. This topic can serve as a mutual concern that can foster closer relations between Muslims and Christians.

Contemporary humanity faces a pressing need to acknowledge and embrace "love" as the shared message of divine religions. Our world is plagued by wars, bloodshed, hatred, grudges, arrogance, and selfishness. Those who tried to create a better world ultimately brought nothing but hatred and hostility. However, as hatred increases, human peace, serenity, and security decrease. Yet, this was not humanity's intended fate. God created humans to experience love, and they, in turn, should extend love to others with generosity.

God wants us to be kind towards each other, yet humans have lost their way. Mistakenly, they believe that more war and hostility lead to greater comfort in life. However, this mindset only worsens the human condition day by day. Meanwhile, Islam and Christianity offer a remedy for renewing human life.

Neglecting God's commands to spread love has led humans astray from the divine plan of salvation. Instead of a world filled with love and kindness as intended, humans have transformed it into one marked by hatred and violence. This is why true believers must exemplify kindness in their lives.

---

1. Ahmad b. al-Hasan al-Barqi, al-Mahasin, vol. 1, p. 263.

Love and Kindness in Islamic and Christian Scriptures

Furthermore, despite accusations leveled against religions, it is crucial to demonstrate how the spirit of love is present in all faiths. Each prophet brings forth new, more comprehensive teachings regarding the tradition of love and kindness for humanity.

Moreover, due to misconduct by certain purportedly Islamic extremist factions and extensive media propaganda, numerous misunderstandings and misjudgments have arisen about Islam among many Christians. This has led many Western thinkers to wrongly accuse Islam of inherent violence.

Philip W. Sutton and Stephen Vertigans argue that in the West, Islam is often depicted as a "religion of the sword," a picture accompanied by stereotypes of war, aggression, fundamentalism, and terrorism.[2]

According to statistical studies conducted by LifeWay Research, affiliated with the Southern Baptist Convention, two out of every three Protestant pastors in the US perceive Islam as a religion of violence.[3]

While this negative conception is directly tied to violent actions of Jihadist and excommunicationist groups such as ISIS and al-Qaeda, it is nevertheless a misconception of Islam.

Conversely, Muslims have often failed to develop a precise understanding of Christianity, leading to various prejudices about this religion.

All of these factors highlight the necessity for a comprehensive examination of perspectives within the sacred texts of Islam and Christianity concerning love and kindness. This need ultimately gave rise to the creation of the present book, *Love and Kindness in Islamic and Christian Scriptures*.

This research aims to compare the portrayal of love and kindness in the sacred texts of Islam and Christianity, with the objective of uncovering points of agreement and disagreement, as well as assessing the significance of these themes within Islamic and Christian scriptures.

The findings of this research show the importance of love and kindness in both Islam and Christianity, revealing both their similarities and differences in relation to mutual love between humans and God, as well as among humans themselves, within their respective sacred texts.

It is important to note that this research is not intended to address questions regarding violence in Islam and Christianity. Rather, the research is specifically limited to teachings related to love and kindness, or actions based on love and kindness. The scope of the

---

2. Philip W. Sutton and Stephen Vertigans, Resurgent Islam: A Sociological Approach, p. 7.
3. Adelle M. Banks, "Survey: Two-thirds of Protestant pastors consider Islam 'dangerous'."

research encompasses the sacred revealed texts of both Islam and Christianity.

Our aim is to study religions based on their authentic origins, namely their scriptures or sacred texts. The research does not involve the views of Muslim and Christian theologians, jurists, exegetes or commentators, mystics, or jurisprudents. Instead, it seeks to explore the revealed texts of the religions to arrive at a prescription about kindness and love for followers of these religions.

The research methodology employed in this study relies on library readings, with a particular focus on scriptures. It is important to note that this research does not offer a historical or field investigation into the behaviors of Christians or Muslims.

The citation method utilized in this book relies on a "direct relationship" approach. This means that it examines Quranic or Biblical verses, as well as other religious narratives (such as hadiths), that provide direct and straightforward teachings on love and kindness concerning the topics being investigated.

Some Islamic or Christian scholars may offer alternative interpretations of certain texts, perhaps in mystical or ethical terms. However, since these interpretations do not directly denote the texts and often require complex analyses to be inferred, we do not rely on them in this research.

I express my gratitude and appreciation to Professor Bartolomeo Pirone, who enthusiastically embraced this collaborative interreligious project. I also extend my thanks to the International Institute for Shia and Global Peace and its esteemed director, Mr. Jafar Hossein Nejad, for facilitating my collaboration with Professor Pirone on this joint endeavor.

Several esteemed scholars and researchers made significant contributions to the formulation of this work. Among them, Hujjat al-Islam Ehsan Soltani Gerdfaramarzi and Professor Farid Dehdar deserve special mention. Additionally, Professors Hassan Shah-Rajabian, Seyed Mohammad Reza Tabatabai, Kazem Esmaili, Seyed Mahdi Taghavi, Mohammad Mahdi Kazemi, Abbas Zamani Deh-Yaghoubi, Morteza Yeganeh, Heidar Najaf, Seyed Ahmad Razavi, Fakhroddin Asadi Toosi, and Abbas Asghari played crucial roles in researching specific parts of this work. Their contributions are deeply appreciated.

Moreover, esteemed colleagues Ahmad Ramezani, Morteza Movahedian, Mohammad Hashem Nematollahi, Ali Rahimian Mohaghegh, and Reyhaneh Mirjafari collaborated and assisted in language editing and proofreading of the work. I express my gratitude to all of them.

I pray for the continued success of all my colleagues and friends, with blessings from the Creator of Love and Kindness.

◆ **Mohammad Sahaf Kashani** ◆

Introduction

The current writing aims to extract data from the sacred texts of Islam and Christianity to foster a culture of compassion, mercy, love, and kindness in society. Prior to delving into the subject matter, it is essential to outline the objectives, methods, concepts, and scope of this research.

1. Objectives

1. Love and kindness are among the shared virtues of both Islam and Christianity. This research aims to foster dialogues between these two Abrahamic religions over these shared virtues, as per the Quranic emphasis on interfaith dialogues over common grounds: "O People of the Book! Come to a common word between us and you" (Quran 3:64).
2. Through comparative studies of Islamic and Christian scriptures, we aim to bring the attention of Muslim and Christian communities closer to religious moral virtues. This will pave the way for more cohesive and successful religious communities. Especially in a world where secularism and atheism are prevalent, religious communities bear a greater responsibility in upholding and promoting religious and human values.
3. This research can serve as a valuable resource for future studies on the similarities and distinctions between Islam and Christianity regarding morality. It can demonstrate how the sacred texts of these two religions emphasize and promote love and kindness, as well as highlight the similarities and differences in their perspectives.
4. In our contemporary world, there are many misunderstandings and misconceptions about religions, often due to a lack of knowledge about their true origins. Focusing on the sacred texts of these religions and seeking to understand them through their authentic sources, rather than relying solely on the actions and behaviors of their followers, can lead to a more accurate understanding of the truths about these religions.
5. This type of comparative study can also be expanded to include other religions beyond Islam and Christianity. By doing so, we can foster a deeper understanding among various religious traditions. This will contribute to establishing a valuable religious tradition aimed at reforming and improving social behaviors in human societies.

Love and Kindness in Islamic and Christian Scriptures

2. Methodology

Given the limited scope of this book, we were unable to cite all the relevant texts within Islamic and Christian scriptures pertaining to the moral concepts under study. In making selections from these texts, we adhered to the following guiding principles:

1. **Direct relationship:** In this research, we focused solely on collecting data directly related to the topic at hand. We did not attempt to extract indirect data through implications, entailments, generalizations, etc.
2. **Focus on scriptural texts:** The primary focus of this research is on the scriptural texts of Islam and Christianity. We primarily rely on narrating the sacred texts of these two religions, trying to minimize citations from material outside of these texts, such as commentaries and interpretations by Muslim or Christian scholars.
3. **Avoiding interpretation:** In this research, we strictly use information that directly and explicitly emerges from the relevant scriptural texts, without requiring attempts to make interpretations or inferences. It is important to note that, to prevent confusion and misunderstanding, we provide a brief explanation at the beginning of each section.
4. **Fragmentation of scriptural texts:** In this research, for the sake of brevity, we only cite relevant fragments of scriptural texts such as Biblical or Quranic passages or hadiths, avoiding citations in their entirety.
5. **Accessibility to the general public:** Given that the topics of this research concern daily, ordinary issues of society, we have chosen material that is accessible and understandable to the general public. We refrain from delving into topics solely of interest to specialized readers. Consequently, this research does not encompass all the information extractable from Islamic and Christian scriptures.

3. The Concepts

Before delving into our discussion of love and kindness in Islamic and Christian scriptures and sacred texts, it is necessary to elucidate the concept of love (in Arabic, *mahabba*) and to define what constitutes scripture or sacred text in Islam and Christianity. With this foundation laid, we will start our comparative study of love in the sacred texts of Islam and Christianity.

Concepts of Love and Kindness

The central focus of this research is on love and kindness; however, it is essential to establish a clear understanding of what we mean by these terms.

Love and Kindness in Islamic and Christian Scriptures

■ The Concept of Love in Islam

In the Quran, several words are used to convey the concept of love. One of the most significant terms is "mahabba," derived from the root h-b-b, which signifies love or friendship[1] and stands in contrast to hostility and hatred.[2]

The term " mahabba " may refer to one of the following meanings: (1) a heartfelt or emotional connection between two individuals, or (2) compassionate and kind treatment of an individual, as opposed to violent treatment.[3] Thus, the concept of "mahabba" is sometimes understood as an emotion and sometimes as a behavior. The term and its cognates are mentioned 83 times in the Quran and numerous times in hadiths.

Another commonly used term in the Quran that signifies love is "mawadda," which is synonymous with "mahabba." It originates from the Arabic root w-d-d, denoting the love of something and having aspirations to achieve it.[4] It stands in opposition to enmity and hostility.[5]

This term and its cognates have been used 28 times in the Quran and numerous times in hadiths. Generally, "mawadda" is considered to denote a higher degree of love than "mahabba," as the former requires outward expression to solidify love and friendship.[6]

The third word used in the Quran to denote love is "khulla." It is derived from "khalal," which literally means a gap or opening between two things.[7]

Words derived from the root kh-l-l appear 13 times in the Quran and numerous times in hadiths. "Khulla" denotes devoted friendship, perhaps named so because love creates an opening in the heart and infiltrates one's soul, akin to an arrow piercing the heart.[8] Another possible reason for this naming could be that a friend shares their secrets with their friend, creating a sense of closeness as if the friend is situated in the center of one's heart.[9]

The fourth word used in the Quran to denote love is "raghba." Its verb form "raghib/raghab" signifies to desire or love when used with the preposition "fi," but with the preposition "'an," it conveys the opposite meaning, indicating turning away from or

---

1. Muhammad b. Mukarram Ibn al-Manzur, Lisan al-ʿArab, vol. 1, p. 289.
2. Khalil b. Ahmad al-Farahidi, Kitab al-ʿayn, vol. 1, p. 336.
3. Al-Husayn b. Muhammad al-Raghib al-Isfahani, Tarjumih va tahqiq-i Mufradat alfaz Qurʾan.
4. Seyed Gholamreza Khosravi Hosseini, Tarjumih va tahqiq-i Mufradat alfaz Qurʾan.
5. "The opposite of mawadda is hostility … and the opposite of hubb is hatred" (Muhammad b. Yaʿqub al-Kulayni, al-Kafi, vol. 1, p. 22).
6. "When you love (ahbabta) someone, tell him about it, as this would establish the love (mawadda) between the two of you" (Muhammad b. Yaʿqub al-Kulayni, al-Kafi, vol. 2, p. 644).
7. Muhammad b. Mukarram Ibn al-Manzur, Lisan al-ʿArab, the word "khalal."
8. Al-Husayn b. Muhammad al-Raghib al-Isfahani, Mufradat, the word "khalil."
9. Muhammad b. Mukarram Ibn al-Manzur, Lisan al-ʿArab, the word "khalal."

being disinclined to someone or something.[10] "Raghba" also signifies an emphatic inner desire.[11] Words derived from the root r-gh-b have been used 8 times in the Quran. *Raghba* is indeed a special kind of love (*mahabba*), namely, a very intense form of it.

The final word used in the Quran to signify love is "wilaya." Literally, it carries numerous meanings, one of which is love and friendship. Originally, it denotes a strong connection between two or more things, such that nothing else comes between them. Therefore, *wilaya* is a special kind of *mahabba*.[12] Words derived from the root w-l-y appear 231 times in the Quran and numerous times in hadiths, encompassing various meanings, some of which denote friendship.[13]

The Concept of Love in Christianity

"Love" is a frequently used term in the Two Testaments. In the Old Testament, the Hebrew word אָהֵב (*aheb*) is used to convey love and friendship. According to the Book of Deuteronomy, "The Lord your God is testing you to find out whether you love (אָהֵב/*aheb*) him with all your heart and with all your soul" (Deuteronomy 13:3). The word *aheb* and its cognates appear 209 times in the Two Testaments.

When the New Testament was being compiled, the prevailing culture in Palestinian territories was the Greek culture, where the words referring to love include: *agape* (spiritual love), *eros* (appetitive love, bodily and physical love), *philia* (friendship and affection), *storge* (a fundamental love inherent at the bottom of human existence), and *xenia* (respect and honor). Early Christians, influenced by the predominant Greek culture, often used these Greek words in reference to the notion of love.[14] The most significant love-related terms in the New Testament can be divided into three categories.[15] While there are other kinds of love, they all go back to these three types.[16]

- Philia (φιλία)

Philia means friendship, companionship, fraternal love,[17] or whishing the best for someone or something else, without expecting a reward or interest.[18] Aristotle

---

10. Al-Fadl b. al-Hasan al-Tabarsi, Majmaʿ al-bayan fi tafsir al-Qurʾan, vol. 1, p. 369.
11. Hasan al-Mustafawi, al-Tahqiq fi kalimat al-Qurʾan al-karim.
12. Muhammad b. Mukarram Ibn al-Manzur, Lisan al-ʿArab, the word "wali."
13. These are some of the Quranic verses where "wilaya" or its cognates are used: 10:62, 41:34, 60:1, and 62:1.
14. R. Chervin, Chutch of Love, pp. 9, 10, 19, 62
15. Alexander Moseley, Philosophy of love, pp. 10-13.
16. R.O. Johann, "Love" in New Catholic Encyclopedia, p. 1040.
17. Anders Theodor Samuel Nygren, Eros and Agape (first published in Swedish, 1930–1936).
18. Gene Ourka, "Love," Encyclopedia of Ethics vol. 12, p. 1012.

introduced this type of love, referring to it as benevolence. The Epistle to James reads: "You adulterous people, don't you know that friendship (*philia*) with the world means enmity against God? Therefore, anyone who chooses to be a friend of the world becomes an enemy of God" (James 4:4). This term was used 29 times in the New Testament.

- *Agape (ἀγάπη)*

Agape is the most significant love-related term in the New Testament. It refers to a kind of love that follows principles rather than emotions. *Agape* is not a mere expression of love out of personal affection. Rather, it refers to the highest form of love, particularly God's love of people and their love of Him.[19] *Agape* is the highest possible degree of love,[20] which is unconditional.[21] When John wrote, "The Father loves the Son" (3:35), he used a cognate of the term "agape." According to 2 Peter, "[Make every effort] to godliness, mutual affection; and to mutual affection, love (*agapēn* = ἀγάπην)" (2 Peter 1:7).

This term appears 116 times in the New Testament. Karl Barth, a prominent Christian theologian of the nineteenth century, distinguishes between *agape* and *eros*, with the former referring to non-physical love that involves no expectation from the object of love.[22]

Since the focus of this research is love and kindness in Islam and Christianity, it was imperative to explore all relevant words in religious sources of these two religions. This includes terms such as compassion, friendship, mercy, companionship, infatuation, intimacy, affection, affectionateness, fraternal love, support, fraternity, and others. Additionally, it was necessary to examine antonyms of these terms, including enmity, hostility, hatred, grudge, despise, and similar concepts. However, even with such exploration, the obtained results may not offer a comprehensive understanding of kind behavior in these religions. This is because in many cases, the religious texts of Islam and Christianity include commands to kindness and love, which may not be explicitly found through searches for the word "love" and its synonyms. This includes actions such as kissing and hugging, which directly relate to love.

---

19. Henry George Liddell, Robert Scott (2010), An Intermediate Greek-English Lexicon: Founded Upon the Seventh Edition of Liddell and Scott's Greek-English Lexicon, Benediction Classics, p. 4.
20. Henry George Liddell, Robert Scott (2010), An Intermediate Greek-English Lexicon: Founded Upon the Seventh Edition of Liddell and Scott's Greek-English Lexicon, Benediction Classics, p. 4.
21. Henry George Liddell, Robert Scott (2010), An Intermediate Greek-English Lexicon: Founded Upon the Seventh Edition of Liddell and Scott's Greek-English Lexicon, Benediction Classics, p. 6.
22. Church Dogmatics IV.2, translated by G. W Bromiley (1958), p. 745.

Love and Kindness in Islamic and Christian Scriptures

4. Research Scope (Sacred Texts)

The scope of this research is limited to sacred revealed texts. It is important to note that this study does not aim to explore the views of Muslim and Christian theologians, exegetes or commentators, psychologists, religious sociologists, ethicists, or mystics regarding love and kindness. Furthermore, it does not seek to conduct a statistical study of social behaviors within Muslim and Christian communities in response to commands to love and kindness. Additionally, it does not intend to undertake a historical study of instances of kindness and love in Islamic or Christian history. This research is focused solely on texts considered sacred and revealed from the perspective of Christians and Muslims in general.

In the following discussion, we explain what is meant by the sacred revealed texts of Islam and Christianity.

Sacred Texts in Islam

- *The Quran*

The Quran is the most important sacred text in Islam. It is believed that God conveyed the Quran to Prophet Muhammad, peace be upon him and his household, through an angel of revelation, as stated in the Quran: "[This book is] brought down by the Trustworthy Spirit" (Quran 26:193).

The Quran was revealed to people by the Prophet, peace be upon him and his household, over a period of 23 years. Within the Islamic perspective, the Quran is regarded as an infallible book, with both its words and meanings believed to be revealed from God. As the Quran states, "Indeed We have sent down the Reminder, and indeed We will preserve it" (Quran 19:9).

Furthermore, God challenges all of humanity by stating: "And if you are in doubt concerning what We have sent down to Our servant, then bring a surah like it" (Quran 2:23).

- *Hadith*

Muslims believe that the Quran is not the only sacred revealed text. Alongside the Quran, there is another significant source known as the "Tradition" or "Sunnah," which encompasses the words, actions, and confirmations of Infallible figures in Islam—Prophet Muhammad, peace be upon him and his household, his rightful successors, and earlier prophets. After the Quran, such traditions or hadiths are considered the most important revealed sacred texts among Muslims. While all Muslims agree that the Prophetic tradition is an authoritative revealed source, there is disagreement regarding the traditions of the twelve Imams or the Prophet's companions. Shias regard hadiths from their Imams as credible sources of religious knowledge and view them as sacred revealed texts. Additionally, Sunni Muslims uphold the righteousness of all companions of the Prophet (Sahaba), believing them to be reliable transmitters of the Prophetic tradition. Some Sunni Muslims go further, considering the tradition of Sahaba as valuable in itself, not merely as a reliable report of the Prophetic tradition. They often attribute such status only to the early caliphs—Abu Bakr, ʿUmar, ʿUthman, and ʿAli.

But why do Muslims believe that the hadiths of the Prophet, peace be upon him and his household, and other Infallibles are sacred and revealed? The Quran explicitly acknowledge that it has numerous hidden layers, although it claims to have explained and elucidated everything: "We have sent down the Book to you as a clarification of all things" (Quran 16:89). Elsewhere, the Quran says, "nor anything fresh or withered but it is in a manifest Book" (Quran 6:59). Thus, there is an explanation of everything in the Quran, but those are within its hidden layers. As the Quran explicitly states, only a select few have been taught those hidden layers of the Quran, which is called the esoteric interpretation and the inner meanings of the Quran: "Then We made those whom We chose from Our servants heirs to the Book" (Quran 35:32) and "Indeed, it is [present as] manifest signs in the breasts of those who have been given knowledge" (Quran 29:49). The Quran explicitly states that these inner meanings are not accessible to the general public: "Indeed it is a glorious Quran, in a preserved tablet" (Quran 85:21-22), where the "preserved tablet" is a stage higher than the Quran, which is not accessible just like the Quran itself: "This is indeed a noble Quran, in a guarded Book—no one touches it except the purified ones" (Quran 56:77-79).

The term "guarded Book" refers to a protected and inaccessible book, while "touching" the Book implies accessing its underlying secrets and truths, which are only available to the "purified ones" (note that this is different from "pure ones" as this refers to those who have been purified by God). The concept of purification is mentioned in the Quran, particularly in relation to the People of the Household: "Indeed Allah desires to repel all impurity from you, O People of the Household, and purify you with a thorough purification" (Quran 33:33).

This verse refers to those who have been purified by God. Many Shiite scholars and some Sunni scholars believe, as indicated by numerous hadiths in both Shiite and Sunni sources, that the "Household" mentioned in this verse includes the Prophet, his daughter

Love and Kindness in Islamic and Christian Scriptures

Fatima, Imam ʿAli, Imam al-Hasan, and Imam al-Husayn (peace upon them),[23] and according to some hadiths, all twelve Shiite Imams.[24]

Consequently, the only way people can have access to those inner meanings of the Quran is through the words of those who are given knowledge of the Book and have been purified from any evils by God. Thus, the Quran commands the Prophet, peace be upon him and his household, to interpret and explain the Quran to Muslims: "We have sent down the reminder to you so that you may clarify for the people that which has been sent down to them" (Quran 16:44).

As mentioned before, the Quran has inner meanings and esoteric interpretations. This verse indicates that the words of the Prophet, peace be upon him and his household, signify those inner meanings, so these words are sacred and count as revelations from God. This is why in Surah al-Najm, God describes all the words spoken by the Prophet as revealed from God: "Nor does he speak out of [his own] desire: it is just a revelation that is revealed [to him], taught to him by one of great powers" (Quran 53:3-5).

Moreover, the Quran equates obedience to the Prophet with obedience to God: "Whoever obeys the Apostle certainly obeys Allah" (Quran 4:80).

According to Shiite beliefs, along with the hadiths and teachings transmitted from Prophet Muhammad, peace be upon him and his household, the words of other Infallibles, including past prophets and Prophet Muhammad's rightful successors, are considered revealed sources if they are transmitted from one of the prophets or the Fourteen Infallibles (Prophet Muhammad, his daughter Fatima, Imam ʿAli, and the eleven Shiite Imams from his progeny) through reliable chains of transmission. These teachings serve as credible evidence for religious beliefs and rulings. Prophet Muhammad himself, peace be upon him and his household, emphasized the importance of both the Quran and his Household, stating, "I leave among you two weighty things

---

23. Umm Salama, the Prophet's wife, reports that the verse "Indeed Allah desires to repel all impurity from you, O People of the Household, and purify you with a thorough purification" was revealed in her house. When it was revealed, the Prophet sent for ʿAli, Fatima, al-Hasan, and al-Husayn, and then said, "These are my Household" (Muhammad b. ʿAbd Allah al-Hakim al-Nishaburi, al-Mustadrak, vol. 3, p. 158, hadith no. 4705).
24. Imam al-Sadiq was quoted as saying about this Quranic verse, "this means the Imams and their guardianship. He who enters their guardianship enters the Prophet's Household" (Muhammad b. Yaʿqub al-Kulayni, Usul al-kafi, vol. 1, p. 423).

(*thaqalayn*): the Book of Allah the Glorified and Esteemed and my Household."[25] This hadith equates the reliability and authority of the Prophet's Household with that of the Quran.

The Quran contains numerous verses commanding believers to obey prophets and Infallibles. For instance, it states, "They are the ones whom Allah has guided. So follow their guidance" (Quran 6:90). Additionally, it emphasizes, "Obey Allah and obey the Apostle and those vested with authority among you" (Quran 4:59). In Shia Islam, "those vested with authority" (*Ulu al-Amr*) refer to the Fourteen Infallibles, including Prophet Muhammad, peace be upon him and his household, his daughter Fatima, Imam ʿAli, and the eleven Shiite Imams from his progeny.[26]

Accordingly, the words of the Prophet's Household are also considered to be revealed, just like those of the Prophet. Regarding the Imam's connection with revelation, there is a hadith from the Prophet in which he states that "revelation (*wahy*) was made to me and inspiration (*ilham*) was made to ʿAli."[27] In a hadith from Imam al-Rida, the eighth Shiite Imam, the Imams are described as truthful, endowed with understanding (*mufahham*), and are "muhaddath."[28] Imam ʿAli defines "muhaddath" as "those to whom the angel comes and instills knowledge in their heart."[29]

Additionally, Zurara, one of the companions of the sixth Shiite Imam al-Sadiq, asked him about the status and place of Imamate. The Imam replied, "He hears the voice [of the angel] but does not see him and does not face him."[30]

In another hadith, Imam al-Rida, the eighth Shiite Imam, says, "The Imam is one who hears the words [of the angel] but does not see the [angel's] person."[31]

Moreover, apart from inspiration, there are other channels through which the Imam is linked to revelation. According to hadiths, these encompass a "pillar of light" extending

---

25. Muslim b. Hajjaj, Sahih Muslim, 2:1873, hadith no. 36-37; Muhammad b. Yaʿqub al-Kulayni, Usul al-kafi, vol. 1, p. 294.
26. In a sermon, Imam al-Hasan emphasizes the obligation to obey the Imams, stating that obedience to them is obligatory and equated with obeying God and His Apostle. Similarly, Imam al-Sadiq affirms the significance of obeying the Imams as those vested with authority, as mentioned in the Quranic verse. He identifies "those vested with authority" as the Imams from the Prophet's Household (al-Qunduzi, Yanabiʿ al-mawadda, vol. 1, p. 341; Ibn Shahrashub al-Mazandarani, Manaqib Al Abi Talib ʿalayhim al-salam, vol. 3, p. 15).
27. Muhammad b. al-Hasan al-Tusi, al-Amali, p. 408.
28. Muhammad b. al-Hasan al-Tusi, al-Amali, p. 425.
29. Muhammad b. al-Hasan al-Tusi, al-Amali, p. 407.
30. Muhammad b. Yaʿqub al-Kulayni, al-Usul min al-Kafi, vol. 1, p. 176.
31. Muhammad b. Yaʿqub al-Kulayni, al-Usul min al-Kafi, vol. 1, p. 176.

from heaven to the Imam, the Imam being entrusted with Prophetic knowledge, and possessing the original authentic versions of scriptures from earlier prophets such as Abraham's scriptures, Moses's tablets, the Torah, and the Gospel. Additionally, the Imam is believed to have access to God's Greatest Name and the "Knowledge of the Book," all of which signify his connection to revelation.

The teachings transmitted from the Infallibles are documented in collections of "hadiths." These compilations span from the first year of the Prophetic mission (13 years before Hijra—Muslims' migration from Mecca to Medina) until 260 after Hijra, marking the beginning of the Major Occultation of the final Shiite Imam al-Mahdi, whose awaited reappearance is anticipated by Shia Muslims. These hadiths are preserved in various sources. The Fourteen Infallibles comprise Prophet Muhammad, the first Shiite Imam ʿAli ibn Abi Talib, his wife Lady Fatima al-Zahra, their sons Imam al-Hasan al-Mujtaba and Imam al-Husayn, the second and third Shiite Imams, respectively, along with Imam al-Sajjad, Imam al-Baqir, Imam al-Sadiq, Imam al-Kazim, Imam al-Rida, Imam al-Jawad, Imam al-Hadi, Imam al-Hasan al-ʿAskari, and Imam al-Mahdi, the twelfth and final Imam, who entered the Major Occultation (peace be upon them).

It is important to note that unlike the Quran, where every word is considered the exact words of God as conveyed to the Prophet, not all hadiths are reliable and authentic. Over time, there have been numerous unreliable hadiths. Some transmitters failed to convey them with precision due to carelessness, biases, conflicts of interest, or even fabrication. To address this, scholars have developed various methodologies for discerning reliable from unreliable hadiths. These methods include scrutinizing the chains of transmission, evaluating the content, assessing the frequency of transmission (*tawatur*), among others.

Nevertheless, due to disagreements regarding the means and methodologies for discerning reliable from unreliable hadiths, and in line with maintaining a fair and impartial stance in this research, questionable hadiths have not been examined or verified. Instead, they have been set aside for the purposes of this study.

---

32. Muhammad b. al-Hasan al-Tusi, al-Amali, 425.
33. Muhammad b. Yaʿqub al-Kulayni, al-Usul min al-Kafi, vol. 1, p. 293, vol. 1, pp. 222-238; Muhammad b. ʿAli Ibn Babawayh, ʿUyun akhbar al-Rida ʿalayh al-salam, vol. 2, p. 122.
34. Al-Saffar, Basair al-darajat, p. 135.
35. Al-Saffar, Basair al-darajat, pp. 212-219, particularly 214.
36. See ʿAbd al-Husayn al-Amini, Al-Waddaʿun wa-ahadithum al-mawduʿa (Fabricators and their fabricated hadiths).

Love and Kindness in Islamic and Christian Scriptures

Other sources of Islamic beliefs, such as reason and consensus among Muslims, are indeed considered reliable or confirmed sources, but they are not deemed revealed sacred texts. Therefore, for the purposes of this research, they have not been taken into consideration.

According to the culture of the Prophet's Household, in addition to hadiths passed down to us from the Prophet, those from other Infallibles, including earlier prophets or Prophet Muhammad's successors, are authoritative and can be treated as reliable sources of religious knowledge if they are transmitted from a prophet or one of the Fourteen Infallibles through a reliable chain of transmission.

The Christian Scripture

- *The Bible*

The Christian scripture consists of two parts: the Old Testament and the New Testament. "Testament" means a pledge or covenant between God and humans. The Old Testament is a covenant of Sharia laws, while the New Testament is a covenant of faith. Overall, the Old Testament consists of 39 books divided into three parts: history, preaching, and wisdom literature and prophecies.[37] The books of the Old Testament are considered sacred by both Jews and Christians.

The New Testament comprises 27 books and essays, including the four Gospels (which detail the history and fate of Christ), the Acts of the Apostles (narratives of Jesus's disciples and the apostles after Christ), the Epistle of the Apostles (21 letters), and John's Revelation (a mysterious text concerning the events of the end times).[38] This collection is considered sacred only by Christians.

Christians believe that these books were written and compiled by various prophets or scribes over a time span ranging from 1500 BC to 100 AD under the guidance of the Holy Spirit. They are considered a legacy passed down from the prophets of antiquity and the apostles of the New Testament.[39]

---

37. Here are the books of the Old Testament: Genesis, Exodus, Leviticus, Numbers, Deuteronomy, Joshua, Judges, Ruth, 1 Samuel, 2 Samuel, 1 Kings, 2 Kings, 1 Chronicles, 2 Chronicles, Ezra, Nehemiah, Esther, Job, Psalms, Proverbs, Ecclesiastes, Song of Solomon, Isaiah, Jeremiah, Lamentations, Ezekiel, Daniel, Hosea, Joel, Amos, Obadiah, Jonah, Micah, Nahum, Habakkuk, Zephaniah, Haggai, Zechariah, Malachi.
38. Here are the books of the New Testament: Matthew, Mark, Luke, John, Acts, Romans, 1 Corinthians, 2 Corinthians, Galatians, Ephesians, Philippians, Colossians, 1 Thessalonians, 2 Thessalonians, 1 Timothy, 2 Timothy, Titus, Philemon, Hebrews, James, 1 Peter, 2 Peter, 1 John, 2 John, 3 John, Jude, Revelation.
39. See Mohammad Kashani, Lectures on Christianity: an introduction to the Two Testaments.

Love and Kindness in Islamic and Christian Scriptures

The books of the Old Testament are attributed to 25 prominent prophets and scribes who lived over a period of 1000 years, including Moses, Joshua, Samuel, Jeremiah, Nehemiah (or Mordecai), Job, Isaiah, Ezekiel, Daniel, Hosea, Joel, Amos, Obadiah, Jonah, Micah, Nahum, Habakkuk, Zephaniah, Haggai, Zechariah, and Malachi. The books of the New Testament are attributed to 8 disciples of Christ and apostles, written over a span of 60 years. These figures include Matthew, Mark, Luke, John, Paul, James, Peter, and Jude.

It is worth noting that Christians disagree over the number of sacred books. In addition to the above 66 books, Catholics and Orthodox Christians consider additional books as sacred texts: Tobit, Judith, Wisdom of Solomon, Sirach (also known as Ecclesiasticus), Baruch, 1 Maccabees, and 2 Maccabees. These are known as the Deuterocanonical or secondary canon. The Council of Trent endorsed their authenticity for Catholics.[40] However, Protestants do not consider these books canonical,[41] referring to them as the "Apocrypha," meaning hidden or secret, and they are not included in their biblical canon.[42]

Although Christians no longer adhere to the Sharia laws of the Old Testament after the crucifixion of Jesus (Galatians 5:2-4), this does not diminish the revealed, theological, or moral value of the Old Testament. In the New Testament, in a letter to his pupil Timothy, Paul refers to the Old Testament as the word of God, stating, "All Scripture is God-breathed" (2 Timothy 3:16). The teachings of the Catholic Church affirm this perspective, stating:

> The Old Testament is an indispensable part of Sacred Scripture. Its books are divinely inspired and retain a permanent value, for the Old Covenant has never been revoked. ... Christians venerate the Old Testament as true Word of God. the Church has always vigorously opposed the idea of rejecting the Old Testament under the pretext that the New has rendered it void (Marcionism). ... it must not make us forget that the Old Testament retains its own intrinsic value as Revelation reaffirmed by our Lord himself. Besides, the New Testament has to be read in the light of the

---

40. Council of Trent, 4th Session (8th April 1546).
41. Reid, George, "Apocrypha," The Catholic Encyclopedia, vol. 1.
42. Since this research extracts Christian data from studies conducted by Christian research centers and tools based on the Bible, it is important to note that these centers typically rely on the canonical 66 books accepted by all Christian sects, including Catholic, Orthodox, and Protestant, without including the Apocrypha. As a result, the present research does not include data on love and kindness from the Apocrypha.

Old. Early Christian catechesis made constant use of the Old Testament. As an old saying put it, the New Testament lies hidden in the Old and the Old Testament is unveiled in the New.[43]

The Two Testaments, or the Bible, are considered divine revelation for Christians. The belief in the infallibility of the Bible is an ancient, unchangeable belief held by the Church.[44] Protestant theologians also fundamentally and radically underscore the theory of Biblical infallibility.

The Chicago Statement on Biblical Inerrancy asserts that "We affirm that a confession of the full authority, infallibility, and inerrancy of Scripture is vital to a sound understanding of the whole of the Christian faith."[45]

---

43. Catechism of the Catholic Church, sections 121-129.
44. See Mohammad Haghani Fazl, Biblical infallibility, p. 266.
45. The Chicago Statement on Biblical Inerrancy, 1978.

Love and Kindness in Islam Scriptures

Significance and Etiquettes of Love

In Islamic moral commands, there are numerous rulings related to showing kindness and love towards others. However, before delving into specific directives regarding recipients of this love, it is essential to consider the place and significance of love and kindness within the ethical system of Islam. According to Quranic verses and hadiths, in Islamic culture, love is regarded as a transcendent value and the foremost factor contributing to proximity to God. Demonstrating love and kindness to others holds a significant place within this framework, as outlined below.

Significance of Showing Love
Religion is Love

According to Islamic hadiths, religion is encapsulated in the essence of love and kindness. In fact, if we were to distill religion into a single word, that word would be "love." Imam al-Baqir, the fifth Shiite Imam, briefly expresses this point by stating: "Religion is love, and love is religion."[1] Imam al-Sadiq, the sixth Shiite Imam, rhetorically asks: "Is religion but love?"[2]

Burayd b. Muʿawiya al-ʿIjli recounts an encounter with Abu Jaʿfar (referring to Imam al-Baqir, the sixth Imam). A traveler from Khorasan presented his worn-out feet, evidence of his arduous journey on foot. Expressing his devotion, he attributed his journey solely to his love for the Prophet's Household. In response, Abu Jaʿfar affirmed the profound nature of love, stating that even inanimate objects, like a stone, would be resurrected alongside them on the Day of Judgment if they harbored love for the Prophet's Household. The Imam then added, "Is religion but love?"[3]

---

1. Ahmad b. Muhammad al-Barqi, al-Mahasin, vol. 1, p. 263.
2. Ahmad b. Muhammad al-Barqi, al-Mahasin, vol. 1, p. 263.
3. Muhammad b. Masʿud al-Samarqandi, Tafsir al-ʿAyyashi, vol. 1, p. 167, hadith no. 27.

Love and Kindness in Islamic and Christian Scriptures

Moreover, Imam al-Baqir also said, "faith is love and enmity."[4]

Prophet Muhammad, peace be upon him and his household, also underscored the importance of love and kindness towards others as integral components of religion and religiosity, stating: "Kindness is half of religion."[5]

In a similar vein, the first Imam, ʿAli Amir al-Muʾminin (Commander of the Faithful), advises: "Do not hate each other, as this diminishes [the faith]."[6]

▪ Love: Purpose of Human Creation

According to Quranic teachings, echoed by the Persian poet Hafiz, humans and all other creatures exist for the sake of love's existence. God, in His kindness and love, created humans to manifest His kindness and love towards them. The Quran states: "Had your Lord willed, He would have made mankind one community, but they continue to differ except those on whom your Lord has mercy—and that is why He created them" (Quran 11:118-119). This verse explicitly states that God has created people for the sake of "mercy"—which means kindness and love.

▪ God, Creator of Love

The Quran attributes the creation of love among humans to God: "Remember Allah's blessing upon you when you were enemies, then He brought your hearts together, so you became brothers with His blessing" (Quran 3:103).

Imam al-Baqir, the fifth Shiite Imam, emphasizes that closeness of hearts—love and kindness among people—is from God, whereas division is from Satan, as Satan hates what God permits.[7]

▪ Love: The Best Treasure

Since ancient times, there were those who risked their lives searching for treasures hidden in mountains and caves, longing to acquire precious wealth. However, Imam ʿAli stresses that the greatest treasure lies in winning the hearts of others through acts of love and kindness. He asserts: "The most beneficial treasure is the affection of hearts."[8]

---

4. Al-Hasan b. ʿAli Ibn Shuʿba al-Harrani, Tuhaf al-ʿuqul, p. 295.
5. Al-Hasan b. ʿAli Ibn Shuʿba al-Harrani, Tuhaf al-ʿuqul, p. 60.
6. Muhammad b. al-Husayn al-Sharif al-Radi, Nahj al-balagha, p. 118, sermon 86.
7. Muhammad b. al-Hasan al-Tusi, Tahdhib al-ahkam, vol. 7, p. 410.
8. ʿAbd al-Wahid b. Muhammad al-Tamimi al-Amidi, Tasnif ghurar al-hikam wa-durar al-kilam, p. 413, hadith no. 9419.

Love and Kindness in Islamic and Christian Scriptures

■ Love as Sign of Chivalry

Chivalry or magnanimity is considered a commendable trait, one that has long been admired in heroic figures. Imam ʿAli asserts that true chivalry requires demonstrating love towards others, stating: "The essence of chivalry begins with a cheerful demeanor and ends in displaying kindness to people."[9] In another instance, Imam ʿAli asserts, "The magnanimous individual exhibits more affection than even one's own relatives."[10]

■ Love as Sign of Rationality

Imam al-Rida, the eighth Shiite Imam, praises those who exhibit kindness towards others as the most rational individuals, asserting, "After faith, the cornerstone of rationality lies in kindness and friendship with others."[11]

Moreover, Prophet Muhammad, peace be upon him and his household, is quoted as saying, "Displaying kindness towards people constitutes half of reason [rationality]"[12] or "The start of rationality lies in displaying kindness."[13]

■ Friendship is better than Kinship

In the past, one of the primary sources of power lay in having a large family or tribe. Those with superior lineages and extensive tribal connections enjoyed stronger security and prestige. Consequently, individuals sought to expand their networks of relatives. Imam ʿAli noted that forming bonds of friendship with people serves as a method to broaden one's circle of support, akin to extending one's family. He remarked, "Friendship is an acquired form of kinship."[14]

He also says, "Friendship is one of the two forms of kinship."[15]

From the Islamic standpoint, the kinship forged through love and friendship holds greater importance and significance than blood ties. Imam ʿAli emphasizes this notion, stating that "Friendship is the most intimate kinship."[16]

---

9. ʿAbd al-Wahid b. Muhammad al-Tamimi al-Amidi, Tasnif ghurar al-hikam wa-durar al-kilam, p. 258, hadith no. 5495.
10. Al-Sayyid al-Radi, Nahj al-balagha, p. 511, saying 247.
11. Muhammad b. Zayn al-Din Ibn Abi Jumhur, ʿAwali al-liʾali al-ʿAziziyya fi al-ahadith al-diniyya, vol. 1, p. 291.
12. Muhammad b. Yaʿqub al-Kulayni, al-Kafi, vol. 2, p. 543.
13. ʿAbd al-Wahid b. Muhammad al-Tamimi al-Amidi, Tasnif ghurar al-hikam wa-durar al-kilam, p. 189, hadith no. 95.
14. Muhammad b. al-Husayn al-Sharif al-Radi, Nahj al-balagha, p. 506, saying no. 211.
15. ʿAbd al-Wahid b. Muhammad al-Tamimi al-Amidi, Tasnif ghurar al-hikam wa-durar al-kilam, p. 87, hadith no. 1657.
16. ʿAbd al-Wahid b. Muhammad al-Tamimi al-Amidi, Tasnif ghurar al-hikam wa-durar al-kilam, p. 28, hadith no. 339.

Love and Kindness in Islamic and Christian Scriptures

Conversely, the absence of friends in life or the loss of friendships can result in feelings of desolation, isolation, and a loss of support. Imam ʿAli aptly expresses this point, stating that "The absence of friends brings desolation."[17]

For this reason, in the will he wrote to his senior son Imam al-Hasan, Imam ʿAli says, "The desolate is one who has no friends."[18]

■ Refraining from Showing Love is Worthy of Blame

A person who shows love and kindness towards others deserves praise and admiration. Conversely, one who displays hostility and hatred, neglecting companionship, friendship, kindness, and love, is worthy of blame. Imam al-Sadiq, the sixth Shiite Imam, emphasizes that "those who withhold kindness do not deserve praise."[19]

Advantages of Love

According to the sacred texts of Islam, displaying love towards others brings about numerous blessings and rewards, several of which are outlined in this section.

■ Love as a Source of Peacefulness

Love, friendship, and companionship foster peacefulness and serenity in our interactions with others. According to a hadith transmitted from Imam al-Sadiq, the sixth Shiite Imam, Prophet David was curious about the extent of Solomon's wisdom. To measure this, he asked, "What is the sweetest thing?" Solomon responded, "Love, for it is the peace bestowed by God upon His servants." David was greatly pleased by Solomon's response.[20]

Conversely, the loss of friends disrupts one's peace, as Imam ʿAli expresses: "Three things are disheartening: the loss of friends, poverty in exile, and prolonged hardship."[21]

■ Love as a Source of Esteem

Love is a factor that contributes to one's superiority and esteem, as Imam ʿAli stated, "The most superior individuals in terms of benevolence are those who initiate with love and kindness."[22]

---

17. Muhammad b. al-Husayn al-Sharif al-Radi, p. 479, saying no. 65.
18. Muhammad b. al-Husayn al-Sharif al-Rad, p. 404, letter 31.
19. Al-Hasan b. ʿAli Ibn Shuʿba al-Harrani, Tuhaf al-ʿiqul, p. 364.
20. Muhammad b. Yaʿqub al-Kulayni, Usul al-kafi, vol. 1, p. 383.
21. ʿAbd al-Wahid b. Muhammad al-Tamimi al-Amidi, Tasnif ghurar al-hikam wa-durar al-kilam, p. 332, hadith no. 26.
22. ʿAbd al-Wahid b. Muhammad al-Tamimi al-Amidi, Tasnif ghurar al-hikam wa-durar al-kilam, p. 413, hadith no. 9422.

Love and Kindness in Islamic and Christian Scriptures

Indeed, Islam introduces the display of love and kindness as a criterion of superiority, as Prophet Muhammad, peace be upon him and his household, stated, "When two believers meet, the most superior is one who shows stronger love for his fellow believer."[23]

■ Love as a Source of Blessing

According to Islamic teachings, showing love and friendship with others result in blessings, as Imam 'Ali says, "Friendship is [a source of] blessing."[24]

■ Love as Sign of Loving One's Religion

The more we express love towards our friends, the deeper our love for our religion turns out to be. Imam al-Kazim, the seventh Shiite Imam, was asked by one of his companions, 'Ali b. Ja'far, "Who among us loves his religion more?" The Imam replied: "The one who loves his friends more."[25]

■ Love as a Source of Happiness

Loving others and showing kindness to them brings about happiness. Imam al-Rida, the eighth Shiite Imam, cites Prophet Muhammad, peace be upon him and his household, as saying that a sign of happiness is having love for others: "My nation (Ummah) will be happy as long as they love each other, exchange gifts, and honor each other's trusts."[26]

Another hadith states, "There is no life [that is, no happiness] for one who is separated from his friends."[27]

■ Love as a Source of Divine Mercy

Showing love and kindness to others attracts divine mercy. Imam al-Sadiq, the sixth Imam, says: "God bestows mercy upon a servant who attracts people's love and friendship towards himself."[28]

---

23. Muhammad b. Ya'qub al-Kulayni, Usul al-kafi, vol. 2, p. 127.
24. 'Abd al-Wahid b. Muhammad al-Tamimi al-Amidi, Tasnif ghurar al-hikam wa-durar al-kilam, p. 19, hadith no. 80.
25. 'Ali b. Ja'far al-'Aridi, Masail 'Ali b. Ja'far wa-mustadrakatuha, p. 341.
26. Muhammad b. 'Ali Ibn Babawayh, 'Uyun akhbar al-Rida 'alayh al-salam, vol. 2, p. 29.
27. 'Abd al-Wahid b. Muhammad al-Tamimi al-Amidi, Tasnif ghurar al-hikam wa-durar al-kilam, p. 777, hadith no. 224.
28. Muhammad b. Ya'qub al-Kulayni, al-Kafi, vol. 2, p. 223.

Love and Kindness in Islamic and Christian Scriptures

▪ Reunion with Loved Ones on the Day of Resurrection

From the Islamic perspective, individuals will be reunited with those they love on the Day of Resurrection. Prophet Muhammad, peace be upon him and his household, said, "One who loves a group of people will be resurrected alongside them."[29]

Imam al-Baqir asserts, "I swear to God that if a stone loves us, God will reunite it with us on the Day of Resurrection."[30]

▪ Paradise as the Place of Kind and Loving Individuals

Islam asserts that Paradise is the abode of loving and kind individuals and serves as a reward for those who practice benevolence. Prophet Muhammad, peace be upon him and his household, stated, "You will not enter Paradise unless you believe, and you will not truly believe unless you love one another."[31]

Furthermore, hastening to restore broken friendships is considered virtuous and can lead to Paradise. Prophet Muhammad, peace be upon him and his household, stated, "A Muslim is not permitted to sever ties with their Muslim brother for more than three days. The one who hastens to reconcile will be the one who hastens towards Paradise."[32]

Etiquettes of Expressing Love

Islamic texts provide guidance on the etiquette of possessing and demonstrating love, as detailed below.

▪ Sincere Love

Love should be sincere, as Imam ʿAli advises, "Give all of your love to your friend, but do not give him all of your trust."[33]

Imam al-Sajjad, the fourth Imam, prays to God: "O God! … replace for me the attachment of flatterers with love set right."[34]

Once, someone asked the Prophet, "Who among the people is superior in faith?" and he replied, "Those with the most sincere love."[35]

---

29. Muhammad Baqir al-Majlisi, Bihar al-anwar, vol. 68, p. 131.
30. Muhammad b. Masʿud al-Samarqandi, Tafsir al-ʿAyyashi, vol. 1, p. 167, hadith no. 27.
31. Masʿud b. ʿIsa al-Warram b. Abi Firas, Majmuʿat al-Warram, vol. 1, p. 127.
32. Muhammad b. al-Hasan al-Tusi, al-Amali, p. 391.
33. Muhammad b. ʿAli al-Karajaki, Kanz al-fawaʾid, vol. 1, p. 93.
34. Al-Sahifat al-Sajjadiyya, p. 94, supplication 20.
35. Ahmad b. ʿAli al-Qummi, Jamiʿ al-ahadith, p. 205.

Love and Kindness in Islamic and Christian Scriptures

Love should be sincere and pure. In describing the characteristics of true believers, Imam ʿAli told Hammam, one of his close companions, "O Hammam! A true believer is ... sincere in love and friendship."[36]

Persistence in Love

Love is not merely a fleeting emotion that fades quickly. Instead, it should endure persistently. Imam ʿAli emphasizes, "The greatest chivalry is to preserve love and friendship."[37]

Outward Expression of Love

When we love someone, it is advisable to express our affection to them. Imam ʿAli believes that openly acknowledging love strengthens friendship: "When one of you loves his religious brother, he had better let him know, as this is better to solidify their bond."[38]

Another hadith states, "Love is solidified by expression of friendship."[39]

Moderation in Love

Love should not be taken to extremes, as Imam ʿAli advises, "Do not let your love become a burden [for the other person], and do not let your hatred lead to destruction [of other people's possessions]. Love your loved one to the right degree, and hate your enemy to the right degree."[40]

In another hadith, Imam ʿAli emphasizes, "The essence of intimacy lies in refraining from burdening others."[41]

Prophet Muhammad, peace be upon him and his household, cautioned, "Some people have ruined themselves due to their love for others. Do not be like them."[42]

Luqman, the renowned wise man to whom a Quranic chapter is devoted, advised his son: "O my son! Do not become overly attached to others, which may result in your alienation from them, and do not distance yourself too much from others, lest you be [overlooked and] humiliated."[43]

---

36. Muhammad b. Yaʿqub al-Kulayni, al-Kafi, vol. 2, pp. 226-228.
37. ʿAbd al-Wahid b. Muhammad al-Tamimi al-Amidi, Tasnif ghurar al-hikam wa-durar al-kilam, p. 258, hadith no. 5498.
38. Al-Husayni al-Rawandi, Nawadir al-Rawandi, p. 12.
39. Abu al-Hasan ʿAli b. Abi Nazzal al-Laythi al-Wasiti, ʿUyun al-hikam wa-l-mawaʿiz, p. 186.
40. Muhammad b. al-Hasan al-Tusi, al-Amali, p. 703.
41. Al-Laythi al-Wasiti, ʿUyun al-hikam wa-l-mawaʿiz, p. 298.
42. Al-Muttaqi al-Hindi, Kanz al-ʿummal, vol. 9, p. 45.
43. Qasas al-anbiyaʾ, p. 190/239.

Love and Kindness in Islamic and Christian Scriptures

■ Love with Affability

Love should be coupled with affability, kind treatment, and courteous behavior. It is inconsistent to claim love while treating others poorly. Imam ʿAli emphasized, "Friendship endures through kind treatment."[44]

Another hadith advises: "Accustom your tongue to gentle speech and warm greetings, so that your circle of friends expands and your adversaries diminish."[45]

■ Love in Practice

Love goes beyond mere verbal flattery; it must manifest in action. Its true essence is revealed when we make sacrifices and prioritize our loved ones over ourselves. Imam ʿAli counsels, "Be willing to sacrifice your life and possessions for your friend, offer your support and presence to your acquaintances, share your cheerful demeanor and love with all people, and demonstrate your justice and fairness even to your enemy. However, never compromise your faith or reputation for anyone."[46]

Furthermore, Imam ʿAli is also quoted as saying: "Express love to your friend so that he also loves you."[47]

■ Facial Expression of Love

When someone loves another, that affection is evident in their countenance and gaze. Imam ʿAli affirms, "Friendship is conveyed through words, while love is expressed through the eyes."[48]

■ Avoiding Those Other than the Loved One

When someone loves another, they distance themselves from the loved one's rivals. Explaining the essence of love, Imam al-Sadiq, the sixth Imam, states, "The foundation of love lies in the avoidance of anyone other than the beloved."[49]

■ Alerting Loved Ones to their Deficiencies

When we love someone and notice flaws or deficiencies in them, it is important to

---

44. Al-Laythi al-Wasiti, ʿUyun al-hikam wa-l-mawaʿiz, p. 187, hadith no. 3820.
45. Al-Laythi al-Wasiti, ʿUyun al-hikam wa-l-mawaʿiz, p. 340, hadith no. 5793.
46. Muhammad b. ʿAli Ibn Babawayh, al-Khisal, vol. 1, p. 147.
47. Al-Laythi al-Wasiti, ʿUyun al-hikam wa-l-mawaʿiz, p. 203.
48. ʿAbd al-Wahid b. Muhammad al-Tamimi al-Amidi, Tasnif ghurar al-hikam wa-durar al-kilam, p. 3471.
49. Misbah al-Shariʿa (attributed to Imam al-Sadiq), p. 194.

communicate these observations to them so they can address and improve upon them. Imam ʿAli remarked, "When someone points out your flaws to you, he is your true friend."[50]

Imam al-Husayn, the third Shiite Imam, conveys, "Those who love you will offer criticism, while those who hate you will indulge in flattery."[51]

It is important to distinguish between pointing out a friend's flaws with the intention of helping them improve and simply finding faults in them.

▪ Love with Respect

Another aspect of the etiquette of love is to show respect for those you love and those who love you. Imam ʿAli advises: "Respect those who love you and pardon your enemies, thus completing your virtue."[52]

▪ Love without Expectation

Luqman, the renowned wise man, delineates the types of friends ("brothers") for his son and emphasizes that the best friend is the one who is "interested," which he elucidates as follows: "The interested friend is one who has tendency to build relationships with you without any expectations."[53]

▪ Friendship with Peers

Luqman advises to establish friendships with one's peers, those who are equals or counterparts, or as the saying goes, birds of a feather. He advises, "O son! Every creature seeks its own kind, and humans naturally gravitate towards their counterparts. Do not share your belongings except with those who genuinely seek it. Just as there is no companionship between a wolf and a sheep, there is no friendship between the righteous and the transgressors."[54]

▪ Supporting a Friend Through Mutual Hardships

When two individuals who love each other encounter a mutual hardship, they provide each other with reassurance and comforting words. Luqman's son inquired about the

---

50. Al-Laythi al-Wasiti, ʿUyun al-hikam wa-l-mawaʿiz, p. 444.
51. Muhammad b. ʿAli al-Karajki, Kanz al-fawáid, vol. 1, p. 279.
52. ʿAbd al-Wahid b. Muhammad al-Tamimi al-Amidi, Tasnif ghurar al-hikam wa-durar al-kilam, p. 138, hadith no. 144.
53. Muhadarat al-udabá, vol. 3, p. 8.
54. Qasas al-anbiyá, p. 190/239.

most comforting thing, to which he replied, "Your friend when the same door is closed to both of you," meaning that having a companion who shares your struggles can be immensely comforting.[55]

■ Praying for Love

In numerous supplication texts within Islamic sources, believers ask God to grant them love. In one such supplication, Imam al-Sadiq, the sixth Imam, prays to God: "O God! I seek from You beauty, adornment, and love, and I seek refuge in You from evil, enmity, and grudges."[56]

---

55. Rawdat al-ʿuqalā, p. 342.
56. Muhammad b. Yaʿqub al-Kulayni, al-Kafi, vol. 6, pp. 519, 520; al-Hasan b. Fadl al-Tabarsi, Makarim al-akhlaq, p. 47.

Love and Kindness towards Others

Islam commands us to extend our love to all people without regard for their skin color, wealth, or social status. In this chapter, we explore some of the recommendations, effects, consequences, and etiquettes of showing love and kindness towards others.

Islam encourages us to exhibit love and mercy towards all individuals without discrimination. Imam ʿAli advises, "Commit yourself to friendship and love, and endure the burdens of others with patience."[1]

Furthermore, he expresses, "Blessed are those who form close bonds with others, and people form close bonds with them in the path of obedience to God."[2]

Such love and kindness should encompass all people regardless of their skin color or religious inclinations, as Imam ʿAli advises Malik al-Ashtar in a letter where he provides instructions and counsel for rulers, having appointed Malik as the ruler of Egypt: "Cultivate in your heart a sense of love for your people, and let it be the source of kindness and blessing towards them."[3]

According to a hadith transmitted from Imam al-Sadiq, God instructed Jesus Christ: "Do not do to others what you dislike to be done to you."[4]

One way to show kindness to others is by displaying a cheerful face when interacting with them. Imam ʿAli advised, "Give... all people your cheerful demeanor and love."[5]

Another way to express love to people is by giving gifts to them. Gifts foster love, dispel hatred and hostility, and ease hardships. Prophet Muhammad, peace be upon him and his household, advised: "Exchange gifts, even if it is only a branch of cedar, so that friendship and love may continue among you."[6]

Imam al-Sadiq, the sixth Imam, emphasized: "Exchange gifts to cultivate mutual love."[7]

---

1. Muhammad b. ʿAli Ibn Babawayh, al-Khisal, vol. 1, p. 147.
2. Al-Hasan b. ʿAli Ibn Shuʿba al-Harrani, Tuhaf al-ʿuqul, p. 217.
3. Muhammad b. al-Husayn al-Sharif al-Radi, Nahj al-balagha, p. 427, letter 53.
4. Muhammad b. ʿAli Ibn Babawayh, al-Amali, p. 366.
5. Muhammad b. ʿAli Ibn Babawayh, al-Khisal, p. 147, hadith no. 178.
6. Muhammad b. Yaʿqub al-Kulayni, al-Kafi, vol. 5, p. 144, hadith no. 13. It should be noted that in this hadith, the branch of cedar metaphorically represents the most inexpensive gift. Therefore, the hadith implies that even if you cannot afford to purchase expensive gifts, you can still give something simple like a branch of cedar to foster love and friendship.
7. Muhammad b. ʿAli Ibn Babawayh, Man la-yahduruh al-faqih, vol. 3, p. 299.

Love and Kindness in Islamic and Christian Scriptures

◉ Significance and Impacts of Showing Love to Others

In Islamic sources of hadiths, there is significant emphasis on kindness and demonstrating love towards others, as elaborated below.

■ Love as Sign of Rationality

Kindness and love towards others are signs of rationality. Prophet Muhammad, peace be upon him and his household, states, "After belief in God the Glorified and Exalted, the cornerstone of rationality is friendship and kindness towards others."[1]

In a hadith from Imam 'Ali, it is emphasized that "friendship with others is the cornerstone of rationality."[2]

■ Best People are those who Show Love to Others

Prophet Muhammad, peace be upon him and his household, declares that the best of people are those who show kindness and love towards others: "The best among you are those with the best temperament, who form close bonds with others, and with whom people readily form close bonds."[3]

In another hadith, the Prophet says, "The most virtuous actions, after believing in God, is forming friendships with others."[4]

The Prophet regards the failure to establish intimate bonds with others as a sign of lacking blessings: "There is no blessing for one who does not form close bonds, and with whom no one forms close bonds."[5]

■ Popularity as Reward for Showing Love

Displaying love towards others tends to increase one's popularity. Imam 'Ali noted, "People's hearts are like untamed beasts. They are drawn to those who tame them [through kindliness]."[6]

Imam al-Baqir, the fifth Imam, recounted an incident where an Arab from the Banu Tamim clan sought advice from Prophet Muhammad, peace be upon him and his

---

1. Muhammad b. 'Ali Ibn Babawayh, al-Khisal, vol. 1, p. 15.
2. 'Abd al-Wahid b. Muhammad al-Tamimi al-Amidi, Tasnif ghurar al-hikam wa-durar al-kilam, p. 72, hadith no. 1391.
3. Al-Hasan b. 'Ali Ibn Shu'ba al-Harrani, Tuhaf al-'uqul, p. 45.
4. Abolghasem Payandeh, Nahj al-fasaha, p. 228, hadith no. 387.
5. Muhammad b. al-Hasan al-Tusi, al-Amali, p. 462.
6. Muhammad b. al-Husayn al-Sharif al-Radi, Nahj al-balagha, p. 477, saying no. 50.

Love and Kindness in Islamic and Christian Scriptures

household. Among his counsel, the Prophet advised: "Show love [or friendliness] to people so that they love you."[7]

■ Heavenly Mercy as Reward for Showing Love

Kindness towards people attracts heavenly mercy. Prophet Muhammad, peace be upon him and his household, said, "Show mercy towards those on Earth so that the One in Heaven may show mercy upon you."[8]

■ Security as a Fruit of Love

Friendliness, kindness, and displaying love towards people contribute to enhanced safety and security. Luqman, the renowned wise man, advised his son: "O son! Extend love and kindness to people, for this fosters safety, whereas displaying hostility towards them breeds fear [and insecurity]."[9]

■ Paradise as Reward for Love

Showing love and kindness to people is among the reasons for which individuals enter Paradise in the afterlife. Prophet Muhammad, peace be upon him and his household, said, "There are five qualities that only a true believer possesses, ensuring their entry into Paradise, [including] love and kindness towards people and maintaining a cheerful countenance."[10]

---

7. Muhammad b. Ya'qub al-Kulayni, al-Kafi, vol. 2, p. 642.
8. Muhammad b. 'Ali Ibn Babawayh, Man la-yahduruh al-faqih, vol. 4, p. 379.
9. Nathr al-durr, vol. 7, p. 37.
10. Al-Karajaki, Kanz al-fawaid, vol. 2, p. 10.

Love towards Believers

Believers are those who adhere to a religion, and in Islamic sacred texts, there is immense emphasis placed on showing love and kindness to fellow believers.[1] In the Islamic perspective, believers hold a special reverence and respect, beyond their inherent human dignity, as they are connected to God. Respecting a believer is, in essence, showing respect to God. Believers deserve this respect because God holds them in esteem. There are recommendations to show mercy and love towards believers. For example, the Quran states: "Those who were settled in the land and [abided] in faith before them, who love those who migrate toward them" (Quran 59:9). This verse refers to the Ansar or Helpers in Medina during the early years of Islam, who supported and demonstrated love and kindness to persecuted Muslims (known as al-Muhajirun) who migrated to their city from Mecca.

The Prophet encourages those who extend their love to others for the sake of God: "Blessed are those who love each other mutually on the path of God."[2]

Imam ʿAli, the Commander of the Faithful, is quoted as advising: "Glorify God the Exalted... and befriend [or love] His friends."[3]

Another hadith attributed to him states: "Blessed are those who purify … their love and their hatred for God."[4]

Moreover, Imam ʿAli said, "Establish friendship with others for the sake of God."[5]

Imam al-Sadiq, the sixth Imam, frequently cautioned his companions by saying: "Fear God and be good brothers to each other. Love each other for the sake of God, maintain mutual bonds, and show mercy towards one another. Visit each other and gather together."[6]

The Imam also emphasized: "Purify your love and friendship for your fellow believers."[7]

---

1. In compiling this chapter, we drew upon the book, Friendship in the Quran and Hadiths (in Persian) by Mohammad Mohammadi Reyshahri.
2. Ahmad b. Muhammad b. Khalid al-Barqi, al-Mahasin, vol. 1, p. 265.
3. ʿAbd al-Wahid b. Muhammad al-Tamimi al-Amidi, Tasnif ghurar al-hikam wa-durar al-kilam, p. 728, hadith no. 44.
4. Al-Laythi al-Wasiti, ʿUyun al-hikam wa-l-mawaʿiz, p. 314.
5. Al-Laythi al-Wasiti, ʿUyun al-hikam wa-l-mawaʿiz, p. 504.
6. Muhammad b. Yaʿqub al-Kulayni, al-Kafi, vol. 2, p. 175.
7. Muhammad b. ʿAli Ibn Babawayh, Man la-yahduruh al-faqih, vol. 4, p. 404.

Love and Kindness in Islamic and Christian Scriptures

One duty that believers have towards each other is to forgive each other's mistakes and wrongs with kindness. In describing the characteristics of believers, Prophet Muhammad, peace be upon him and his household, states: "A believer is kind and gracious towards the mistakes of their fellow believer and upholds the rights of longstanding companionship."[8]

In addition, there are numerous hadiths suggesting that believers are like brothers to one another and sympathize with each other. For instance, Prophet Muhammad, peace be upon him and his household, stated: "The believers in their mutual mercy, kindness, and compassion are like a single body; when one part of the body suffers, the whole body responds with sleeplessness and fever."[9]

Such love entails that believers should refrain from making accusations against each other and should not deceive their fellow believers. ʿAbd al-Muʾmin al-Asari reports that he visited Imam Musa b. Jaʿfar, the seventh Imam, and Muhammad b. ʿAbd Allah al-Jaʿfari was present there before the Imam. He says, "I smiled upon seeing Muhammad." Imam Musa al-Kazim asks, "Do you love him?" I said, "Yes, and I love him only because of you." The Imam replied, "He is your brother, and indeed believers are each other's true brothers. Cursed are those who make accusations against their brothers. Cursed are those who deceive their brothers. Cursed are those who are not benevolent towards their brothers. Cursed are those who prefer someone else over their brothers. Cursed are those who hide themselves from their brothers. Cursed are those who backbite against their brothers behind their backs."[10]

In accordance with Islamic teachings on love and friendship among believers, when the bond between two believers is firm and deep-rooted, there is a recommended practice of establishing a covenant of brotherhood between them. In this practice, two fellow believers enter into a formal agreement of brotherhood. This practice is strongly recommended in Islam and was first initiated between 45 members of the Ansar (Helpers in Medina) and 45 members of the Muhajirun (migrants from Mecca to Medina) after the Battle of Badr during the time of Prophet Muhammad, peace be upon him and his household.[11]

Damra b. Saʿid, a second-generation Muslim who was a companion of the Prophet's companions, reports that when the Prophet arrived in Medina, he established formal

---

8. Muhammad b. Hammam b. Suhayl al-Iskafi, al-Tamhis, p. 75.
9. Abolghasem Payandeh, Nahj al-fasaha, p. 382.
10. Al-Husayn b. Muhammad b. al-Hasan b. Nasr al-Halawani, Nuzhat al-nazir wa-tanbih al-khatir, p. 124.
11. Muhammad Baqir al-Majlisi, Bihar al-anwar, vol. 19, p. 130.

contracts of brotherhood among the Muhajirun themselves and between them and the Ansar. Under these contracts, they pledged to uphold each other's rights, support each other, and inherit from one another. These contracts involved a total of ninety individuals: 45 from the Muhajirun and 45 from the Ansar. In some accounts, this number is stated as one hundred, with 50 from each group. This event occurred prior to the Battle of Badr between the Muslims and the polytheists of Mecca. After the Battle of Badr, Allah revealed the following verse: "The relatives are more entitled to inheritance in the decree of Allah. Indeed, Allah is Knowing of all things" (Quran 8:75). This verse nullified the previous ruling that allowed fellow believers who had entered into formal brotherhood contracts to inherit from each other. Inheritance was now restricted to blood relatives as outlined in this verse.[12]

Within an Islamic society, social interactions among believers should be founded upon love and kindness. Imam al-Sadiq, the sixth Imam, emphasized: "Muslims are each other's brothers. ... It is the duty of Muslims ... to be compassionate and concerned about each other, following the example of the Ansar during the time of the Prophet, peace be upon him and his Household."[13]

Believers should extend help and support to each other during times of hardship. ʿIsa b. Sumaʿa, a companion of the sixth Imam, narrates that he asked Imam al-Sadiq about those who possess surplus goods while their brothers are in dire need and zakat charities do not cover them. Can they indulge themselves while their brothers go hungry? The Imam responded, "Muslims should exert effort to be kind and provide solace to those in need, showing empathy towards them. In accordance with God's command, they should demonstrate mercy towards one another.[14] They should exhibit kindness towards each other and take an interest in their well-being, following the example of the Ansar during the time of the Prophet, peace be upon him and his Household."[15]

Imam ʿAli said: When the Prophet sent me on a mission to Yemen, I asked him how I should lead congregational prayer among those people. The Prophet said, "Lead the prayer in accordance to the prayer of the weakest among them and be merciful towards believers."[16]

---

12. Muhammad Baqir al-Majlisi, Bihar al-anwar, vol. 19, p. 130.
13. Muhammad b. Yaʿqub al-Kulayni, al-Kafi, vol. 4, p. 50.
14. This is a reference to the Quranic verse, "Muhammad, the Apostle of Allah, and those who are with him are hard against the faithless and merciful amongst themselves" (Quran 48:29).
15. Muhammad b. Yaʿqub al-Kulayni, al-Kafi, vol. 4, p. 50.
16. Al-Sayyid al-Radi, Nahj al-balagha, p. 440, letter 53.

Love and Kindness in Islamic and Christian Scriptures

In the Quran, God praises Christians for their love and friendship towards Muslim believers: "Surely You will find the most hostile of all people towards the faithful to be the Jews and the polytheists, and surely you will find the nearest of them in affection to the faithful to be those who say 'We are Christians.' That is because there are priests and monks among them, and because they are not arrogant" (Quran 5:82). This verse indicates that Christians, due to their lack of arrogance, expressed love and sympathy towards Muslims during the time of the Prophet.

Each person belongs to a family, the household where they were born. However, they also belong to a larger household, which is the household of God. The Quran refers to the relationship between two believers as that of brotherhood, stating: "The faithful are indeed brothers" (Quran 49:10).

Imam al-Baqir, the fifth Imam, underscores this relationship of brotherhood to such an extent that he states: "A believer is a believer's brother as if they are from one and the same father and mother."[17]

Imam ʿAli emphasizes that friendship for the sake of God holds greater significance than blood ties, stating: "Friendship for the sake of God is the closest kinship."[18]

Believers are not only each other's brothers; above that, they are parts of the same body, not distinct individuals but one and the same entity, as Prophet Muhammad, peace be upon him and his household, said, "The believers in their mutual mercy, kindness, and compassion are like a single body; when one part of the body suffers, the whole body responds with sleeplessness and fever."[19]

Imam ʿAli, the Commander of the Faithful, is quoted as saying: "The best of brothers are those whose friendship is for the sake of God."[20]

He is also quoted as saying: "All that is good is encompassed in [three things:] friendship for the sake of God, enmity for the sake of God, and love for the sake of God."[21]

Prophet Muhammad, peace be upon him and his household, told a man: "Would you like me to guide you to the criterion of what leads you to the good of this world and the hereafter? Be committed to the companionship of those who remember God. And when you are alone, engage your tongue in remembrance of God as much as you can. Love for the sake of God and hate for the sake of God."[22]

---

17. Muhammad b. Yaʿqub al-Kulayni, al-Kafi, vol. 2, p. 166.
18. Al-Laythi al-Wasiti, ʿUyun al-hikam wa-l-mawaʿiz, p. 28.
19. Abolghasem Payandeh, Nahj al-fasaha, p. 382.
20. Al-Laythi al-Wasiti, ʿUyun al-hikam wa-l-mawaʿiz, p. 240.
21. Al-Laythi al-Wasiti, ʿUyun al-hikam wa-l-mawaʿiz, p. 223.
22. Ibn al-ʿAsakir, Tarikh Madina Dimashq, vol. 13, p. 317.

Love and Kindness in Islamic and Christian Scriptures

Imam al-Sadiq quotes Prophet Muhammad, peace be upon him and his household, as saying: "Would you like me to inform you about those among you who are most similar to me?" They said, "yes, O Messenger of Allah!" He said, among other things: "Those who have the greatest love for their religious brothers."[23]

Failure to show love and kindness towards believers will result in loss. In an interpretation of the Quranic verse, "those who break the covenant made with Allah after having pledged it solemnly... it is they who are the losers" (Quran 2:27), Imam al-Hasan al-'Askari, the eleventh Imam, said: "The verse refers to those who had pledged to be committed to God's Lordship, Muhammad's prophethood, 'Ali's Imamate, and love and respect for the followers of Muhammad and 'Ali."[24] Thus, those who break these covenants, including those who fail to show love and kindness to believers, are deemed losers.

Significance and Effects of Showing Love to Believers

In Islamic sources of hadith, there is a strong recommendation for showing love and kindness to believers. Some of these teachings are outlined in the following sections.

Kindness towards Believers as a Religious Obligation

Showing love and kindness towards believers is a religious obligation. From an Islamic perspective, one's heart is considered the abode of God, and it is a divine duty to harbor God's friends within one's heart. Prophet Muhammad, peace be upon him and his household, emphasized this principle, stating: "Love for the sake of God is an obligation."[25]

One should befriend others on the path of God and sever relations with others on the path of God. According to a hadith, "Believers have seven rights upon each other, which have been obligated by God the Glorified and Esteemed, including harboring each other's love in their hearts."[26]

Hafs b. al-Bakhtari, a close companion of the sixth Imam al-Sadiq, also known as Abu 'Abd Allah, reports: I was in the presence of Abu 'Abd Allah, peace be upon him. A man entered. The Imam asked me if I loved that man. I said yes. He then told

---

23. Muhammad b. Ya'qub al-Kulayni, al-Kafi, pp. 240-241.
24. Muhammad Baqir Majlisi, Bihar al-anwar, vol. 24, p. 389.
25. Muhammad b. Muhammad al-Shu'ayri, Jami' al-akhbar, p. 128.
26. Muhammad b. 'Ali Ibn Babawayh, Man la-yahduruh al-faqih, vol. 4, p. 398.

me, "Why would you not love him? He is your brother and your fellow believer, your supporter against your enemy, while he does not burden you in his livelihood."[27]

Showing Love to Believers as honoring God's Right

It is indeed a right that God has upon us to show love and friendship to His friends and supporters. Imam al-Jawad, the ninth Imam, reports that Prophet Muhammad, peace be upon him and his household, stated: "God the Exalted revealed to one of His prophets to convey to a devout worshiper: 'With your asceticism, you have already made the moment of your death easier, and you have honored Me by isolating yourself for My sake. But what have you done for the right I have upon you?' The worshiper asked, 'O Lord! What is the right that You have upon me?' God replied, 'Have you taken anyone as an enemy for My sake and taken anyone as a friend for My sake?'"[28]

To love someone who has faith in God is to love God indeed. When one shows love and kindness to a believer, one is indeed showing love to God, as Prophet Muhammad, peace be upon him and his household, says, "When a servant loves another servant of God, he has indeed honored his Lord, the Glorified and Esteemed."[29]

Imam al-Rida, the eighth Imam, said, "Those who loved and befriended each other for the sake of God will enter the divine court on the Day of Resurrection, and God will address them, 'O my servants, my creatures, my visitors, who loved each other for Me! Welcome to the abode of my honor.'"[30]

Attaining the Peak of Faith by Kindness to Believers

The most virtuous humans are those who entrust God with the house of their hearts, and thus their friendship or enmity is not due to personal desires and interests but for the sake of God. Prophet Muhammad, peace be upon him and his household, said, "Love and friendship towards believers for the sake of God is one of the greatest branches of faith."[31]

Moreover, the Commander of the Faithful, Imam ʿAli, is quoted as saying: "The highest degree of religiosity is to love for the sake of God and hate for the sake of God."[32]

---

27. Muhammad b. Yaʿqub al-Kulayni, al-Kafi, vol. 2, p. 166.
28. Al-Hasan b. ʿAli Ibn Shuʿba al-Harrani, Tuhaf al-ʿuqul, pp. 455-456.
29. Al-Muttaqi al-Hindi, Kanz al-ʿummal, vol. 9, p. 4, hadith no. 24647.
30. Muhammad b. Muhammad al-Shuʿayri, Jami al-akhbar, p. 118.
31. Muhammad b. Yaʿqub al-Kulayni, al-Kafi, vol. 2, p. 125.
32. ʿAbd al-Wahid b. Muhammad al-Tamimi al-Amidi, Tasnif ghurar al-hikam wa-durar al-kilam, p. 231, hadith no. 164.

Love and Kindness in Islamic and Christian Scriptures

Another hadith from Prophet Muhammad, peace be upon him and his household, states: "The firmest handle of faith is to love for the sake of God and hate for the sake of God."[33]

Those who love and befriend God's friends will taste the ultimate truth and peak of faith, as Prophet Muhammad, peace be upon him and his household, is quoted as saying: "No servant of God will grasp the pure essence of faith until he loves for the sake of God and hates for the sake of God. When he loves for the sake of God the Blessed and Exalted and hates for the sake of God the Blessed and Exalted, he will deserve friendship with God."[34]

Imam al-Sadiq also said, "Those who love for the sake of God, hate for the sake of God, and donate for the sake of God are among those who have perfected their faith."[35]

Prophet Muhammad, peace be upon him and his household, stated, "There are three characteristics. Whoever has them all will taste the savor of faith. One of them is to love others only for the sake of God."[36]

Another hadith from the Prophet says, "Those who would like to find the sweetness of faith must love others only for the sake of God, the Glorified and Esteemed."[37]

▪ Kindness to Believers as Sign of Loving the Religion

Displaying kindness and love to believers is regarded as a sign of affection and devotion to religion. Imam al-Sadiq stated, "Part of one's love for religion is the love for one's religious brothers."[38]

Samaʿa b. Mihran, a companion of the sixth Imam al-Sadiq, reports that one day the Imam asked him about his love for his religious brothers. He replied, "May I be sacrificed for you! I swear to God that I love them and have affection towards them." The Imam responded, "O Samaʿa! When someone strongly loves his religious brothers, then he likewise strongly loves his religion."[39]

▪ Kindness to Believers as Sign of Righteousness

While all individuals like to be regarded as righteous, not everyone embodies righteousness

---

33. Muhammad b. ʿAli Ibn Babawayh, Man la-yahduruh al-faqih, vol. 4, p. 362, hadith no. 5762.
34. Ahmad b. Hanbal, Musnad Ahmad, vol. 24, pp. 316-317, hadith no. 15549.
35. Muhammad b. Yaʿqub al-Kulayni, al-Kafi, vol. 2, pp. 124-125, hadith no. 1.
36. Abu al-Fadl ʿAli al-Tabarsi, Mishkat al-anwar fi ghurar al-akhbar, p. 123.
37. Al-Muttaqi al-Hindi, Kanz al-ʿummal, vol. 9, p. 10, hadith no. 24679.
38. Muhammad b. ʿAli Ibn Babawayh, al-Khisal, vol. 1, p. 3.
39. Ibn Hayyun, Sharh al-akhbar fi fadaʾil al-aʾimma al-athar ʿalayhim al-salam, vol. 3, p. 436.

Love and Kindness in Islamic and Christian Scriptures

and uprightness. Prophet Muhammad, peace be upon him and his household, said, "There are ten signs of the righteous, including love and friendship for the sake of God."[40]

Imam al-Baqir, the fifth Imam, said, "If you wish to ascertain whether there is a blessing within you, examine your heart. If it loves those who obey God and hates sinners, then there is indeed a blessing within you, and God loves you. ... A person is with those whom they love."[41]

Prophet Muhammad, peace be upon him and his household, is quoted as saying: "A believer's love and friendship toward another believer for the sake of God is one of the greatest branches of faith. Beware! Those who love for the sake of God, hate for the sake of God, give for the sake of God, and withhold for the sake of God are among those chosen by God."[42]

The best believers are those who show love and kindness to other believers, as the Prophet also said, "The best of believers is one who forms close bonds with other believers. There is no blessing in those who do not form close bonds with anyone, and with whom no one forms close bonds."[43]

▪ To Love Believers is to Love God and the Prophet

According to hadiths, those who love God and the Prophet also love others who love God and the Prophet. The Commander of the Faithful, Imam ʿAli, said, "Those who love God will also love the Prophet, and those who love the Prophet also love us, and those who love us will also love our Shias (followers)."[44]

▪ Loving the Believers as a Divine Gift

God in the Quran states that love and close bonds among believers are divine gifts: "Hold fast, all together, to Allah's cord, and do not be divided [into sects]. Remember Allah's blessing upon you when you were enemies, then He brought your hearts together, so you became brothers with His blessing" (Quran 3:103).

Imam ʿAli also affirms that God has created love within the hearts of believers: "God the Exalted has graced this nation by creating a bond of intimacy and closeness among them, under the shadow of which they enjoy peace. This blessing is of the greatest price and of greatest importance."[45]

---

40. Al-Hasan b. ʿAli Ibn Shuʿba al-Harrani, Tuhaf al-ʿuqul, p. 21.
41. Muhammad b. Yaʿqub al-Kulayni, al-Kafi, vol. 2, pp. 126-127.
42. Muhammad b. Yaʿqub al-Kulayni, al-Kafi, vol. 2, p. 125, hadith no. 3.
43. Muhammad b. al-Hasan al-Tusi, al-Amali, p. 462.
44. Abu al-Qasim Furat al-Kufi, Tafsir Furat al-Kufi, p. 128.
45. Al-Sayyid al-Radi, Nahj al-balagha, p. 298-299, sermon 192.

Love and Kindness in Islamic and Christian Scriptures

■ Continued Prosperity through Kindness to Believers

Imam al-Rida, the eighth Imam, quotes the Prophet as saying that kindness towards friends is a factor contributing to continued prosperity and blessings from God: "My nation will always be prosperous as long as they love one another, exchange gifts, and uphold each other's trusts."[46]

■ Kindness and Affection towards Believers as a Religious Act

Displaying love and kindness towards believers is considered a religious act, for which God rewards in the afterlife. The Commander of the Faithful, Imam ʿAli, is quoted as saying: "A believer's glance upon the face of his religious brother out of affection and love is an act of worship."[47]

Loving the believers is indeed one of the most commendable religious acts or acts of worship, as Prophet Muhammad, peace be upon him and his household, said, "The most virtuous deed is to love for the sake of God and to dislike for the sake of God."[48]

■ Divine Rewards for Loving the Believers

A person who loves a believer for the sake of God will benefit from divine rewards. Imam ʿAli is quoted as saying: "Those who establish brotherhood for the sake of God will be rewarded, while those who establish brotherhood for worldly gain will be deprived."[49]

This raises a question: what if we are uncertain whether someone is truly a believer or a transgressor? Should we harbor love for such an individual? Imam al-Baqir, the fifth Imam, said, "If a person loves another for the sake of God, then God will reward them for his love, even if, in God's knowledge, the loved one deserves the fire of Hell."[50]

Furthermore, according to Hadiths, loving others is a virtue. For instance, the sixth Imam al-Sadiq is quoted as saying: "A person's virtue before God is his love for his brothers."[51]

■ Liberation from the Difficulties of the Day of Resurrection through Kindness to Believers

While everyone is concerned and anxious on the Day of Resurrection, those who have

---

46. Muhammad b. ʿAli Ibn Babawayh, ʿUyun akhbar al-Rida ʿalayh al-salam, vol. 2, p. 29.
47. Al-Hasan b. ʿAli Ibn Shuʿba al-Harrani, Tuhaf al-ʿuqul, p. 282.
48. Muhammad Baqir al-Majlisi, Bihar al-anwar, vol. 66, p. 252.
49. ʿAbd al-Wahid b. Muhammad al-Tamimi al-Amidi, Tasnif ghurar al-hikam wa-durar al-kilam, p. 423, hadiths no. 9702 and 9703.
50. Muhammad b. Yaʿqub al-Kulayni, al-Kafi, vol. 2, p. 127.
51. Muhammad b. ʿAli Ibn Babawayh, Thawab al-aʿmal wa-ʿiqab al-aʿmal, p. 185.

loved and befriended the friends of God will experience peace and comfort. Prophet Muhammad, peace be upon him and his household, is quoted as saying: "Those who loved each other for the sake of God will rise on the Day of Resurrection on a ground paved by green peridot under the shadow of God's Throne from the right side. Their faces shine intensely, more than the rising sun. Every archangel and every prophet will envy their position. People will ask, 'Who are these?' And it will be said, 'These are those who loved each other for the sake of God.'"[52]

Another Hadith states: "When two individuals love each other for the sake of God, then God will give them a chair on the Day of Resurrection. They will sit on it until God the Glorified and Esteemed finishes His reckoning [of people's actions]."[53]

On the Day of Resurrection, all will be overcome by an intense thirst except those who quench their thirst from the Pond of Kawthar. According to a hadith attributed to Prophet Muhammad, peace be upon him and his household, "The first of those who arrive at the pond on the Day of Resurrection are those who loved one another for the sake of Allah, the Glorified and the Exalted."[54]

On the Day of Resurrection, there will be no shade except the shade of divine mercy. Those who loved the friends of God will find peace and tranquility under this shade, for it is reported that the Prophet stated, "On the Day of Resurrection, God will ask: Where are those who loved one another for My sake? Today, I shall shade them under My shade, on a day when there is no shade but Mine."[55]

Imam al-Sadiq quoted Prophet Muhammad's words, stating: "Those who honor and dignify their Muslim brothers with a kind word and alleviate their distress will remain under the shade of God's mercy, which encompasses them as long as they continue to do so."[56]

■ Paradise and Salvation as Rewards of Showing Love to Believers

The reward for those who demonstrate love and kindness towards fellow believers is the attainment of Paradise. God promises to reward those who show mercy and kindness to believers with blessings in Paradise. In the Quran, God emphasizes that those who display love towards believers will achieve salvation: "[They are as well] for those who were

---

52. Muhammad b. Ya'qub al-Kulayni, al-Kafi, vol. 2, p. 126.
53. Al-Muttaqi al-Hindi, Kanz al-'ummal, vol. 9, p. 5, hadith no. 24649.
54. Al-Muttaqi al-Hindi, Kanz al-'ummal, vol. 9, p. 18, hadith no. 24715.
55. Al-Muttaqi al-Hindi, Kanz al-'ummal, vol. 9, p. 6, hadith no. 24655.
56. Muhammad b. Ya'qub al-Kulayni, al-Kafi, vol. 2, p. 206.

settled in the land and [abided] in faith before them, who love those who migrate toward them... it is they who are the felicitous" (Quran 59:9).

Furthermore, God will grant them attendants in Paradise who will serve them with foods, refreshing drinks, and all manner of comforts. Prophet Muhammad, peace be upon him and his household, asserted: "If someone within my community (Ummah) shows any form of kindness to their fellow believer for the sake of God, then God will assign the servants of Paradise to serve them."[57]

In another hadith, the Prophet describes a scene on the Day of Resurrection: God will gather all beings in one vast field. Then, a caller, representing God the Glorified and Exalted, will address them. His voice will reach those at the forefront as clearly as it reaches those at the back. He will ask, "Where are the neighbors of God, Exalted is His Status?" A group of people will stand up, welcomed by a host of angels. The angels inquire, "What deeds did you perform in the world that earned you the privilege of being neighbors to the Exalted God in His abode?" They respond, "We loved one another for the sake of God, supported each other for His sake, and visited each other for His sake." Then, a caller announces on behalf of God, "My servants have spoken the truth. Clear their path so they may enter the neighborhood of God in Paradise without their deeds being scrutinized." Thus, they proceed towards Paradise without being held to account for their deeds. Abu Ja'far [Imam al-Baqir who quoted the Prophet's words] added, "These are the neighbors of God. While others are fearful [on the Day of Resurrection], they are not. While others are being held to account for their deeds, they are exempt."[58]

According to hadiths, those who love and befriend the allies of God will be elevated to the rank of the Prophet in Paradise. For instance, it is narrated that Prophet Muhammad, peace be upon him and his household, said: "I know of individuals who will share the same status as mine before God on the Day of Resurrection. They are neither prophets nor martyrs, yet their rank will be envied by prophets and martyrs." When asked about them, he replied, "They are those who treated each other as brothers in the spirit of God, not for the purposes of worldly gains, nor because of close kinship. I swear by the One in whose hand is my life, there is radiance upon their faces, and they are enveloped in light. They do not grieve when others grieve, nor do they fear when others are afraid." He then recited the Quranic verse, "Behold! Indeed, the friends of Allah will have no fear nor will they grieve" (Quran 10:62).[59]

---

57. Muhammad b. Ya'qub al-Kulayni, al-Kafi, vol. 2, p. 206.
58. Muhammad b. al-Hasan al-Tusi, al-Amali, p. 103.
59. Al-Hasan b. Muhammad al-Daylami, A'lam al-din fi sifat al-mu'minin, p. 280.

Love and Kindness in Islamic and Christian Scriptures

■ Liberation from Hell as a Reward for Kind Treatment of Believers

In a hadith, the fifth Imam al-Baqir recounted that Prophet Moses asked God, "O God! What is the reward for those who, out of their love for You, love those who obey You?" God responded, "O Moses! I will make My fire forbidden to them."[60]

■ Kindness to Believers and Liberation from Evil's Dominion

Evil seeps through the heart's vulnerabilities. If it gains mastery over the heart, it can control the individual. However, if one surrenders their heart solely to God before evil's infiltration, and teaches their heart to love for God's sake and to hate for His sake, then evil will be unable to dominate their heart. Once, Prophet Muhammad, peace be upon him and his household, addressed his companions, saying: "Shall I not inform you of something that, if you know it, evil will distance itself from you like the distance between the east and the west?" They eagerly responded, "Yes, please." The Prophet replied, "Love for the sake of God and cooperation in performing righteous deeds will sever the grip of evil."[61]

Furthermore, the fifth Imam al-Baqir is quoted as saying: "Your love shall be for the sake of God, and you should foster affection and collaborate in performing righteous deeds. This will break the hold of both the tyrant ruler and evil."[62]

■ Persistence of Friendships even on the Day of Resurrection

On the Day of Resurrection, a profound sense of dread grips everyone, causing children to flee from their parents and parents to flee from their children. Each individual becomes absorbed in their own concerns, as described in the Quran: "The day when a man will flee from his brother, his mother and his father, his wife and his children. Each one of them, that Day, will have enough concern (of his own) to make him indifferent to the others" (Quran 80:34-37). Moreover, friends will not only fail to aid and support one another, but they will even become adversaries, except for those who were friends for the sake of God. The Quran states: "On that Day, friends will be enemies to one another, except the righteous" (Quran 43:67). Interpreting this verse, Imam ʿAli explains: "People may be brothers, but if their brotherhood is not for the

---

60. Muhammad Baqir al-Majlisi, Bihar al-anwar, vol. 66, p. 413.
61. Muhammad b. Yaʿqub al-Kulayni, al-Kafi, vol. 4, p. 62.
62. Al-Hasan b. ʿAli Ibn Shuʿba al-Harrani, Tuhaf al-ʿuqul, p. 298.

sake of God, it will transform into enmity, which is the essence of God's statement, 'friends will be one another's enemies, except for the righteous.'"[63]

Those who love each other for the sake of God will reunite in Paradise, as Prophet Muhammad, peace be upon him and his household, declared: "If two individuals love each other for the sake of God, with one residing in the east and the other in the west, God will bring them together on the Day of Resurrection."[64]

The fourth Imam al-Sajjad, renowned for his extensive supplications to God, prayed fervently: "My Master, have mercy upon me at my resurrection and uprising and on that day, appoint my standing place with Your friends, my place of emergence with Your beloveds, and my dwelling in Your neighborhood! O Lord of the worlds!"[65]

The Prophet's Interception as a Reward for Kindness to Believers

On the Day of Resurrection, Prophet Muhammad, peace be upon him and his household, will intercede for those who showed kindness towards believers, as he affirmed, "I intercede for any two individuals who became brothers for the sake of God from the beginning of my mission until the Day of Resurrection."[66]

On that fateful day, God will grant certain believers the ability to intercede for others, seeking forgiveness for their sins and admission into Paradise. These believers will intercede on behalf of their friends and relatives. This shows the importance of companionship with fellow believers, who can save one from Hell on the Day of Resurrection. Hence, the Quran recounts the regret of the inhabitants of Hell: "Now we have no intercessors, nor do we have any compassionate friends" (Quran 26:101). Interpreting this verse, the sixth Imam al-Sadiq explained, "The status of a friend is so esteemed that even the inhabitants of Hell seek their aid and call upon them before reaching out to their own kin."[67]

Divine Mercy as a Reward for Kindness towards Believers

Kindness and love towards believers hold such immense value in the eyes of God that it garners His affection. God extends His mercy to all who exhibit love and friendship towards fellow believers. Prophet Muhammad, peace be upon him and his household,

---

63. Muhammad b. ʿAli al-Karajaki, Kanz al-fawāid, vol. 1, p. 93.
64. Muhammad b. Muhammad al-Shuʿayri, Jamiʿ al-akhbar, p. 128.
65. Al-Sahifat al-Sajjadiyya, p. 258, supplication no. 53.
66. Al-Muttaqi al-Hindi, Kanz al-ʿummal, vol. 9, p. 4, hadith no. 24644.
67. Muhammad b. al-Hasan al-Tusi, al-Amali, p. 517, hadith no. 1133.

Love and Kindness in Islamic and Christian Scriptures

emphasized this, saying: "Those who honor and dignify their Muslim brothers with a kind word and alleviate their distress will remain under the shade of God's mercy, which encompasses them as long as they continue to do so."[68]

Asking God for the Opportunity for Friendship with Believers

While it is crucial to try hard to show kindness, love, and earn the friendship of believers, it is equally important to ask God for the privilege of befriending His chosen ones. This is why various supplication texts within Islamic sources beseech God for the blessing of companionship with His friends. For example, it is reported that Prophet Muhammad, peace be upon him and his household, supplicated to God, saying: "O God! Make us companions of Your friends and adversaries of Your enemies, so that with Your love, we may love those who love You, and with Your enmity, we may oppose those who oppose You."[69]

In the renowned "Minor Supplication" handed down from the Prophet, he implores God: "O God! In Your service, guide us to seek Your servants and Your chosen ones in all quarters. Make us companions of the purified friends of Yours and allies of those who seek Your presence, appealing to Your door."[70]

Moreover, the fourth Imam al-Sajjad supplicates: "My Master, have mercy upon me at my resurrection and uprising and on that day, appoint my standing place with Your friends, my place of emergence with Your beloveds, and my dwelling in Your neighborhood! O Lord of the worlds!"[71]

Overall, n supplications, it is encouraged to pray for our hearts to be filled with love for fellow believers. The Quran underscores this sentiment: "Our Lord! ... do not place in our hearts resentment toward those who have believed" (Quran 59:10).

According to hadiths, it is advisable to recite the following supplication during the *qunut* section of Islamic prayers, wherein one stands upright and raises hands in prayer to God: "O God! ... You are aware of the affection and love I hold in the depths of my heart for Your friends."[72]

---

68. Muhammad b. Ya'qub al-Kulayni, al-Kafi, vol. 2, p. 206.
69. Muhammad b. 'Ali Ibn Abi Jumhur al-Ihsai, 'Awali al-li'ali, vol. 1, p. 194.
70. Muhammad Baqir al-Majlisi, Bihar al-anwar, vol. 91, p. 128.
71. Al-Sahifat al-Sajjadiyya, p. 258, supplication no. 53.
72. Al-Fiqh al-mansub ila al-Imam al-Rida 'alayh al-salam, p. 404.

Love for Followers of Other Religions

From a religious perspective, humanity is often categorized into believers and non-believers. While the preceding section focused on the importance of showing love and kindness to fellow believers, it is essential to explore directives regarding love and kindness towards non-believers and all people, irrespective of their religious beliefs. In Islam, Muslims are urged to display love and kindness not only towards their fellow Muslims but also towards non-believers. The Quran emphasizes this principle: "Allah does not forbid you from dealing kindly and justly with those [polytheists] who have not fought against you because of religion and have not driven you out of your homes. Indeed, Allah loves the just" (Quran 60:8).

Islamic leaders have consistently emphasized the importance of Muslims demonstrating kindness and love towards non-Muslims. In a letter addressed to Malik al-Ashtar, whom he appointed as the ruler of Egypt, the Commander of the Faithful Imam ʿAli articulated instructions on governance and the treatment of people. He advised: " Cultivate in your heart a sense of love for your people, and let it be the source of kindness and blessing towards them. Do not conduct yourself toward them in a harsh manner, nor wrongfully claim what is rightfully theirs. Remember that the citizens of the state fall into two categories: they are either your brethren in faith or your brethren in humanity."[1]

The sixth Imam al-Sadiq remarked, "May God have His mercy upon a person who draws the love and affection of others towards us [the Imams], speaking to them about things they see appropriate and abstaining from discussing matters that they find inappropriate."[2]

Muʿammar b. Khallad, a companion of the eighth Shiite Imam al-Rida, once asked him, "Should I supplicate for my parents even if they do not embrace the truth [that is, Shiite belief]?" The Imam responded, "Indeed, pray for them, donate on their behalf,

---

1. Muhammad b. al-Husayn al-Sharif al-Radi, Nahj al-balagha, p. 427, letter 53.
2. Muhammad b. al-Hasan al-Tusi, al-Amali, p. 86.

and if they are alive and remain unconvinced, continue to treat them with kindness and love. For the Messenger of God [Muhammad] stated, 'Truly, God has tasked me with mercy, not with ingratitude [which includes severing ties with parents and family].'"

The importance of honoring kindness promised to non-Muslims should not be underestimated. Imam ʿAli emphasizes this by stating, "Do not underestimate a kindness you have pledged to them [non-Muslims], even if it seems insignificant."

In Islam, there exists a principle of kindness towards non-believers known as "reconciliation of the hearts" (*tâlif al-qulub*). According to this principle, Muslims are encouraged to show kindness to non-Muslims. As a strategic approach regarding the rights of minorities, this principle seeks to foster close bonds and genuine affection with opponents of Islam. An example of its application in Islamic jurisprudence is the allocation of funds from "zakat," which is collected from Muslims, to perform acts of favor and kindness towards non-Muslims. This practice is recommended in the Quranic verse: "The charities are only for the poor and the needy, and those employed to collect them, and those whose hearts are to be reconciled, and for [the freedom of] the slaves and the debtors, and in the way of Allah, and for the traveler. [This is] an ordinance from Allah, and Allah is all-knowing, all-wise" (Quran 9:60). Muslim jurists explicitly state that the phrase "those whose hearts are to be reconciled" includes unbelievers.

Imam ʿAli advocated for the equal treatment and protection of the life and property of non-Muslims residing under an Islamic government, akin to the treatment of Muslims. Additionally, just as Muslims contribute to the expenses for the security and development of the Islamic government, non-Muslims are also expected to contribute. Explaining the rationale behind minorities paying "jizya" (a special tax for non-Muslims under an Islamic government), Imam ʿAli explained, "They pay *jizya* so that their property may be safeguarded like our own, and their lives may be protected equally to ours."

---

3. Muhammad b. Yaʿqub al-Kulayni, al-Kafi, vol. 2, p. 159.
4. Muhammad b. al-Husayn al-Sharif al-Radi, Nahj al-Balagha, p. 433.
5. Muhammad b. al-Hasan al-Tusi, al-Mabsut fi fiqh al-Imamiyya, vol. 1, p 249: "Those entitled to receive zakat include those whose hearts are to be reconciled, a category we believe encompasses unbelievers who, by receiving a portion of the charitable funds, may be inclined towards Islam."
6. Al-Dhahabi, Tarikh al-Islam, vol. 52, p. 77.

Love for One's Spouse

In Islamic sacred texts, there are emphatic recommendations advocating kindness and compassion towards one's spouse. Prophet Muhammad, peace be upon him and his household, addressing a woman named Hawla, stated: "O Hawla! A man has rights upon his wife to maintain the home, show affection towards him, love him, and be kind to him."[1]

The fourth Imam al-Sajjad is quoted as emphasizing the importance of a wife's rights, stating: "The wife's right is for you to recognize that God, the Glorified and Esteemed, has appointed her as a source of peace and an intimate companion. Therefore, acknowledge this as a blessing from God and honor her accordingly, being kind and compassionate towards her."[2]

In another hadith, Imam al-Sajjad asserted, "She has the right to receive kindness and intimate companionship, and finding solace in her presence fulfills the inevitable pleasure, which is of great significance."[3]

Imam al-Sajjad also emphasized, "The man's right upon the woman is for her to maintain the home, be affectionate towards him, love him, and show compassion towards him."[4]

Women are encouraged to love their husbands deeply. According to a hadith attributed to Imam ʿAli, Luqman, the renowned wise man, advised his son regarding the selection of a wife. He categorized women into four groups, distinguishing between the righteous and the less righteous. Regarding the former group, he described them as "affectionate," likening them to "a merciful mother who shows love to older children and compassion to younger ones. Such a wife loves her husband's children, even if they are from another mother."[5]

One might forget many things, but the love and affection for one's spouse are never forgotten. As the Prophet said, "When the man tells the woman 'I love you,' those words would never fade from her heart."[6]

---

1. Husayn b. Muhammad Taqi al-Nuri al-Tabarsi, Mustadrak al-wasáil wa-mustanbat al-masáil, vol. 14, p. 244, hadith no. 16604.
2. Muhammad b. ʿAli Ibn Babawayh, Man la-yahduruh al-faqih, vol. 2, p. 621.
3. Al-Hasan b. ʿAli Ibn Shuʿba al-Harrani, Tuhaf al-ʿuqul, p. 262.
4. Husayn b. Muhammad Taqi al-Nuri al-Tabarsi, Mustadrak al-wasáil wa-mustanbat al-masáil, vol. 14, p. 244.
5. Muhammad Baqir al-Majlisi, Bihar al-anwar, vol. 13, p. 429.
6. Muhammad b. Yaʿqub al-Kulayni, al-Kafi, vol. 5, p. 569, hadith no. 59.

Love and Kindness in Islamic and Christian Scriptures

The sixth Imam al-Sadiq stated, "A wife finds fulfillment in her relationship with her harmonious husband through three key characteristics: [including] expressing love to him in a captivating manner, and maintaining a pleasant appearance in his eyes."[7]

Man and woman should exchange love. ʿUthman b. Mazʿun[8] was a companion of the Prophet who always engaged himself in prayer and worship. According to a hadith, "ʿUthman b. Mazʿun's wife approached the Prophet, peace be upon him and his Household, and said, 'O Messenger of God! ʿUthman fasts during the days and stays vigilant during the night [performing prayers].' The Prophet, peace be upon him and his Household, left angrily while he held his shoes in his hands until he met ʿUthman. He found him performing prayers. When he saw the Prophet, peace be upon him and his Household, ʿUthman cancelled his prayer. The Prophet told him, 'O ʿUthman! Allah the Exalted has not sent for monasticism but sent me for the tolerant convenient way of piety. I fast, I perform prayers, and I fulfil my marital duties towards my wives. He who loves my wife should comply with my tradition, and marriage is part of my tradition.'"[9]

In another hadith, Safwan b. Yahya, a companion of the eighth Imam al-Rida, asked him about a man who refrains from being intimate with his young wife, avoiding her for months or even a year. He does not want to bother or punish her by this, but in fact, a tragedy has befallen them [which makes him reluctant to have an intercourse]. Is this considered a sin? The Imam responded that if he avoids her for four months, he would indeed be considered a sinner thereafter, unless such avoidance is with her explicit consent.[10]

One of the duties of men is companionship and communication with their wives, as a hadith passed down from Prophet Muhammad, peace be upon him and his household, states: "A man sitting beside his wife is more endearing and beloved to God than worshipful stay in my mosque here."[11]

---

7. Al-Hasan b. ʿAli Ibn Shuʿba al-Harrani, Tuhaf al-ʿuqul, p. 323.
8. ʿUthman b. Mazʿun (d. second century AH) was a companion of the Prophet Muhammad and his step-brother through breastfeeding, as his mother had nursed the Prophet when he was a baby. He was among the earliest converts to Islam. Alongside his brother ʿAbd Allah and his son Saib, he migrated to Abyssinia during the early years of Islam, later joining the migration to Medina. He also participated in the Battle of Badr. Renowned for his devotion and asceticism, ʿUthman was held in high esteem by both the Prophet Muhammad and Imam ʿAli. In his honor, Imam ʿAli named one of his sons ʿUthman.
9. Muhammad b. Yaʿqub al-Kulayni, al-Kafi, vol. 5, p. 494.
10. Muhammad b. ʿAli Ibn Babawayh, Man la-yahduruh al-faqih, vol. 3, p. 405.
11. Masʿud b. ʿIsa al-Warram b. Abi Firas, Majmuʿat al-Warram, vol. 2, p. 122.

Love and Kindness in Islamic and Christian Scriptures

In an account of the mutual rights of wives and husbands, Imam al-Sajjad states, "The wife's right is for you to recognize that God, the Glorified and Esteemed, has appointed her as a source of peace and an intimate companion."[12]

One Islamic instruction for attracting the companionship, intimacy, and love of one's wife is to dye one's hair to look younger. Imam al-Sadiq stated, "Dyeing [hair and beard] black leads to intimacy with women."[13]

Moreover, in Islamic culture, husbands are recommended to tolerate women's jealousy because it stems from their love and affection for their husbands. Ishaq b. ʿAmmar, a companion of Imam al-Sadiq, asked him about a woman who displays jealousy towards her husband and troubles him. The Imam replied, "That is out of love."[14]

Leaders of Islam have asserted that it is unfit for underage children to get married, as was practiced among certain tribes. Hisham b. al-Hakam, another companion of Imam al-Sadiq, asked him about the marriage of underage boys and girls. He replied, "When their marriage occurs in childhood, they are less likely to become intimate [after reaching adulthood]."[15]

Significance and Effects of Expressing Love to One's Spouse

In sources of hadiths, there is much emphasis on expressing love and kindness to one's spouse. Below are selected narratives highlighting this importance.

Loving One's Spouse as a Divine Gift

Quranic verses suggest that it is God who creates bonds of love and affection between wives and husbands: "And of His signs is that He created for you mates from your own selves that you may find tranquility in them, and He placed between you affection and mercy. Surely, there are signs in this for those who reflect" (Quran 30:21).

Love of Spouse as a Prophetic Trait

Showing love to one's spouse is a trait and practice of righteous people and divine prophets. Imam al-Sadiq, the sixth Imam, is quoted as saying: "A trait of prophets, peace be upon them, is love for women."[16]

---

12. Muhammad b. ʿAli Ibn Babawayh, Man la-yahduruh al-faqih, vol. 2, p. 621, hadith no. 3214.
13. Muhammad Baqir al-Majlisi, Bihar al-anwar, vol. 73, p. 100.
14. Muhammad b. Yaʿqub al-Kulayni, al-Kafi, vol. 5, p. 506.
15. Muhammad b. Yaʿqub al-Kulayni, al-Kafi, vol. 5, p. 398.
16. Muhammad b. Yaʿqub al-Kulayni, al-Kafi, vol. 5, p. 320, hadith no. 1.

Love and Kindness in Islamic and Christian Scriptures

Moreover, Prophet Muhammad, peace be upon him and his household, said, "Seven traits are bestowed upon us, the Household, which were not given to anyone before us nor will be given to anyone after us, [including] the love of women."[17]

Love of One's Spouse as a Sign of Faith

There is a direct relationship between faith and love for one's spouse. Those who harbor greater affection for their spouses tend to exhibit stronger faith and religious commitment. Imam al-Sadiq is quoted as stating: "The more one loves women, the greater the virtue of their faith will be."[18]

In another hadith, Imam al-Sadiq asserted: "Those who have a stronger love for us [the Imams] also have a strong love for women."[19]

Love of One's Spouse as a Sign of Virtue

Among all criteria of value within Islam, one of the most important is the love for one's spouse and family, which serves to distinguish the goodness or badness of individuals. Prophet Muhammad, peace be upon him and his household, stated, "The best of people in terms of faith are those with the best moral character and the kindest to their families, and I am the kindest among you to my family."[20]

In another hadith, the Prophet said, "I do not believe that a man can increase the virtue of his faith except by increasing his love for women [namely, his wife]."[21]

Greater love for one's wife or husband is considered a sign of virtue and superiority over others. Prophet Muhammad, peace be upon him and his household, said, "The most virtuous women among you are those with the greatest affection and kindness towards their husbands."[22]

In another hadith, the Prophet also emphasizes that a woman's love for her husband is the criterion of her virtue and superiority: "The most virtuous women are those who are affectionate and fertile."[23]

---

17. Muhammad Baqir al-Majlisi, Bihar al-anwar, vol. 66, p. 403.
18. Muhammad b. ʿAli Ibn Babawayh, Man la-yahduruh al-faqih, vol. 3, p. 384.
19. Ibn Idris al-Hilli, al-Saraʾir al-hawi li-tahrir al-fatawi, vol. 3, p. 636; al-Shaykh al-Hurr al-ʿAmili, Wasaʾil al-Shiʿa, vol. 20, p. 24.
20. Muhammad b. ʿAli Ibn Babawayh, ʿUyun akhbar al-Rida ʿalayh al-salam, vol. 2, p. 38.
21. Muhammad b. Yaʿqub al-Kulayni, al-Kafi, vol. 5, p. 320.
22. Ibn Hayyun, Daʿaim al-Islam, vol. 2, p. 195.
23. Ibn Hayyun, Daʿaim al-Islam, vol. 2, p. 191.

Love and Kindness in Islamic and Christian Scriptures

▪ Reward for Love

According to hadiths, God grants the reward of martyrs—those who sacrifice their lives for the cause of God—to those who love sincerely. Prophet Muhammad, peace be upon him and his household, stated, "He who falls in love, conceals his love, preserves his chastity, and then dies will die as a martyr."[24]

Moreover, Paradise is the reward of chaste love, as another hadith from the Prophet, peace be upon him and his household, states, "He who falls in love, conceals his love, preserves his chastity, and remains patient, God will forgive his sins and admit him to Paradise."[25]

Chaste love serves as expiation for one's sins. Abu Saʿid al-Khudri, a companion of Prophet Muhammad, peace be upon him and his household, quotes him as saying: "Pure, untainted love is an expiation for one's sins."[26]

God forgives one's sins when one holds and expresses love towards one's spouse. Prophet Muhammad, peace be upon him and his household, said, "When the faithful servant takes his wife's hand, God, the Glorified and Esteemed, will write for him ten good deeds and erase ten of his bad deeds. If he kisses her, God will write for him one hundred good deeds and erase one hundred of his bad deeds."[27]

---

24. Al-Muttaqi al-Hindi, Kanz al-ʿummal, vol. 3, p. 372.
25. Al-Muttaqi al-Hindi, Kanz al-ʿummal, vol. 3, p. 373.
26. Al-Daylami al-Hamdhani, al-Firdaws, vol. 3, p. 94.
27. Ibn Hayyun, Daʿaim al-Islam, vol. 2, p. 190.

Love for Children

All humans need to be loved, but it is of essential importance to prioritize showing love and kindness to children. If children are deprived of love, they cannot achieve proper educational and moral development. This is why Islamic sacred texts place significant emphasis on showing love and kindness to children. There are numerous religious directives and instructions regarding kind treatment of children. Prophet Muhammad commanded, "Show love to children and have mercy and compassion towards them."[1]

The Commander of the Faithful, Imam 'Ali, is quoted as saying, "Within your family, show mercy toward the younger ones and show respect and dignity towards the older ones."[2]

This love is not a transaction or exchange but a gift. Parents have the obligation to show love to their children even though children may not reciprocate with mutual love towards them.

Sacred Islamic texts often highlight the importance of showing kindness and compassion towards children as one of the most virtuous human practices. In a hadith narrated by Imam al-Sadiq, Prophet Moses, son of Amram, asked God, "O Lord, which action is the most virtuous for You?" To which the reply came, "Showing love to children, for I have built their nature on My unity."[3]

Imam 'Ali, the Commander of the Faithful, emphasized, "It is incumbent upon you to show compassion to your children even more than they show compassion to you."[4]

In another hadith, Imam al-Sadiq asserted that those who fill their children with love and affection will undoubtedly be covered by God's mercy and forgiveness, stating, "Truly, God the Glorified and Esteemed will bestow mercy upon a person who harbors deep love and affection for his child."[5]

---

1. Muhammad b. Ya'qub al-Kulayni, al-Kafi, vol. 6, p. 49, hadith no. 3.
2. Al-Shaykh al-Mufid, al-Amali, p. 222.
3. Ahmad b. Muhammad b. Khalid al-Barqi, al-Mahasin, vol. 1, p. 293; al-Hasan b. Fadl al-Tabarsi, Makarim al-akhlaq, p. 237.
4. Ibn Abi al-Hadid, Sharh nahj al-balagha, vol. 20, p. 272, wisdom no. 152.
5. Muhammad b. 'Ali Ibn Babawayh, Man la-yahduruh al-faqih, vol. 3, p. 482.

Love and Kindness in Islamic and Christian Scriptures

A hadith transmitted from Prophet Muhammad states: "The best of people in terms of faith are those with the best moral character and the kindest to their families, and I am the kindest among you to my family."[6]

According to the Quran, it is an instinctive desire in human nature to feel love and affection towards their children and family: "The love of ... women and children ... has been made appealing to people" (Quran 3:14). However, it should be controlled lest it affects one's religious life.

Kissing the hands of one's children is the sign of the peak of affection and love towards them. Therefore, numerous hadiths strongly recommend the practice of kissing children's hands as a gesture of love. In one such hadith, the Messenger of God was seen kissing his grandsons, al-Hasan and al-Husayn (peace be upon them). A companion of the Prophet—one account, it was 'Uyayna, and on another, it was al-Aqra' b. Habis—remarked that despite having ten children, he had never kissed any of them. The Prophet, peace be upon him and his household, responded, "He who does not show mercy will not receive mercy."[7]

It is recommended that parents observe justice and fairness among their children, even in expressing love and affection. According to a hadith, the Prophet, peace be upon him and his household, was sitting along with a number of his companions. They encountered a man from among the Ansar (Helpers) who had two children. The man kissed one child but neglected the other. The Prophet inquired, "Why do you fail to uphold justice by only kissing one of them?"[8]

There is even a hadith that recommends observing justice in kissing one's children, as this act of justice will lead to God's satisfaction: "Truly, God the Exalted would like you to maintain fairness between your children even in the act of kissing them."[9]

Imam al-Hasan recounts an incident where the Prophet, peace be upon him and his household, was conversing with his companions. A child entered the mosque and headed towards his father, who lovingly wiped his hand over the child's head and seated him on his right knee. Shortly after, the man's daughter entered the mosque. When she approached her father, he also wiped his hand over her head out of compassion but made her sit on the ground rather than on his knee. The Prophet inquired, "Why did you not let her sit on your

---

6. Muhammad b. 'Ali Ibn Babawayh, 'Uyun akhbar al-Rida 'alayh al-salam, vol. 2, p. 38.
7. Ibn Shahrashub al-Mazandarani, Manaqib Al Abi Talib 'alayhim al-salam, vol. 3, p. 384.
8. Ibn Fahd al-Hilli, 'Uddat al-da'i wa-najah al-sa'i, p. 89; Muhammad Baqir Majlisi, Bihar al-anwar, vol. 101, p. 99, section 2.
9. Abolghasem Payandeh, Nahj al-fasaha, p. 306.

Love and Kindness in Islamic and Christian Scriptures

other knee?" The man promptly made her sit on his other knee. The Prophet then remarked, "Now you have observed justice."[10]

Saʿd b. Saʿd al-Ashʿari, a companion of the eighth Imam al-Rida, peace be upon him, once told him, "May I be sacrificed for you! There is a man who loves his daughters more than he loves his sons." The Imam responded, "Daughters and sons should be equal in love."[11]

Prophet Muhammad, peace be upon him and his household, emphasized the value of even a loving gaze at one's children, which brings them happiness and delight: "When a parent looks at their child with affection, and the child becomes delighted, God will reward the parent as if they have emancipated a slave." When asked, "O Messenger of God! What if the parent looks affectionately at the child three hundred and sixty times?" The Prophet replied, "God is the greatest [meaning God's generosity is vast; such a reward is assured]."[12]

Parents are encouraged to raise and train their children with love and compassion. Prophet Muhammad, peace be upon him and his household, emphasized this, saying, "May God have mercy upon those who, out of piety, aid their children by showing kindness towards them, forming strong bonds to them, teaching them, and educating them with discipline."[13]

There is a notable emphasis in hadiths on showing love and affection towards one's daughters. The Prophet, peace be upon him and his household, said, "God the Exalted is compassionate towards girls. Those who display compassion towards girls are held in the same esteem as those who cry out of fear of God, for those who cry out of fear of God will be forgiven by Him."[14]

However, this love and compassion have their boundaries and limitations. One should never commit sins or transgress religious boundaries for the sake of their children. Prophet Muhammad, peace be upon him and his household, advised one of his companions, Ibn Masʿad, saying: "Compassion for your family and your children should not lead you to commit sins and forbidden acts. For God the Exalted says in the Quran, 'The day when neither wealth nor children will avail [except him who comes to Allah with a sound heart]' (Quran 26:87-88)."[15]

---

10. ʿAbd Allah b. Abi al-Dunya, al-ʿAyal, vol. 1, p. 173, hadith no. 36.
11. Muhammad b. al-Hasan al-Tusi, Tahdhib al-ahkam, vol. 8, p. 114.
12. Fattal al-Nayshaburi, Rawdat al-waʿizin wa-basirat al-muttaʿizin, vol. 2, p. 369; Muhammad Baqir al-Majlisi, Bihar al-anwar, vol. 71, p. 80.
13. Husayn b. Muhammad Taqi al-Nuri al-Tabarsi, Mustadrak al-wasāil wa-mustanbat al-masāil, vol. 15, p. 169.
14. Al-Sharif al-Radi, Tanbih al-ghafilin, p. 352, hadith no. 526.
15. Al-Hasan b. Fadl al-Tabarsi, Makarim al-akhlaq, p. 457.

Love and Kindness in Islamic and Christian Scriptures

Significance and Effects

In sacred Islamic texts, numerous teachings emphasize the importance and impacts of showing love and affection toward children. Some of these teachings are outlined in the following sections.

Loving Children as a Characteristic of the Prophet's Followers

Those who fail to show mercy and affection towards children are distant from the teachings of Prophet Muhammad, peace be upon him and his household. He explicitly stated, "Those who show no mercy to young children and do not respect and honor the elderly are not from us."[16]

Conversely, those who demonstrate love and compassion towards children can achieve the esteemed status of companionship and friendship with the Prophet. He advised one of his close companions, Anas b. Malik, saying: "O Anas! Show mercy to young children ... so that you may be among my friends."[17]

Kindness towards Children Drawing Divine Mercy

Mercy and kindness towards children will indeed draw God's mercy upon us. As transmitted from Imam al-Sadiq in a hadith: "God will have mercy upon a servant of His who deeply loves his children."[18]

Loving Children as an Act of Worship

Showing love and affection towards one's child is not merely a maternal or paternal emotion; it is, in fact, an act of worshiping God. According to hadiths, Prophet Muhammad said, "He who kisses his child, God will inscribe for him a good deed [in the record of his actions]."[19]

In another hadith, the Prophet states, "Kiss your children, for with every kiss, there will be a degree for you in Paradise."[20]

The same is true when children show love and affection towards their children. The Prophet asserts, "When a pious child looks at his parents with the gaze of mercy, with each glance he will be rewarded the equivalent of an accepted hajj pilgrimage." He was asked,

---

16. Attributed to the Sixth Imam al-Sadiq, Misbah al-Shari'a, p. 69.
17. Sulayman b. Ahmad al-Tabarani, al-Mu'jam al-awsat, vol. 5, p. 328.
18. Muhammad b. Ya'qub al-Kulayni, al-Kafi, vol. 6, p. 50, hadith no. 5.
19. Muhammad b. Ya'qub al-Kulayni, al-Kafi, vol. 6, p. 49, hadith no. 1.
20. Al-Hasan b. Fadl al-Tabarsi, Makarim al-akhlaq, p. 220.

Love and Kindness in Islamic and Christian Scriptures

"O Messenger of God! What if he looks one hundred times a day?" He responded, "Yes, God is the greatest [meaning God's generosity is vast; such a reward is assured]."[21]

Showing love to children is not only an act of worship but one of the most virtuous acts. According to a hadith, Prophet Moses, son of Amram, asked God, "O Lord, which action is the most virtuous for You?" To which the reply came, "Showing love to children, for I have built their nature on My unity. If I take the life of children, I will take them to My Paradise with My mercy."[22]

▪ Neglecting Children Leading to Hell

Loving and caring for children is immensely valuable, attracting God's satisfaction and potentially saving parents from Hell, ensuring their good fate. Conversely, neglecting children, lacking kindness and love towards them, and perpetrating violence against them will lead to God's anger. Without repentance and seeking forgiveness from the child, such actions may lead to Hell.

In this regard, Imam al-Rida, the eighth Imam, recounted that a man approached Prophet Muhammad and confessed that he had never kissed a child. The Prophet, peace be upon him and his household, responded, "The one who shows no compassion towards children will be among the inhabitants of Hell."[23]

In contrast, showing love and affection to children will serve as a shield against the fires of Hell, as Prophet Muhammad, peace be upon him and his household, said, "Loving children will be a veil against the fire of Hell."[24]

▪ Paradise as a Reward for Kindness to Children

Children, especially at very young ages, perceive love and affection from others through kissing, which is a natural expression of love. Imam al-Sadiq recommended, "Frequently kiss your children, for with every kiss, you will earn a degree in Paradise, where each degree takes five hundred years to travel."[25]

Furthermore, showing affection towards one's children is believed to yield happiness on the Day of Resurrection. Prophet Muhammad, peace be upon him and

---

21. Fattal al-Nayshaburi, Rawdat al-waʿizin wa-basirat al-muttaʿizin, vol. 2, p. 368; Abu al-Fadl ʿAli al-Tabarsi, Mishkat al-anwar fi ghurar al-akhbar, p. 162.
22. Ahmad b. Muhammad b. Khalid al-Barqi, al-Mahasin, vol. 1, p. 293.
23. Muhammad b. al-Hasan al-Tusi, Tahdhib al-ahkam, vol. 8, p. 113.
24. Al-Sharif al-Radi, Tanbih al-ghafilin, p. 344.
25. Fattal al-Nayshaburi, Rawdat al-waʿizin wa-basirat al-muttaʿizin, vol. 2, p. 369.

his household, emphasized this by stating, "he who kisses his child will earn a good deed [recorded in his actions], and he who brings joy to his child, God will bring him joy on the Day of Resurrection."[26]

■ Neglecting Children as a Sign of Ignorance

Neglecting to show love to children is regarded as a manifestation of ignorance. Imam ʿAli, peace be upon him, admonished, "The elderly should exhibit compassion and affection towards the younger ones, and should not be like the cruel people of the [pre-Islamic] period of ignorance."[27]

---

26. Muhammad b. Yaʿqub al-Kulayni, al-Kafi, vol. 6, p 49.
27. Al-Sayyid al-Radi, Nahj al-balagha, sermon 166, p. 240.

Love and Kindness towards Parents

Father and mother are the very foundation of one's existence. From the helpless stages of infancy, through childhood, adolescence, youth, and into adulthood, parents consistently provide us with the utmost love and care. Therefore, they rightfully deserve the highest level of affection from us. Islam has outlined numerous instructions and directives emphasizing the obligation of kindness and respect towards parents, which we will explore in this section.

A beautiful manifestation of showing love to parents is to regard them with a gaze of mercy and affection, as advised by the sixth Imam al-Sadiq: "Do not cast your eyes upon your parents except with feelings of mercy and compassion."[1]

Islam even promises divine rewards for a kind and affectionate gaze towards one's parents. A hadith transmitted from Prophet Muhammad states: "A child's loving glance at their parents is considered an act of worship."[2]

The divine reward for this action is so great that every single loving gaze towards parents is said to carry the equivalent reward of performing a Hajj pilgrimage, a significant highly rewarded act of worship in Islam conducted in Mecca around the Kaaba.

An essential etiquette of showing love and kindness towards parents is to treat them with humility and modesty. Individuals should interact respectfully with their parents, dignifying them and refraining from any display of arrogance in their presence. As the Quran instructs, "Lower the wing of humility to them, mercifully" (Quran 17:24).

Another duty of children towards their parents to pray for them. A person asked the eighth Imam al-Rida whether he should pray for his parents even though they do not recognize the path of truth and are not committed to the right religious path. In response Imam al-Rida said, "Indeed, pray for them, donate on their behalf, and if they are alive and remain unconvinced, continue to treat them with kindness and love. For the Messenger of God [Muhammad] stated, 'Truly, God has tasked me with mercy, not with ingratitude [and unkindness].'"[3]

---

1. Muhammad b. Ya'qub al-Kulayni, al-Kafi, vol. 2, p. 158, hadith no. 1.
2. Al-Hasan b. 'Ali Ibn Shu'ba al-Harrani, Tuhaf al-'uqul, p. 46.
3. Muhammad b. Ya'qub al-Kulayni, al-Kafi, vol. 2, p. 159, hadith no. 8; Abu al-Fadl 'Ali al-Tabarsi, Mishkat al-anwar fi ghurar al-akhbar, p. 159.

Love and Kindness in Islamic and Christian Scriptures

In the Quran, God teaches us how to pray for our parents: "and say, 'My Lord! Have mercy on them, just as they reared me when I was [a] small [child]!'" (Quran 17:24).

In a supplication to God, the fourth Imam al-Sajjad prays: "O God, instill in me a profound reverence for my parents, akin to the awe one feels towards a powerful ruler, and grant me the dedication to them resembling the devotion of a compassionate mother! May my obedience and devotion to them bring greater joy to my heart than sleep to the weary and greater refreshment to my soul than drink to the thirsty. Help me prioritize their desires over my own, and may their satisfaction be more precious to me than my own."[4]

It is recommended that we also demonstrate love and kindness to the friends of our fathers. Luqman, the renowned wise man, advised his son: "Love your friend and the friend of your father."[5]

According to hadiths, daughters often exhibit more love towards their parents because God has created girls inherently inclined towards affection. Prophet Muhammad, peace be upon him and his household, said, "What blessings daughters are! They are graceful, supportive of their parents, close companions, and a source of blessings and affection."[6]

Significance and Effects of Love and Kindness towards Parents

Islamic teachings strongly emphasize the significance of love and kindness towards parents. In the following sections, we will explore some of these teachings.

Satisfaction of Parents linked with God's Satisfaction

Love and kindness towards parents not only brings about their satisfaction but also leads to the satisfaction of God. Prophet Muhammad describes the satisfaction of one's parents as intertwined with the satisfaction of God, stating: "God's satisfaction is linked with the satisfaction of the parents, and God's displeasure is linked with the displeasure of the parents."[7]

Consequently, according to the Prophet, those who seek to attain God's satisfaction must prioritize earning the satisfaction of their parents: "He who pleases his parents has indeed pleased God."[8]

---

4. Al-Sahifat al-Sajjadiyya, p. 116, supplication 24.
5. Al-Bidaya wa-l-nihaya, vol. 2, p. 128.
6. Muhammad b. Yaʿqub al-Kulayni, al-Kafi, vol. 6, p. 5.
7. Fattal al-Nayshaburi, Rawdat al-waʿizin wa-basirat al-muttaʿizin, vol. 2, p. 368.
8. Abolghasem Payandeh, Nahj al-fasaha, p. 760.

Love and Kindness in Islamic and Christian Scriptures

■ Kindness towards Parents as the Greatest Act of Worship

Kind treatment of one's parents is considered an act of worship, as Prophet Muhammad stated, "A child's affectionate glance at the face of his parents out of love for them is indeed an act of worship."[9]

Even a compassionate glance at one's parents carries a reward equivalent to that of performing a Hajj pilgrimage, as Prophet Muhammad stated. "When a pious child looks at his parents with the gaze of mercy, with each glance he will be rewarded the equivalent of an accepted hajj pilgrimage." He was asked, "O Messenger of God! What if he looks one hundred times a day?" He responded, "Yes, God has more and better than these rewards."[10]

■ Kindness towards Parent Leading to Friendship with the Prophet's Household

A person who shows love and kindness to their parents will be loved by the Prophet's Household and Shiite Imams. One day, a person approached Imam al-Sadiq, the sixth Shiite Imam, and spoke of his child's kind treatment of him and his wife. The Imam said, "I already loved him and now I love him even more."[11]

■ Kindness towards Parents Leading to Divine Mercy

Kind treatment of one's parents opens the doors of divine mercy, as Prophet Muhammad, peace be upon him and his household, said, "The doors of heaven open with mercy on four occasions: when it rains, when a child lovingly glances at the faces of his parents..."[12]

■ Failing to Show Love to Parents Leading to God's Anger

Islamic texts strongly caution against breaking the hearts of parents and causing them anger. According to these teachings, as long as parents are not pleased, God's pleasure is not attained. Prophet Muhammad states, "God's displeasure is linked with the displeasure of the parents."[13]

---

9. Muhammad b. Muhammad Ibn Ash'ath, Ja'fariyyat (al-Ash'athiyyat), p. 187; Al-Hasan b. 'Ali Ibn Shu'ba al-Harrani, Tuhaf al-'iqul, p. 46.
10. Muhammad b. al-Hasan al-Tusi, al-Amali, p. 307.
11. Muhammad b. Ya'qub al-Kulayni, al-Kafi, vol. 2, p. 161, hadith no. 12.
12. Muhammad b. Muhammad al-Shu'ayri, Jami al-akhbar, p. 101.
13. Fattal al-Nayshaburi, Rawdat al-wa'izin wa-basirat al-mutta'izin, vol. 2, p. 368.

Love and Kindness in Islamic and Christian Scriptures

■ Kindness to Parents as a Requirement for Acceptance of Worships

A prerequisite for the acceptance of acts of worship by God is to respect one's parents and treat them with love and kindness. Imam al-Sadiq states: "Even if one has been treated cruelly by their parents, God will not accept their prayers if they look at them angrily and hatefully."[14]

■ Unkindness to Parents leading to Humility in the World

One worldly consequence of unkindness towards one's parents is disgrace, dishonor, and humility in this world. According to a hadith transmitted from the Prophet, "There are three groups, if you are unkind to them, you will experience humiliation, including one's father."[15]

■ Neglecting One's Parents and Deprivation of Paradise

Those who are unkind and ungrateful to their parents will be deprived of admission to Paradise, as Imam al-Sadiq states, "Those who disrespect their parents will not enter Paradise."[16]

■ Unkindness to Parents leading to Shortened Life

One consequence of being unkind to parents is a shortened lifespan, as Prophet Muhammad stated, "Disrespecting parents shortens life."[17]

---

14. Muhammad b. Ya'qub al-Kulayni, al-Kafi, vol. 2, p. 349.
15. Muhammad b. 'Ali Ibn Babawayh, al-Khisal, vol. 1, p. 195.
16. 'Abd Allah b. Ja'far al-Himyari, Qurb al-isnad, p. 82; al-Shaykh al-Hurr al-'Amili, Wasail al-Shi'a, vol. 9, p. 454.
17. Al-Husayn b. Muhammad b. al-Hasan b. Nasr al-Halawani, Nuzhat al-nazir wa-tanbih al-khatir, p. 37; Husayn b. Muhammad Taqi al-Nuri al-Tabarsi, Mustadrak al-wasail wa-mustanbat al-masail, vol. 12, p. 334.

Love and Kindness towards Relatives

In addition to parents, spouse, and children, there are other relatives towards whom we should show kindness and compassion. This includes brothers, sisters, maternal and paternal uncles and aunts, their children, as well as the relatives of one's spouse.

It is a divine command to act kindly towards relatives. Observance of this directive leads to the attraction of divine mercy and increased livelihood. As transmitted in a hadith from the Prophet, "For one who promises one thing I promise four things: one who establishes relationships with relatives will secure four things: God's love, expansion of livelihood, lengthening of life, and admission into the paradise He has promised."[1]

Maintaining positive relationships with relatives can prevent grudges and foster love in hearts. Prophet Muhammad is quoted as saying: "Maintaining ties with relatives leads to increased wealth, love among family and relatives, and may delay death."[2]

In a hadith transmitted from the Commander of the Faithful Imam ʿAli, it is stated that "maintaining ties with relatives fosters love and diminishes the power of enemies."[3]

He is also quoted as saying, "Maintaining ties with relatives fosters compassion towards each other."[4]

In another hadith from Imam ʿAli, peace be upon him, it is stated, "Love and friendship among fathers pave the way for closeness among their children."[5]

According to a hadith, God the Exalted revealed to Moses, the son of Amram, peace be upon him, "O Moses! ... I created family and relatives out of My mercy and grace so that My servants may be compassionate towards them."[6]

Moreover, according to sacred Islamic texts, Imam ʿAli, peace be upon him, said, "Those who show kindness to their relatives will always receive love and friendship from them."[7]

---

1. Muhammad b. ʿAli Ibn Babawayh, ʿUyun akhbar al-Rida ʿalayh al-salam, vol. 2, p. 37.
2. Al-Husayn b. Saʿid al-Kufi, al-Zuhd, p. 41.
3. Al-Laythi al-Wasiti, ʿUyun al-hikam wa-l-mawaʿiz, p. 304.
4. Al-Laythi al-Wasiti, ʿUyun al-hikam wa-l-mawaʿiz, p. 149.
5. Nahj al-balagha, hadith no. 308.
6. Al-Hasan b. ʿAli Ibn Shuʿba al-Harrani, Tuhaf al-ʿuqul, p. 492.
7. Nahj al-balagha, sermon 23.

Love and Compassion toward Teachers and Students

There are numerous recommendations and directives emphasizing kind treatment of teachers and religious scholars within Islamic sources. In this section, we allude to some of the most significant instructions in this regard.

Those who generously share their knowledge and offer guidance to others deserve the utmost compassion and kindness. Islamic texts contain numerous directives regarding love and kindness towards religious scholars. For instance, the Quran states, "So he turned away from them and said, 'O my people, I had certainly conveyed to you the message of my Lord and advised you, but you do not like advisors.'" (Quran 7:79). This verse underscores the significance of expressing love towards those who offer guidance toward others. Indeed, this verse criticizes Prophet Salih's people for their failure to demonstrate love and kindness towards those who offer advice.

The Commander of the Faithful, Imam 'Ali, is quoted as saying, "The most beloved people to you should be those who show compassion and offer advice."[1]

In another hadith, Imam 'Ali stated, "For the sake of God, love those who strive to correct your religion and help you attain certainty in goodness."[2]

Imam 'Ali also asserted, "The most beloved people to you should be those who guide you toward the right paths and reveal your flaws to you."[3]

Moreover, he said, "There is no compassionate person like a well-wishing friend."[4]

In a description of religious scholars, the Commander of the Faithful, Imam 'Ali, said, "Know that, certainly, those creatures of Allah who preserve His knowledge offer

---

1. 'Abd al-Wahid b. Muhammad al-Tamimi al-Amidi, Tasnif ghurar al-hikam wa-durar al-kilam, p. 416, hadith no. 9503.
2. 'Abd al-Wahid b. Muhammad al-Tamimi al-Amidi, Tasnif ghurar al-hikam wa-durar al-kilam, p. 415, hadith no. 9478.
3. Al-Laythi al-Wasiti, 'Uyun al-hikam wa-l-mawa'iz, p. 404.
4. Al-Laythi al-Wasiti, 'Uyun al-hikam wa-l-mawa'iz, p. 531.

protection to those things which He desires to be protected and make His springs flow for the benefit of others. They interact with friendliness and meet each other with affection. They drink water from cups that quench thirst and return from the watering places fully satiated. Misgiving does not affect them, and backbiting does not gain ground with them. Allah has tied their nature with good manners. Because of this, they love each other and meet each other."[5]

One etiquette of expressing love and kindness towards one's teacher or a scholar is to gaze upon them with affection. Hadiths within Islamic sources stress that even if you do not have any questions, attending the gatherings of religious scholars and simply gazing at their faces may grant you shares of spirituality. For instance, Imam Musa b. Ja'far, peace be upon him, the seventh Shiite Imam, said, "Looking at the face of a religious scholar out of love for him is an act of worshiping God."[6]

The Commander of the Faithful, Imam 'Ali, said, "An hour of sitting in the presence of religious scholars is more beloved to God than one thousand years of worship, and looking at the face of religious scholars is more beloved to God than one year of worshipful stay in the Kaaba."[7]

Moreover, Islamic guidelines and instructions emphasize kindness and respectful treatment towards one's teacher. The Prophet of Islam stated, "Be kind … towards those from whom you learn."[8]

Furthermore, teachers should also show kindness towards their students. Their love and compassion for their students should be evident in their actions. This is why the Prophet said, "Be kind towards those whom you teach."[9]

It is narrated in sources that Prophet Muhammad showed kindness and compassion towards those who learned from him. When learners were sick, sad, or on a journey, he would visit them, alleviate their sadness, and inquire about their well-being and that of their families. If they needed anything, he would provide it, and if they did not, he would still express kindness and affection before bidding them farewell.[10]

---

5. Sharif al-Radi, Nahj al-balagha, p. 331, sermon 214.
6. Muhammad b. Muhammad Ibn Ash'ath, Ja'fariyyat (al-Ash'athiyyat), p. 194.
7. Ibn Fahd al-Hilli, 'Uddat al-da'i wa-najah al-sa'i, p. 75.
8. Al-Laythi al-Wasiti, 'Uyun al-hikam wa-l-mawa'iz, p. 202.
9. Muhammad Baqir al-Majlisi, Bihar al-anwar, vol. 2, p. 62.
10. Al-Shaykh Zayn al-Din al-Jaba'i al-'Amili al-Shahid al-Thani, Munyat al-murid fi adab al-mufid wa-l-mustafid, p. 195.

Love and Kindness in Islamic and Christian Scriptures

Significance and Effects of Showing Love and Kindness towards Teachers and Scholars

Prophet Muhammad emphasized the religious obligation for everyone to learn and expand their knowledge,[1] making knowledge and the love of knowledge among the highest values in Islam. Additionally, Islam places significant importance on love for those who possess and impart knowledge. In this section, we will explore some of the primary effects of demonstrating love and kindness towards teachers and scholars from an Islamic perspective.

Love and Kindness towards Scholars leading to Friendship with God and the Prophet

From the perspective of Islam, respecting scholars is tantamount to respecting God and the Prophet. According to a hadith transmitted from Prophet Muhammad, "O people! … You should love those who carry knowledge of the Quran. You should love your scholars. Do not be hostile towards them, do not be envious of them, and do not find fault in them. Beware! Those who love them love me, and those who love me love God, and those who hate them hate me, and those who hate me hate God. Have I made myself clear?"[2]

Mansur al-Bazraj, a companion of the sixth Imam al-Sadiq, peace be upon him, once said to the Imam, "My master! You frequently mention Salman al-Farsi [a Persian companion of the Prophet]." The Imam replied, "Do not say al-Farsi, but say Salman al-Muhammadi. Do you know why I mention him a lot?" He said no. The Imam said, "For three traits… the third is that he loved knowledge and scholars."[3]

Love and Kindness towards Scholars as an Act of Worshiping God

Showing love and kindness towards scholars is not merely a recommendation within Islam; it is considered an act of worshiping God. Imam Musa b. Jaʿfar, the seventh Shiite Imam, said, "Looking at the face of a religious scholar is an act of worshiping God."[4] Thus, even gazing upon one's teacher or a religious scholar can be regarded as a worshipful practice that leads to divine rewards.

Imam ʿAli advised his close companion Kumayl b. Ziyad, "Showing love towards scholars… leads to attaining divine obedience during life."[5]

---

1. Muhammad b. Yaʿqub al-Kulayni, al-Kafi, vol. 1, p. 30, hadith no. 1.
2. Nasr b. Muhammad al-Samarqandi, Tanbih al-ghafilin fi al-mawʿiza bi-ahadith sayyid al-anbiyaʾ wa-l-mursalin, p. 553, hadith no. 898.
3. Muhammad b. al-Hasan al-Tusi, al-Amali, p. 133.
4. Muhammad b. Muhammad Ibn Ashʿath, Jaʿfariyyat (al-Ashʿathiyyat), p. 194.
5. Al-Hasan b. ʿAli Ibn Shuʿba al-Harrani, Tuhaf al-ʿuqul, p. 170.

Love and Kindness in Islamic and Christian Scriptures

There is a divine reward for showing love and kindness towards scholars. Imam ʿAli, peace be upon him, addressed his companion Kumayl b. Ziyad al-Nakhaʿi once again, stating, "O Kumayl b. Ziyad! Love towards scholars is a religious practice that will be rewarded."

■ Love and Kindness towards Scholars leading to Salvation

According to the teachings of Prophet Muhammad, peace be upon him and his household, humanity can be classified into four distinct groups. Those not falling within these categories are deemed wretched, while those within them will attain salvation. The Prophet advised, "Be either a scholar [possessor of knowledge], a learner, a listener, or a lover of these groups. Do not be outside of these categories, lest you find yourself among the wretched."

■ Love and Kindness towards Scholars leading to Good Reputation

According to hadiths, expressing love and kindness towards scholars can result in a favorable reputation after one's passing. Imam ʿAli advised his companion Kumayl b. Ziyad, stating, "Showing affection to scholars... leads to a good reputation in the afterlife."

■ Unkindness towards Scholars resulting in Loss of Blessing

If a community mistreats scholars and those who provide counsel and guidance, it will miss out on their blessings and be deprived of other forms of blessings too. The Commander of the Faithful, Imam ʿAli, is quoted as saying, "A community devoid of guidance and devoid of love for those who offer guidance knows no blessing."

---

6. Al-Hasan b. ʿAli Ibn Shuʿba al-Harrani, Tuhaf al-ʿuqul, p. 170.
7. Muhammad b. ʿAli al-Karajaki, Kanz al-fawaʾid, vol. 2, p. 31.
8. Al-Hasan b. ʿAli Ibn Shuʿba al-Harrani, Tuhaf al-ʿuqul, p. 170.
9. Al-Laythi al-Wasiti, ʿUyun al-hikam wa-l-mawaʿiz, p. 535.

Showing Love and Kindness to Friends[1]

Love and kindness should be offered to all, yet friends deserve a special depth of affection. Indeed, within the bonds of friendship, there exists an expectation of heightened compassion and warmth, as friendship is essentially based on mutual love.

In Islamic moral teachings, friendship holds significant importance alongside the rights of friends. Believers are encouraged to extend kindness and compassion towards their companions. Certain hadiths advise that genuine friendship implies expressions of love and affection, while also cautioning against revealing every secret to one's friends. Imam ʿAli, the Commander of the Faithful, wisely advised, "Offer your friend all your affection, but do not offer him your complete trust."[2]

In Islamic teachings concerning believers' mutual love and friendship, when the bond between two believers strengthens, it is advised that they formalize their relationship through a brotherhood covenant. In this customary ritual, the two individuals recite a brotherhood contract and then regard each other as brothers. This practice holds great significance in Islam, which originally took place after the Battle of Badr during the early years of Islam. Prophet Muhammad established brotherhood covenants between forty-five individuals from the Ansar (Helpers) and forty-five from the Muhajirun (Migrants).[3]

Friends have an obligation to share sympathy and empathy with each other. The Commander of the Faithful, Imam ʿAli, wisely stated, "Offer all of your affection to your friend... and offer all of your empathy to him."[4]

Furthermore, the Imam also affirmed, "Sympathy towards friends is a sign of noble lineage."[5]

---

1. In crafting this chapter, we relied on the book Friendship in the Quran and Hadiths (in Persian) authored by Mohammad Mohammadi Reyshahdi.
2. Muhammad b. ʿAli al-Karajaki, Kanz al-fawāid, vol. 1, p. 93.
3. Muhammad Baqir al-Majlisi, Bihar al-anwar, vol. 19, p. 130.
4. Muhammad b. ʿAli al-Karajaki, Kanz al-fawāid, vol. 1, p. 93.
5. Al-Laythi al-Wasiti, ʿUyun al-hikam wa-l-mawāʿiz, p. 143, hadith no. 3193.

Love and Kindness in Islamic and Christian Scriptures

At times, one may harbor love for another yet have difficulty in expressing it. However, Islamic teachings emphasize the importance of openly expressing affection towards loved ones. Prophet Muhammad explains this etiquette, stating, "When one of you loves their companion or brother, they should convey this love openly."[6]

Such expression of love results in the strength of friendship. Imam al-Sadiq, the sixth Imam, advised, "When you love someone, express it, as this strengthens the bond of friendship between you."[7]

One manifestation of love is to greet the loved one with a cheerful smile. According to a hadith transmitted from Imam al-Baqir, the fifth Imam, a man once sought advice from Prophet Muhammad. Among his counsel, the Prophet advised, "Meet your brother with a cheerful face."[8]

In another hadith, it is stated that "a man's smile in the face of his religious brother is a good deed [warranting divine rewards], and removing trash from his way is also a good deed. God is not worshipped with anything more beloved than bringing joy into a believer's heart."[9]

Smiling at someone's face holds profound importance in Islamic teachings, as Imam al-Sadiq also emphasized, "When someone smiles at their religious brother, it counts as a good deed [which warrants divine rewards]."[10]

A fundamental expression of love is found in the humility and modesty one exhibits towards their beloved. Within a compilation of poems attributed to the Commander of the Faithful, Imam ʿAli, there exists a verse that beautifully encapsulates this point: "Lower the wing of humility for your friend, and be as kind to them as a father is to his children."[11]

Another aspect of love and friendship is showing love and affection for the friends of our friends. If we truly love someone, we should not harbor animosity towards their companions. Imam ʿAli aptly remarks, "When you befriend someone, be friendly with his friends, yet there is no need to adopt their enemies as your own."[12]

True friends are willing to point out each other's faults and imperfections. Imam al-Husayn, the third Imam, wisely noted, "When someone truly loves you, he will guide you through criticism, but when someone hates you, he will flatter you."[13]

---

6. Ahmad b. al-Hasan al-Barqi, al-Mahasin, vol. 1, p. 266.
7. Muhammad b. Yaʿqub al-Kulayni, al-Kafi, vol. 2, p. 644.
8. Muhammad b. Yaʿqub al-Kulayni, al-Kafi, vol. 2, p. 103.
9. Muhammad b. Yaʿqub al-Kulayni, al-Kafi, vol. 2, p. 206.
10. Muhammad b. Yaʿqub al-Kulayni, al-Kafi, vol. 2, p. 206.
11. Diwan mansub Amir al-Muʾminin ʿalayh al-salam, p. 49.
12. Ibn Abi al-Hadid, Sharh nahj al-balagha, vol. 20, p. 331.
13. Muhammad Baqir al-Majlisi, Bihar al-anwar, vol. 75, p. 128.

Love and Kindness in Islamic and Christian Scriptures

According to a Hadith transmitted from Prophet Muhammad, "Three things purify friendship: guiding the friend to their flaws, protecting them during their absence, and assisting them in adversity."[14]

A primary expression of love is honesty within friendship. Hypocritical or deceitful friendships are false unreal forms of love and camaraderie. Imam al-Sadiq quotes the Commander of the Faithful, Imam ʿAli, as saying: "If your friend regards you as a brother... extend to him your genuine loyalty and unwavering sincerity."[15]

God the Exalted revealed to Prophet David, peace be upon him, "My servants display friendship with their tongues while harboring hatred and animosity in their hearts. They outwardly seek worldly gains while concealing their deceit and trickery."[16]

Thus, loyalty is often considered a sign of friendship, as love rooted in loyalty is genuine sincere love.

In a friendship guided by honesty and sincerity, flattery becomes unnecessary. The Commander of the Faithful, Imam ʿAli, stated, "Indeed, those who truly love you never resort to flattery."[17]

Friendship extends beyond moments of calm and peace; it holds greater significance during times of suffering and adversity. Imam ʿAli emphasized, "The true helpfulness and empathy of a friend shine through during times of adversity."[18]

Kindness towards friends is demonstrated through good and gentle treatment. Prophet Muhammad, peace be upon him and his household, said, "Gentle treatment fosters friendship." Imam ʿAli, peace be upon him, remarked, "A good temper and gentle treatment not only increase livelihood but also foster intimacy among friends."[19]

Love is also shown by refraining from blaming, reproaching, or making sarcastic remarks towards a friend. The sixth Imam al-Sadiq stated, "When someone shows you their love and friendship, refrain from making sarcastic remarks, and if they err, do not sever ties with them. This is not the behavior of the Apostle of God, peace be upon him and his household, nor of his friends."[20]

---

14. Masʿud b. ʿIsa al-Warram b. Abi Firas, Majmuʿat al-Warram, vol. 2, p. 121.
15. Al-Laythi al-Wasiti, ʿUyun al-hikam wa-l-mawaʿiz, p. 137.
16. Abu al-Fadl ʿAli al-Tabarsi, Mishkat al-anwar fi ghurar al-akhbar, p. 84.
17. Al-Laythi al-Wasiti, ʿUyun al-hikam wa-l-mawaʿiz, p. 177.
18. Al-Laythi al-Wasiti, ʿUyun al-hikam wa-l-mawaʿiz, p. 354.
19. ʿAbd al-Wahid b. Muhammad al-Tamimi al-Amidi, Tasnif ghurar al-hikam wa-durar al-kilam, p. 255, hadith no. 5382.
20. Muhammad b. Yaʿqub al-Kulayni, al-Kafi, vol. 8, p. 150.

Love and Kindness in Islamic and Christian Scriptures

Significance and Effects of Love and Kindness towards Friends

Within Islamic sources, numerous hadiths emphasize the importance and effects of demonstrating love and kindness towards friends. In this section, we will explore some of these hadiths.

Divine Rewards for Love and Kindness towards Friends

Prophet Muhammad, peace be upon him and his household, said, "When two individuals become friends and companions, there will be a great divine reward for their friendship. The one most beloved to God the Exalted and the Esteemed between them is the one who shows more compassion towards his friend."[1]

Friendship as a Form of Kinship

As mentioned previously, family and kinship relations hold great significance within Islamic teachings. Additionally, in Islam, friendship is regarded as a form of acquired kinship.

According to a hadith, "friendship is one of the two forms of kinship,"[2] where one is by blood and the other is acquired.

Another Hadith states that "friendship is the most intertwined form of kinship."[3]

Moreover, Prophet Muhammad is quoted as saying, "The close relative is one who is close through friendship, even if their kinship relation is remote. And a stranger is one who is a stranger in friendship, even if their kinship relation is close."[4]

Unkindness towards Friends resulting in Loss of Ties to the Prophet and His Household

Those who neglect to demonstrate love and kindness towards their friends risk severing their ties to the Prophet of Islam and his household, the Shiite Imams. The sixth Shiite Imam, Jaʿfar al-Sadiq, stated, "Those who do not treat their friends kindly, do not show camaraderie towards their companions, do not share bread with those with whom they break bread, and fail to display good temper to those who show it to them, are not among us [the Prophet's Household]."[5]

---

1. Muhammad b. Yaʿqub al-Kulayni, al-Kafi, vol. 2, p. 120.
2. ʿAbd al-Wahid b. Muhammad al-Tamimi al-Amidi, Tasnif ghurar al-hikam wa-durar al-kilam, p. 87, hadith no. 1657.
3. Muhammad b. Muhammad al-Mufid, al-Irshad fi maʿrifa hujaj Allah ʿala al-ʿibad, vol. 1, p. 298.
4. Muhammad b. Yaʿqub al-Kulayni, al-Kafi, vol. 2, p. 643.
5. Ibn Idris al-Hilli, al-Saràir al-hawi li-tahrir al-fatawi, vol. 3, p. 578.

Love and Kindness in Islamic and Christian Scriptures

■ Supplicating to God to enable us to Show Love to Friends

In his supplications to God, in the book *Al-Sahifat al-Sajjadiyya*, Imam al-Sajjad, the fourth Imam, prays about his relations with his neighbors and friends as follows: "O God, enable me to respond to their (that is, my neighbors' and friends') evil with goodness, to endure their wrongdoing with patience. Grant me a positive opinion of each of them, devote myself to their needs, show humility by lowering my gaze before them, demonstrate gentleness and kindness in my interactions, show compassion to those who are suffering, and bring joy to them in their absence through my affection."

Love and Kindness towards Servants and Subordinates

Within the ethical framework of Islam, there is significant emphasis on upholding the rights of and showing kindness towards workers, laborers, servants, and subordinates. For example, it is stressed that employers should treat their employees with kindness and compassion. The Commander of the Faithful, Imam ʿAli, peace be upon him, articulated in his policy guidelines for his close companion Malik al-Ashtar, upon appointing him as the ruler of Egypt, "That commander of the army should have such a position before you that he renders help to them equitably and spends from his money on them and on those of their families who remain behind so that all their worries converge on the one worry for fighting the enemy. Your kindness to them will turn their hearts to you."[1]

One of the duties of a governor or ruler is to select and appoint officials and agents who demonstrate kindness and gentleness towards their subordinates. In the same covenant addressed to Malik al-Ashtar, Imam ʿAli also offers this advice: "Put in command of your forces the man who in your view is the best well - wisher of Allah, His Prophet and your Imam. The chastest of them in heart and the highest of them in endurance is he who is slow in getting enraged, accepts excuses, is kind to the weak and is strict with the strong; violence should not raise his temper and weakness should not keep him sitting. Also associate with considerate people from high families, virtuous houses and decent traditions, then people of courage, valor, generosity, and benevolence, because they are repositories of honor and springs of virtues. Strive for their matters as the parents strive for their child."[2]

Yet, while emphasizing significant and extensive acts of kindness and care towards subordinates, we should not overlook the importance of attending to minor and everyday

---
1. Al-Sayyid al-Radi, Nahj al-Balagha, p. 433, letter no. 53.
2. Al-Sayyid al-Radi, Nahj al-Balagha, p. 432, letter no. 53.

Love and Kindness in Islamic and Christian Scriptures

instances of care and treatment towards them. In another section of his letter of covenant to Malik al-Ashtar, Imam ʿAli observes: "Do not neglect to attend to their small matters, confining yourself to their important matters, because your small favors will also be of benefit to them while the important ones are such that they cannot ignore them."[3]

Even the smallest acts of kindness and affection can foster empathy among one's subordinates. In that same letter, Imam ʿAli advises Malik al-Ashtar: "Do not regard anything that you do to strengthen them as big nor consider anything that you have agreed to do for them as little (so as to give it up), even though it may be small, because this will make them your well-wishers and create a good impression of you."[4]

---

3. Al-Sayyid al-Radi, Nahj al-Balagha, p. 432, letter no. 53.
4. Al-Sayyid al-Radi, Nahj al-Balagha, p. 432, letter no. 53.

Love and Kindness between Merchants and Customers

Kindness between sellers and buyers, or merchants and their customers, is a crucial factor contributing to success in business. Imam al-Sadiq, the sixth Imam, peace be upon him, said, "The principles of conducting business with people are seven: patience, forgiveness, humility, generosity, compassion, goodwill, justice, and sincerity."[1] Therefore, a businessperson should treat customers with patience and gentleness, overlook their mistakes or unintended offenses, avoid displaying arrogance, show generosity and respect, conduct business with compassion and kindness, approach interactions with good intentions and sincerity, and uphold fairness and justice in all dealings.

Salespeople are encouraged to develop effective communication skills with buyers and foster a sense of empathy between themselves and customers. Imam al-Baqir, the fifth Imam, recounted, "In Kufa, the Commander of the Faithful [Imam 'Ali] would leave his governmental residence every morning and visit each and every market in the city... He would then stand at each market and proclaim, 'O merchants! Fear God, the Exalted and the Esteemed.' Upon hearing his voice, they would set aside their goods and approach him eagerly to listen to his words. He would then advise them, '...cultivate closeness with your buyers.'"[2]

Furthermore, in economic matters, those who exhibit generosity in lending money to others will attract love and popularity within society. Imam al-Sadiq said, "There are three things that foster love: lending money, humility, and donating one's possessions."[3]

Within Islamic culture, lending money to others (without charging interest) is considered superior to donating money outright. Muhammad b. Janab, a prominent Shiite figure, reported that Imam al-Sadiq, the sixth Imam, said, "Indeed, if money is lent, that will be more beloved to me than the money being donated."[4]

---

1. Attributed to the Sixth Imam al-Sadiq, Misbah al-Shari'a, p. 6.
2. Muhammad b. Yaʿqub al-Kulayni, al-Kafi, vol. 5, p. 151.
3. Al-Hasan b. ʿAli Ibn Shuʿba al-Harrani, Tuhaf al-ʿuqul, p. 316.
4. Muhammad b. ʿAli Ibn Babawayh, Thawab al-aʿmal wa-ʿiqab al-aʿmal, p. 138.

Love and Kindness towards Charitable and Benevolent Individuals

Those who exhibit kindness and love towards others are most deserving of receiving kindness and love in return. It is an obligation of gratitude to show even more love and kindness towards charitable and benevolent individuals who have treated us well. According to a hadith from the Commander of the Faithful, Imam ʿAli, "The best course of action is to show love and friendship to good people."[1]

In another Hadith, Imam ʿAli also states, "The most beloved people to you are those who frequently treated you well. If such a person is not around you, then the next most beloved are those whom you frequently treated well."[2]

One characteristic of scholars and knowledgeable individuals is their demonstration of love and kindness towards charitable and benevolent individuals. Imam ʿAli is quoted as saying, "O seekers of knowledge! There are many virtues in knowledge, foremost among them is humility... and next in importance is loving good people."[3]

God will reward those who show love towards benevolent individuals in the Hereafter. According to a hadith transmitted from Imam al-Sadiq, the sixth Imam, "The love of good people for good people brings divine rewards for the good people. The love of bad people for good people is a virtue for the good people. The enmity of bad people towards good people is an adornment for good people, and the enmity of good people towards bad people is a disgrace for the bad people."[4]

Showing love to benevolent people is a sign of unwavering commitment to religious faith. God the Exalted revealed to Prophet Moses, peace be upon him, "O Moses! Do not entrust your children with religious faith unless your child loves righteous people just like you."[5]

---

1. ʿAbd al-Wahid b. Muhammad al-Tamimi al-Amidi, Tasnif ghurar al-hikam wa-durar al-kilam, p. 429, hadith no. 9780.
2. Ibn Abi al-Hadid, Sharh nahj al-balagha, vol. 20, p. 308.
3. Muhammad b. Yaʿqub al-Kulayni, al-Kafi, vol. 1, p. 48.
4. Muhammad b. Yaʿqub al-Kulayni, al-Kafi, vol. 2, p. 640.
5. Al-Hasan b. ʿAli Ibn Shuʿba al-Harrani, Tuhaf al-ʿuqul, p. 490.

Love and Kindness towards Fellow Travelers

During journeys, individuals often find themselves spending time with traveling companions or fellow travelers. The trials and difficulties inherent in travel can sometimes test one's patience. However, it is during these challenging moments that it becomes even more crucial to demonstrate kindness and love towards one's fellow travelers.

It is recommended that we should be intimate, kind, and affectionate towards our traveling companions. Luqman, the renowned wise man, advised his son: "Be kind and affectionate towards your companions, except if they are engaged in sinning against God."[1]

In certain hadiths, it is emphasized that accompanying someone on a journey serves as a significant test for evaluating them as friends. For example, Imam al-Sadiq said, "Do not publicly label someone as your friend until you test them with three things: observe how they react when angered, whether they deviate from truth to falsehood in anger; assess their behavior with dirhams and dinars [money], and accompany them on a journey."[2]

---

1. Ahmad b. Muhammad b. Khalid al-Barqi, al-Mahasin, vol. 2, p. 360.
2. Muhammad Baqir al-Majlisi, Bihar al-anwar, vol. 71, p. 180.

Love and Kindness towards Neighbors

Humans are essentially social beings, and our existence thrives within communities. In order for our collective living to be harmonious, it is crucial to abide by certain laws and moral principles. Failure to do so can result in tension and hardship in our lives. Divine religions have provided guidelines and instructions for fostering better coexistence among humans. One of the fundamental units of this coexistence is the neighborhood. Neighbors should cultivate relationships based on friendship and kindness towards one another.

In a supplication to God, Imam al-Sajjad prays, "O God, enable me to befriend my neigbors. … Grant me a positive opinion of each of them, devote myself to their needs, show humility by lowering my gaze before them, demonstrate gentleness and kindness in my interactions, show compassion to those who are suffering, and bring joy to them in their absence through my affection."[1]

Prophet Muhammad advised Imam ʿAli, saying, "O ʿAli! Show respect to your neighbors, even if they are not Muslims."[2]

It is even recommended to spend money to express kindness towards neighbors. According to a hadith, "Those who seek worldly gains to avoid dependence on others, provide for their families' well-being, and show affection and kindness to their neighbors will meet God the Glorified and Esteemed on the Day of Resurrection, their faces shining like the full moon."[3]

One fundamental moral principle, often referred to as the Golden Rule, emphasizes the importance of loving one's neighbor as oneself. Prophet Muhammad is quoted as saying, "You have not truly believed in Islam unless you love your religious brother... or love for your neighbor what you love for yourself."[4]

---

1. Al-Sahifat al-Sajjadiyya, p. 124, supplication no. 26.
2. Muhammad b. Muhammad al-Shuʿayri, Jamiʿ al-akhbar, p. 84.
3. Muhammad b. Yaʿqub al-Kulayni, al-Kafi, vol. 5, p. 78, hadith no. 5.
4. Ibn Maja, Sunan Ibn Maja, vol. 1, p. 90.

Love and Kindness in Islamic and Christian Scriptures

The highest value in Islam is often considered to be good character traits and a gentle temperament of others. A primary manifestation of such virtues is the kind treatment of one's neighbors. In this context, Imam al-Sadiq advised one of his companions, Dawud b. Sarhan, saying, "O Dawud! Some character traits depend on others, and God distributes them as He sees fit. They may be present in someone without being present in their children, or they may exist in a servant without being present in his master. These traits include maintaining ties with relatives, showing love and friendship towards neighbors and companions, extending hospitality to guests, and the most prominent among them is modesty."[5]

---

5. Muhammad b. al-Hasan al-Tusi, al-Amali, p. 301.

Love and Kindness towards Guests

Within the Islamic religious tradition, there is significant emphasis on hospitality towards one's guests. Believers are recommended to show kindness and generosity to those who visit them.

In his characterization of the traits of true believers, the Commander of the Faithful, Imam ʿAli, affirmed, "Believers... cherish guests."[1]

Prophet Muhammad advised Imam ʿAli, saying, "O ʿAli! Show respect to your guest, even if he is an unbeliever."[2]

Demonstrating love and respect for guests includes offering them quality food. Sulayman al-Sarafi, a companion of Imam al-Sadiq, peace be upon him, reported the Imam's words: "A person's love and care for their religious brother are measured by their generosity in providing food."[3]

The host should be actively engaged in the gathering, maintaining eye contact with the guests, as Prophet Muhammad advised: "When one welcomes guests and [affectionately] meets them eye to eye, their eyes will be shielded from the fires of Hell."[4]

The host ought to greet guests with warmth, cheerfulness, and kindness, according to the remarks of the Commander of the Faithful, Imam ʿAli, who proclaimed, "Half of hospitality is found in cheerfulness."[5]

Another hadith asserts, "The cheerfulness on the face of the host is more beloved to God than the worships performed by one hundred prophets."[6]

In his counsel to Abu Dharr al-Ghifari, a distinguished companion, Prophet Muhammad advised, "O Abu Dharr! Offer your meal to those whom you love for the

---

1. Muhammad b. Muhammad al-Shuʿayri, Jamiʿ al-akhbar, p. 84.
2. Muhammad b. Muhammad al-Shuʿayri, Jamiʿ al-akhbar, p. 84.
3. Muhammad b. Yaʿqub al-Kulayni, al-Kafi, vol. 6, p. 279.
4. Husayn b. Muhammad Taqi al-Nuri al-Tabarsi, Mustadrak al-wasail wa-mustanbat al-masail, vol. 16, p. 258.
5. ʿAbd al-Wahid b. Muhammad al-Tamimi al-Amidi, Tasnif ghurar al-hikam wa-durar al-kilam, p. 434, hadith no. 9930.
6. Muhammad Nabi Tuysirkani, Liʾali al-akhbar, vol. 3, p. 66.

sake of God, and partake in the meal of those who love you for the sake of God, the Glorified and the Exalted."

According to a hadith narrated from Imam al-Rida, the eighth Shiite Imam, peace be upon him, "Visit one another to foster mutual love, shake hands, and refrain from harboring anger towards each other."

The Significance and Effects of Showing Love and Kindness to Guests

Within Islamic teachings, there is a significant emphasis on demonstrating kindness and affection towards guests. These principles are outlined in the following sections.

Partaking in the Host's Meal as a Gesture of Love and Respect

Accepting a host's invitation is a gesture of love and respect towards them. Another indication of such regard is partaking in the host's meal. A narrator recounts an incident where, along with Ibn Abi Ya'fur, a companion of Imam al-Sadiq, the sixth Imam, they visited the Imam along with several others. The Imam, as the host, ordered lunch to be served. They all had the meal, and the Imam joined them. The narrator, being the youngest in the gathering, felt shy about eating. The Imam reassured him, saying, "Eat the meal! Do you not know that a man's love and friendship towards his religious brothers are demonstrated by partaking in their meal?"

'Isa b. Abi Mansur, a companion of Imam al-Sadiq, was hosted by the Imam. The Imam placed roasted meat before 'Isa and remarked, "O 'Isa! It is said that a man's affection for his religious brother is measured by his readiness to eat the meal he has prepared."

Showing Love and Kindness to Guests leading to Continued Blessing

Hospitality towards guests is regarded as a factor contributing to the ongoing blessings and goodness. Prophet Muhammad emphasized this, saying, "My community will be blessed as long as they love one another, fulfill their trusts, abstain from forbidden deeds, honor and respect their guests, uphold prayers, and fulfill their zakat obligations."

---

7. Muhammad b. al-Hasan al-Tusi, al-Amali, p. 535.
8. Muhammad Baqir al-Majlisi, Bihar al-anwar, vol. 75, p. 347.
9. Muhammad b. Ya'qub al-Kulayni, al-Kafi, vol. 6, p. 278.
10. Muhammad b. Ya'qub al-Kulayni, al-Kafi, vol. 6, p. 278.
11. Sahifat al-Imam al-Rida, p. 43.

Love and Kindness in Islamic and Christian Scriptures

■ Hospitable Individuals being God's Friends

God loves and cherishes hospitable individuals, holding them in high regard. A practice greatly beloved by God is the offering of meals to others. Imam al-Baqir, the fifth Shiite Imam, peace be upon him, stated, "Indeed, God loves the act of offering meals."[12]

Imam al-Sadiq, the sixth Imam, recounted an incident where a group of polytheists from Yemen visited Prophet Muhammad. Among them was a man who spoke excessively and engaged in argumentation with the Prophet, leading to visible signs of anger on the Prophet's face. At that moment, Gabriel appeared to the Prophet and conveyed, "Your Lord sends His greetings and says, 'This is a generous man who offers meals to others.'" Upon hearing this, the Prophet's anger calmed down. He then addressed the man, saying, "I would have dismissed you if not for Gabriel reporting through God the Glorified and Esteemed that you are generous, offering meals to others." Intrigued, the man asked, "Does your Lord love generosity?" The Prophet affirmed, "Yes." Upon hearing this, the man immediately declared his faith, bearing witness that there is no god except Allah and that Muhammad is the Messenger of Allah. He then asserted, "I swear by the one who has sent you on the prophetic mission that I never denied anyone of my possessions."[13]

In Islamic tradition, honoring one's guests is synonymous with honoring God, and causing displeasure to a guest is deemed equivalent to displeasing God. Prophet Muhammad emphasized this, saying, "Do not burden yourself excessively for your guests, as it may lead you to resent them. Those who resent guests indeed resent God, and those who resent God will be resented by God."[14]

■ Showing Love and Kindness to Guests as a Sign of Piety

Prophet Muhammad once passed by a cemetery and observed a grave digger toiling to prepare a grave. Inquiring about the deceased, the Prophet learned it was for a particular individual. He then revealed, "He was known for his hospitality towards guests. Indeed, only the pious and God-fearing believers honor their guests."[15]

■ Hospitality towards Guests resulting in Illuminated Resurrection

According to hadiths, on the Day of Resurrection, when the sun dims and darkness dominates everything, the faces of those who showed hospitality towards their guests

---

12. Ahmad b. Muhammad b. Khalid al-Barqi, al-Mahasin, vol. 2, p. 387.
13. Muhammad b. Yaʿqub al-Kulayni, al-Kafi, vol. 4, p. 40.
14. Mulla Muhsin al-Fayd al-Kashani, al-Mahajjat al-baydā, vol. 3, pp. 32-33.
15. ʿAbd Allah b. Jaʿfar al-Himyari, Qurb al-isnad, p. 75.

will radiate like the full moon, illuminating the surroundings. For example, the Commander of the Faithful, Imam ʿAli, said, "Believers who harbor love for their guests will emerge from their graves [on the Day of Resurrection] with faces shining like the full moon."[16]

Showing Love to Guests leading to Forgiveness of Sins

Inviting guests to one's home will lead to the forgiveness of one's sins. The sixth Imam al-Sadiq told one of his companions, "O Husayn! Do you love your religious brothers?" He affirmed, "Yes." The Imam said, "Are you of profit to the poor among them?" He said "Yes." The Imam said, "Sure. You have the obligation to love those who love God. Beware that, I swear by God, when you are of profit to them you will love them. Do you invite them to your home?" He said "Yes. Indeed, I never eat a meal unless there are two or three or more of my religious brothers with me." Imam al-Sadiq then said, "Their grace upon you is greater than yours upon them." He said, "But I invite them to my home, give them from my meal, give them drinks, and they sit on my carpets, and yet they have grace upon me?" The Imam said, "Yes. When they enter your home, they cause your forgiveness and the forgiveness of your family, and when they leave your home, they take away your sins and the sins of your family."[17]

Furthermore, according to another hadith, "Believers who rejoice upon hearing the murmurs and whispers of their guests will find their sins forgiven by God, even if they were as numerous as the space between the earth and the sky."[18]

Showing Love to Guests leading to Protection from Hell

Prophet Muhammad emphasized that a loving and affectionate gaze towards guests serves as a safeguard against the fires of Hell. He stated, "When a person welcomes guests and looks upon their faces with love, God will protect their eyes from the fires of Hell."[19]

---

16. Muhammad b. Muhammad al-Shuʿayri, Jamiʿ al-akhbar, p. 136.
17. Ahmad b. Muhammad b. Khalid al-Barqi, al-Mahasin, vol. 2, p. 390.
18. Muhammad b. Muhammad al-Shuʿayri, Jamiʿ al-akhbar, p. 136.
19. Husayn b. Muhammad Taqi al-Nuri al-Tabarsi, Mustadrak al-wasail wa-mustanbat al-masail, vol. 16, p. 258.

Love and Kindness towards the Elderly

Demonstrating love and respect towards the elderly is a fundamental moral duty, as believers are instructed to uphold reverence for the elderly. One command highlighted in hadiths concerning the rights of the elderly is to display kindness towards them. In an admonition directed to the Shias, Imam al-Sadiq, the sixth Shiite Imam, stated, "You should show affection to the elderly among you and deter the ignorant and those who seek dominance. Otherwise, you will incur my curses until the Day of Resurrection."[1]

---

1. Muhammad b. Yaʿqub al-Kulayni, al-Kafi, vol. 8, p. 158.

Showing Love and Kindness to the Poor

There are individuals who may find themselves unable to fulfill their basic needs and rely on the assistance of charitable individuals. These individuals deserve even greater kindness and affection because they are in a vulnerable position, and their dignity and honor may be at risk. Due to their lack of financial resources, they often receive less respect from others. According to Islamic moral principles, it is not only commanded to help the poor but also to show love and kindness towards them. This is a divine directive addressed to believers. For example, a hadith attributed to Prophet Muhammad states, "My Lord has commanded me to show love to the destitute and the needy."[1]

Furthermore, another hadith emphasizes, "My Lord has commanded me to embody seven characteristics, [including] showing love towards the needy and drawing close to them."[2]

In another hadith, Prophet Muhammad counseled Imam ʿAli, saying, "God has bestowed upon you the love for the poor and the destitute, therefore, be like a brother to them."[3]

A piece of advice given by God to Prophet Jesus, which is emphasized within Islamic tradition, is reported in a hadith where God's communication to Jesus is relayed: "O Jesus! Adorn yourself with piety and love for the destitute, and walk humbly on the earth."[4]

Imam al-Sajjad, the fourth Shiite Imam, peace be upon him, implores God in a supplication, "O God, make companionship with the poor dear to me."[5]

---

1. Muhammad b. Yaʿqub al-Kulayni, al-Kafi, vol. 8, p. 8.
2. Al-Hasan b. Muhammad al-Daylami, Irshad al-qulub ila al-sawab, vol. 1, p. 74.
3. Muhammad b. al-Hasan al-Tusi, al-Amali, p. 561.
4. Muhammad b. Yaʿqub al-Kulayni, al-Kafi, vol. 8, p. 135.
5. Al-Sahifat al-Sajjadiyya, p. 203, supplication no. 30.

Love and Kindness in Islamic and Christian Scriptures

Our duties towards the poor extend beyond just providing financial aid. Additionally, we should hold love for them in our hearts and sincerely care for them. Prophet Muhammad advised his esteemed companion Abu Dharr al-Ghifari, saying, "You should harbor love for the destitute and keep their company."[6]

Mansur al-Bazraj, a companion of the sixth Imam al-Sadiq, peace be upon him, once said to the Imam, "My master! You frequently mention Salman al-Farsi [a Persian companion of the Prophet]." The Imam replied, "Do not say al-Farsi, but say Salman al-Muhammadi. Do you know why I mention him a lot?" He said no. The Imam said, "For three traits... the second is that he loved the poor and preferred them over the wealthy and the privileged."[7]

According to another hadith, it is emphasized that "one should love the destitute and needy among Muslims. Those who degrade them and display arrogance towards them have strayed from the path of God's religion, and God will humiliate and despise them. Our beloved Prophet Muhammad, peace be upon him and his household, said, 'My Lord has commanded me to love the poor among the Muslims.' If anyone humiliates a Muslim individual, God will pour out His hatred and disgrace upon them until they are despised by all. Indeed, God's hatred is the most severe. Therefore, fear God concerning your needy Muslim brothers; they have a right to be loved by you. God has commanded His Prophet, peace be upon him and his household, to love them. Those who do not love those whom God has commanded to be loved have disobeyed God and His Prophet. Those who die in a state of disobedience will be among the misguided."[8]

Imam 'Ali advised his son, Imam al-Hasan, peace be upon them, saying, "Refusing something to your fellow believer with grace and kindness is better than giving something unkindly."[9]

In addition to providing financial assistance and demonstrating love and affection towards the poor, we are also obligated to keep companionship with them. According to a hadith attributed to the Prophet, "Show love to the poor and keep their company."[10]

When we lack the financial means to assist a poor individual who requests our help, it is recommended that we decline their request with utmost kindness. The

---

6. Muhammad b. 'Ali Ibn Babawayh, Ma'ani al-akhbar, p. 335.
7. Muhammad b. al-Hasan al-Tusi, al-Amali, p. 133.
8. Muhammad b. Ya'qub al-Kulayni, al-Kafi, vol. 8, p. 8.
9. Al-Hasan b. 'Ali Ibn Shu'ba al-Harrani, Tuhaf al-'uqul, vol. 2, p. 68.
10. Muhammad b. 'Ali al-Karajaki, Kanz al-fawaid, vol. 6, p. 469, hadith no. 16583.

Love and Kindness in Islamic and Christian Scriptures

Commander of the Faithful, Imam ʿAli, stated, "Whatever you give, give it joyfully, but when you refuse, do so graciously and with legitimate excuses."[11]

A piece of advice given by God to Prophet Jesus, which is emphasized within Islamic tradition, is reported in a hadith where God's communication to Jesus is relayed: "O Jesus! Adorn yourself with piety and love for the destitute, and walk humbly on the earth."[12]

The Significance and Effects of Showing Love and Kindness to the Poor

There is significant emphasis on demonstrating love and affection towards the poor within Islamic sources. Let us review some of these aspects in the following sections.

Loving the Poor as equivalent to Loving God

Those who show kindness to the poor indeed love God. In the Quran, God says, "And be kind, for God loves those who are kind" (Quran 2:195).

The Commander of the Faithful, Imam ʿAli, is quoted as reporting that on the night of ascension, when Prophet Muhammad was elevated to the sky, God told the Prophet: "O Ahmad! Loving Me is equivalent to loving the poor. Therefore, bring the poor closer to you and sit in their proximity. Keep the wealthy away from yourself and avoid their company, for the poor are My friends."[13]

Moreover, Prophet Muhammad stated in a hadith, "The most beloved action to God is the joy that fills the heart of a believer by relieving his hunger or alleviating his sorrow."[14]

In contrast, those who demonstrate unkindness towards the poor will incur God's wrath. Imam al-Sadiq, the sixth Imam, remarked in this regard, "You should show love to the needy among the Muslims. Those who humiliate and show arrogance towards them have strayed from the path of God's religion, and God will humiliate them and display anger and hatred towards them."[15]

Extending Assistance to Others and Garnering Their Affection in Return

According to numerous hadiths, one significant means to cultivate love and affection from others is through acts of generosity and assistance. Imam ʿAli affirms that treating others

---

11. Al-Sharif al-Radi, Nahj al-Balagha, p. 440, letter no. 53.
12. Muhammad b. Yaʿqub al-Kulayni, al-Kafi, vol. 8, p. 135.
13. Al-Hasan b. Muhammad al-Daylami, Irshad al-qulub ila al-sawab, vol. 1, p. 201.
14. Muhammad b. Yaʿqub al-Kulayni, al-Kafi, vol. 2, p. 191.
15. Muhammad b. Yaʿqub al-Kulayni, al-Kafi, vol. 8, p. 8.

with goodness and kindness will result in enduring love and affection: "Those who show kindness to people will continually receive love and affection from them."[16]

In another hadith, Imam ʿAli asserts, "Those who consistently engage in acts of kindness will find themselves beloved by others."[17]

The Imam also affirms that demonstrating love and kindness towards others fosters an increase in affection and inclination towards oneself, stating, "Those who give generously and offer assistance without even being asked will be esteemed and beloved."[18]

Helping the Poor as Sign of Brotherhood

One duty among religious brothers is to provide mutual assistance and sympathy to each other. In a hadith attributed to Prophet Muhammad, it is narrated that a man had an appointment with the Prophet but arrived late. When asked for the reason, he explained, "I did not have clothes." The Prophet inquired further, "Did you not have a neighbor who could have lent you an extra garment?" The man replied, "Yes, O Messenger of God! [But he did not lend me clothes]." Upon hearing this, the Prophet remarked, "He is not your brother."[19]

Showing Love and Kindness to the Poor leading to Salvation

One of the primary outcomes of demonstrating love and compassion towards the poor is achieving salvation on the Day of Resurrection. God states in the Quran: "[And also] for those who were settled in the land and [abided] in faith before them, who love those who migrate to them, and do not find in their hearts any need for what they have been given, but prefer [the immigrants] over themselves, even though they are in need. And whoever is protected from the stinginess of his soul—it is those who will be the successful" (Quran 59:9).

Kindness to the Poor as the Key to Paradise

Paradise awaits those who aid the poor and treat them with kindness. According to a hadith attributed to Prophet Muhammad, "Everything has a key, and the key to Paradise is love and kindness towards the destitute and the poor."[20]

---

16. Al-Laythi al-Wasiti, ʿUyun al-hikam wa-l-mawaʿiz, p. 439, hadith no. 7632.
17. Al-Laythi al-Wasiti, ʿUyun al-hikam wa-l-mawaʿiz, p. 440, hadith no. 7645.
18. Al-Laythi al-Wasiti, ʿUyun al-hikam wa-l-mawaʿiz, p. 440, hadith no. 7645.
19. Muhammad b. ʿAli Ibn Babawayh, Musadaqat al-ikhwan, p. 36.
20. Abolghasem Payandeh, Nahj al-fasaha, p. 633.

Love and Kindness towards Orphaned Children

Orphans are children deprived of the blessing of having both a father and mother. They lack the special attention other children receive from their parents and may consequently suffer from emotional or social deficiencies. Therefore, religious texts in Islam strongly advocate for special care and kindness towards orphaned children. There are unequivocal and firm commands within Islamic sources regarding the compassionate treatment of orphans.

The Quran underscores the importance of upholding the integrity and dignity of orphans and advocates for their kind treatment: "And they ask you about the orphans. … if you associate with them, they are indeed your brothers" (Quran 2:220). This verse implies that orphans should be regarded and treated as one's own siblings.

One of our duties towards orphans is to show them affection and express love by caressing them. The sixth Shiite Imam al-Sadiq states, "If an individual tenderly and compassionately runs his hand over the head of an orphan, God the Glorified and Esteemed will grant him as many lights on the Day of Resurrection as the number of hairs on the orphan's head."[1]

The Prophet of Islam stated, "Be towards orphans like a merciful father, and know that you will reap what you sow."[2]

According to a hadith transmitted from Imam al-Rida, the eighth Imam, "If you encounter an orphan crying, soothe them with kindness and compassion. It is narrated that the 'Scholar' [referring to his father, the seventh Imam Musa al-Kazim] said, 'When an orphan cries, the Divine Throne trembles for them, and then God the Blessed and Exalted will inquire, Who has caused My servant, whose father I took

---

1. Muhammad b. ʿAli Ibn Babawayh, Man la-yahduruh al-faqih, vol. 1, p. 188.
2. Muhammad Baqir al-Majlisi, Bihar al-anwar, vol. 74, p. 171.

during his childhood, to cry? I swear by My dignity, magnificence, and exalted status that if a believer comforts an orphan, I will guarantee Paradise for them.'"[3]

Prophet Muhammad stated that if someone is concerned about how his children will be treated after his death, he should show kindness to other people's orphans. The second part of the above hadith, "Be towards orphans like a merciful father, and know that you will reap what you sow,"[4] implies that by treating other people's orphans kindly, one can expect others to treat their own orphans kindly after their death.

In this regard, the noble Quran states: "Let those fear [the result of mistreating orphans] who, were they to leave behind weak offspring, would be concerned on their account" (Quran 4:9).

It is recommended to treat orphans and widowed women with the kindness and care one would offer to their own family members. Prophet Muhammad, peace be upon him and his household, stated: "Relieve the orphan's hunger and be towards an orphan like a merciful father. Relieve the hunger of a widowed woman and be towards a widowed woman like a compassionate husband. If you do so, then you will be granted as many palaces in Paradise as the number of breaths taken in this world, with each palace being better than the world and all that it contains."[5]

Showing love and kindness towards orphans was a cherished practice embraced by the Prophet's Household, especially the Shiite Imams. Abu al-Tufayl, a companion of Imam ʿAli, the first Imam, recounted, "I witnessed ʿAli calling orphans to himself and feeding them honey, to the extent that some of his companions expressed, 'We wish we were orphans too!'"[6]

One act that invokes God's mercy is aiding orphans. According to a hadith transmitted from Imam al-Sadiq, "If someone seeks to be encompassed by God's mercy, … then he should show compassion and mercy towards orphans."[7]

There are divine rewards for showing kindness towards orphans. The Commander of the Faithful, Imam ʿAli, stated, "If a male or female believer affectionately runs their hand over an orphan's head out of compassion for him, God will record a good deed for each strand of the orphan's hair within their record of deeds."[8]

---

3. Muhammad Baqir al-Majlisi, Bihar al-anwar, vol. 79, p. 80.
4. Muhammad Baqir al-Majlisi, Bihar al-anwar, vol. 74, p. 171.
5. Abu al-Fadl ʿAli al-Tabarsi, Mishkat al-anwar fi ghurar al-akhbar, p. 168.
6. Ibn Shahrashub al-Mazandarani, Manaqib Al Abi Talib ʿalayhim al-salam, vol. 2, p. 75.
7. Muhammad b. ʿAli Ibn Babawayh, al-Amali, vol. 1, p. 389, hadith no. 15.
8. Al-Shaykh al-Hurr al-ʿAmili, Wasaʾil al-Shiʿa, vol. 21, p. 375.

Love and Kindness in Islamic and Christian Scriptures

Another effect of showing kindness towards orphans is the softening and tenderness of one's heart. According to a hadith, Prophet Muhammad advised one of his companions, saying, "Would you like your heart to become tender and your needs to be fulfilled? Show mercy and compassion to orphans, affectionately run your hand over their heads, and share your meal with them. By doing so, your heart will soften, and your needs will be met."[9]

---

9. Abolghasem Payandeh, Nahj al-fasaha, p. 160, hadith no. 27.

Love and Kindness towards the Sick

When someone falls ill and becomes bedridden, unable to work, they require increased attention, care, and love. This is why Islamic sacred texts offer specific recommendations regarding the care and kindness owed to the sick.

Within Islamic culture, there are directives advocating kind treatment and compassion towards the sick. According to a hadith, "God the Glorified and Esteemed revealed, 'I accept prayers only from those who are humble towards My greatness ... provide clothing to those without garments and show mercy to those afflicted with harm.'"[1]

Moreover, if one is the cause of someone's suffering, they should compassionately endeavor to alleviate their distress. A hadith transmitted from the Commander of the Faithful, Imam ʿAli, states: "If you have caused someone's affliction, then it becomes incumbent upon you to compassionately relieve their suffering."[2]

Physicians are encouraged to treat their patients with care and empathy. Prophet Muhammad advised a physician, saying: "Indeed, the true healer of diseases is God the Glorified and Esteemed, but you are a kind and compassionate assistant."[3]

Furthermore, Imam ʿAli is quoted as saying: "Be like a gentle and kind physician who applies medicine where it brings benefit."[4]

In hadiths, kindness and sympathy are often closely associated with medicine, to the extent that they are occasionally used interchangeably. For example, the eighth Shiite Imam, al-Rida, recounts an incident where his father, the seventh Imam Musa b. Jaʿfar, fell ill. During his sickness, "friends and sympathizers," referring to physicians, provided him with medicine.[5]

---

1. Al-Hasan b. ʿAli Ibn Shuʿba al-Harrani, Tuhaf al-ʿuqul, p. 306.
2. ʿAbd al-Wahid b. Muhammad al-Tamimi al-Amidi, Tasnif ghurar al-hikam wa-durar al-kilam, p. 666, hadith no. 1513.
3. Al-Muttaqi al-Hindi, Kanz al-ʿummal, vol. 10, p. 8, hadith no. 28100.
4. Muhammad Baqir al-Majlisi, Bihar al-anwar, vol. 2, p. 53.
5. Al-Shaykh al-Hurr al-ʿAmili, al-Fusul al-muhimma, vol. 3, p. 55.

Love and Kindness in Islamic and Christian Scriptures

In hadiths describing the etiquette of visiting the sick, it is advised that if the sick person is not afflicted with a contagious or dangerous illness, the visitor should gently run their hands over the sick person, touch their body and forehead, and sit nearby. According to a hadith attributed to Prophet Muhammad, "Visiting the sick is perfected by placing your hand on his forehead or hand, asking about his well-being, and greeting him with a handshake."[6]

Furthermore, the visitor should sit in close proximity to the sick person. Ibn ʿAbbas, a companion of the Prophet, recounted that "when the Prophet, peace and blessings be upon him, visited a sick person, he would sit beside their head."[7]

At times, the sick person may display external symptoms that evoke compassion and pity in others, but it is important not to make them uncomfortable by staring with pity for too long. Prophet Muhammad cautioned, "Do not gaze for long at those afflicted with disabilities or leprosy, as it may distress them."[8]

Furthermore, another hadith advises, "Do not look into people's shortcomings as masters do, but rather look into your own shortcomings as servants do. People fall into two categories: the afflicted and the healthy. Show compassion to the afflicted and express gratitude to God for your health."[9]

---

6. Muhammad b. al-Hasan al-Tusi, al-Amali, p. 639.
7. Nur al-Din al-Haythami, Majmaʿ al-zawáid, vol. 2, p. 297.
8. Muhammad Baqir al-Majlisi, Bihar al-anwar, vol. 72, p. 15.
9. Al-Hasan b. ʿAli Ibn Shuʿba al-Harrani, Tuhaf al-ʿuqul, p. 305.

Love and Kindness towards Tragedy-Stricken Individuals

Throughout life, tragedies or disasters may befall individuals within society, such as the loss of a loved one. During these times, it becomes the duty of others to offer sympathy, love, and kindness to those affected by the tragedy. When a believer experiences such hardships, their fellow believers empathize with their pain and suffering. As a hadith states, "The believers in their mutual mercy, kindness, and compassion are like a single body; when one part of the body suffers, the whole body responds with sleeplessness and fever."[1]

Prophet Muhammad said, "Believers are each other's brothers and are like one body; when one part of the body suffers, the rest of the body feels its pain."[2]

Crying during tragedies can serve as a means to alleviate pain. Therefore, hadiths recommend weeping and shedding tears during times of hardship. The Commander of the Faithful, Imam ʿAli, advised, "When a tragedy befalls you, allow yourself to shed tears, as it can bring calmness to you."[3]

When Prophet Muhammad's young son, Ibrahim, passed away, he cried so profoundly that tears flowed down his beard. Some of his companions remarked, "O Messenger of God! You forbid us from weeping, yet you yourself weep?" He responded, "This is not mere weeping, but an expression of mercy. Those who show no mercy will not be shown mercy."[4]

An etiquette of expressing love and kindness towards those facing tragedies, as outlined in Islamic teachings, involves shaking their hands and embracing them, offering solace and comfort to them. It is recommended to extend a handshake to those affected by hardships. When someone asked Prophet Muhammad about the significance

---

1. Husayn b. Saʿid al-Kufi al-Ahwazi, al-Muʾmin, p. 39.
2. Muhammad b. Yaʿqub al-Kulayni, al-Kafi, vol. 2, p. 166.
3. Muhammad b. Yaʿqub al-Kulayni, al-Kafi, vol. 3, p. 250.
4. Muhammad b. Yaʿqub al-Kulayni, al-Kafi, vol. 79, p. 76.

of shaking hands during times of sorrow, he responded, "It brings solace to the believer. Whoever consoles someone afflicted with a tragedy will receive a divine reward equal to theirs." This implies that enduring a tragedy brings divine reward, and comforting someone in such times earns the same divine reward.

From an Islamic perspective, God promises significant rewards to those who endure the trials and tragedies that befall them. Similarly, those who calm down and bring comfort to those facing tragedies will also receive divine rewards.

One divine reward promised to those who console individuals facing tragedy is the attainment of piety and companionship with righteous individuals. Jabir b. ʿAbd Allah, a companion of the Prophet, quotes him as saying, "Whoever consoles a sorrowful individual, God the Glorified and Exalted will clothe them with the garment of piety and will bestow peace and blessings upon their soul among the souls."

Ibn Masʿud, another companion of the Prophet, quotes him as saying, "Whoever consoles and comforts someone afflicted with a tragedy will receive a divine reward equal to his."

Those who bring patience and solace to those afflicted by tragedies will receive true faith from God. According to a hadith in Islamic sources, Prophet Abraham asked God, "O Lord! What is the reward for those who help sorrowful individuals to remain patient for Your sake?" In response, God said, "I will clothe them with the garment of faith, through which they will dwell in Paradise and be shielded from the fires of Hell."

God has promised Paradise to those who console and comfort the individuals afflicted by tragedy. Imam al-Sadiq quotes the Prophet as saying, "Consoling those suffering from a tragedy will lead to Paradise."

Those who bring comfort and solace to tragedy-stricken individuals will receive a Heavenly garment from God.

The soul of the deceased finds solace when their loved ones pray for God's forgiveness and mercy on their behalf. A hadith transmitted from Imam al-Sadiq states, "The deceased person will find joy when prayers for God's mercy and forgiveness are offered for him, much like a living person feels joy upon receiving a gift."

---

5. Zayn al-Din b. ʿAli al-Shhid al-Thani, Musakkin al-fuʾad ʿind faqd al-ahibba wa-l-awlad, p. 115.
6. Zayn al-Din b. ʿAli al-Shhid al-Thani, Musakkin al-fuʾad ʿind faqd al-ahibba wa-l-awlad, p. 115.
7. Al-Muttaqi al-Hindi, Kanz al-ʿummal, vol. 15, p. 658, hadith no. 42608.
8. Zayn al-Din b. ʿAli al-Shhid al-Thani, Musakkin al-fuʾad ʿind faqd al-ahibba wa-l-awlad, p. 117.
9. Muhammad b. ʿAli Ibn Babawayh, Man la-yahduruh al-faqih, vol. 1, p. 174.
10. Muhammad Baqir al-Majlisi, Bihar al-anwar, vol. 85, p. 308.

Kindness of Rulers towards Citizens

When it comes to governance and ruling over people, Islamic teachings underscore the importance of treating citizens with kindness and compassion. During his caliphate, the Commander of the Faithful, Imam ʿAli, appointed his companion Malik al-Ashtar as the governor of Egypt. In a letter of guidance addressed to Malik, certain principles were outlined for just governance and leadership. In one part of this covenant, the Imam advises Malik: " Habituate your heart to mercy for the subjects and to affection and kindness for them. Do not stand over them like greedy beasts who feel it is enough to devour them, since they are of two kinds, either your brother in religion or one like you in creation. They will commit slips and encounter mistakes. They may act wrongly, wilfully or by neglect. So, extend to them your forgiveness and pardon, in the same way as you would like Allah to extend His forgiveness and pardon to you, because you are over them and your responsible Commander (Imam) is over you while Allah is over him who has appointed you. He (Allah) has sought you to manage their affairs and has tried you through them."[1]

Moreover, the Imam recommends Malik: "do not consider anything that you have agreed to do for them as little (so as to give it up), even though it may be small, because this will make them your well-wishers and create a good impression of you."[2]

In another letter addressed to his appointed governor of Egypt, Muhammad b. Abi Bakr, Imam ʿAli advises: "Interact with humility towards the people and maintain a lenient treatment towards them."[3]

A ruler or governor is obligated to treat citizens kindly. The fourth Shiite Imam, al-Sajjad, peace be upon him, emphasizes: "The right of your fellow believers is … to wish for them what you wish for yourself and to dislike for them what you dislike for yourself. Treat the elderly men among them as you would your own father, the young as your brothers, the elderly women as your mothers, and the children as your own."[4]

---

1. Al-Sharif al-Radi, Nahj al-Balagha, p. 427, letter no. 53.
2. Al-Sharif al-Radi, Nahj al-Balagha, p. 433, letter no. 53.
3. Al-Sharif al-Radi, Nahj al-Balagha, p. 383, letter no. 27.
4. Muhammad b. ʿAli Ibn Babawayh, Man la-yahduruh al-faqih, vol. 2, p. 625.

Love and Kindness in Islamic and Christian Scriptures

The Commander of the Faithful, Imam ʿAli, stressed to his appointed rulers the importance of showing sympathy and kindness towards people. Prophet Muhammad, peace be upon him and his household, also said, "Tolerance is the pinnacle of wisdom. O God! If someone takes charge of the affairs of my community and deals with them kindly and patiently, then treat him kindly. But if he deals with them harshly, then treat him harshly."[5]

Imam ʿAli, peace be upon him, wrote to one of his appointed officials: "Add a little harshness to the mixture of leniency and remain lenient where leniency is more appropriate. Adopt harshness when you cannot do without harshness. Bend your wings (in humbleness) before the subjects. Meet them with your face broad and keep yourself lenient (in behaviour) with them. Treat them equally in looking at them with half eyes or full eyes, in signalling and in greeting so that the great should not expect transgression on your part and the weak should not lose hope in your justice; and that is an end to the matter."[6]

Imam al-Sadiq, the sixth Shiite Imam, told one of his companions, ʿAmmar b. Abi Ahwas, regarding the compassionate and kind nature of Shiite Imams as leaders of society: "Have you not observed that the governance of the Umayyad dynasty relied on the sword and injustice, whereas our Imamate or leadership is founded upon kindness, mercy, moderation, respect, good companionship, piety, and efforts? This is why people are drawn towards your religion and your beliefs."[7]

In another hadith, Imam ʿAli states, "Now, it is incumbent upon an official that the status he attains or the wealth with which he has been blessed should not alter his behavior towards those under his authority. Instead, the riches bestowed upon him by Allah should result in his closeness to his people and increase his kindness towards his religious brothers."[8]

Imam al-Sadiq, peace be upon him, declares, "The most virtuous rulers are those who possess three qualities: compassion, generosity, and justice."[9]

Prophet Muhammad, peace be upon him and his household, states, "One does not merit the status of leadership unless he embodies three qualities: a piety that shields him from transgressing against God, a patience that enables him to control his anger,

---

5. Muhammad b. ʿAli Ibn Abi Jumhur al-Ihsai, ʿAwali al-liʾali, vol. 1, p. 371.
6. Al-Sharif al-Radi, Nahj al-Balagha, pp. 420-421, letter no. 46.
7. Muhammad b. ʿAli Ibn Babawayh, al-Khisal, vol. 2, p. 354.
8. Al-Sharif al-Radi, Nahj al-Balagha (edited by Subhi Salih), p. 424, letter no. 50.
9. Al-Hasan b. ʿAli Ibn Shuʿba al-Harrani, Tuhaf al-ʿuqul, p. 319.

and compassionate governance over those under his authority, treating them with the kindness and mercy of a parent."[10]

Another hadith transmitted from Imam al-Sadiq says, "When the Trustworthy Spirit [Gabriel] informed the Prophet of his imminent death, despite being in good health without any illness, he called for a congregational prayer and instructed the Muhajirun [Migrants] and Ansar [Helpers] to bring their weapons. Upon gathering, the Prophet ascended the pulpit and announced his impending departure from this world. He then said, 'I advise those who will lead my community after me to fear God. I caution them to show mercy and kindness to the Muslim community, to honor the elders, to be compassionate towards the weaker individuals, and to respect and dignify the knowledgeable among them.'"[11]

The Prophet has also been quoted as saying, "If someone assumes a position of leadership within my community and treats them with kindness, then God the Exalted will instill awe for him in the hearts of the people. And if he extends goodness towards the people, God will sow love for him in their hearts."[12]

In his letter of covenant addressed to Malik al-Ashtar, whom he had appointed as the governor of Egypt, Imam ʿAli recommends: "If the subjects suspect you of high-handedness, explain to them your position openly and remove their suspicion with your explanation, because this would mean exercise for your soul and consideration to the subjects while this explanation will secure your aim of keeping them firm in truth."[13]

Rulers are advised to show kindness to the people, particularly when collecting taxes from them. In his letter of covenant to Malik al-Ashtar, the Commander of the Faithful, Imam ʿAli, describes leniency in tax collection as an example of the ruler's kindness towards the people, advising: "Look after the revenue (kharaj or land tax) affairs in such a way that those engaged in it remain prosperous because in their prosperity lies the prosperity of all others. The others cannot prosper without them, because all people are dependent on revenue and its payers. You should also keep an eye on the cultivation of the land more than on the collection of revenue because revenue cannot be had without cultivation and whoever asks for revenue without cultivation, ruins the area and brings death to the people. His rule will not last only a

---

10. Muhammad b. Yaʿqub al-Kulayni, al-Kafi, vol. 1, p. 407.
11. Muhammad b. Yaʿqub al-Kulayni, al-Kafi, vol. 1, p. 406.
12. Muhammad b. ʿAli al-Karajaki, Kanz al-fawaʾid, vol. 1, p. 135.
13. Al-Sharif al-Radi, Nahj al-Balagha, p. 442, letter no. 53.

moment. If they complain of the heaviness (of the revenue) or of diseases, or dearth of water, or excess of water or of a change in the condition of the land either due to flood or to drought, you should remit the revenue to the extent that you hope will improve their position. The remission granted by you for the removal of distress from them should not be grudged by you, because it is an investment which they will return to you in the shape of the prosperity of your country and the progress of your domain in addition to earning their praise and happiness for meeting out justice to them. You can depend upon their strength because of the investment made by you in them through catering to their convenience, and can have confidence in them because of the justice extended to them by being kind to them. After that, circumstances may so turn that you may have to ask for their assistance, when they will bear it happily, for prosperity is capable of hearing whatever you load on it."[14]

Furthermore, the Imam advises Malik al-Ashtar to appoint righteous individuals as his agents and advisors, as they are likely to be kind and compassionate towards the people: "The worst minister for you is he who has been a minister for mischievous persons before you, and who joined them in sins. Therefore, he should not be your chief man, because they are abettors of sinners and brothers of the oppressors. You can find good substitutes for them who will be like them in their views and influence, while not being like them in sins and vices. They have never assisted an oppressor in his oppression or a sinner in his sin. They will give you the least trouble and the best support. They will be most considerate towards you and the least inclined towards others. Therefore, make them your chief companions in privacy as well as in public."[15]

Furthermore, in the letter of covenant to Malik al-Ashtar, the Commander of the Faithful, Imam ʿAli, offers the following guidance: "That commander of the army should have such a position before you that he renders help to them equitably and spends from his money on them and on those of their families who remain behind so that all their worries converge on the one worry for fighting the enemy. Your kindness to them will turn their hearts to you."[16]

Certain hadiths affirm that when God intends to bless a nation, He bestows upon them a kind and compassionate ruler. For example, Imam al-Sadiq, peace be upon him, said,

---

14. Al-Sharif al-Radi, Nahj al-Balagha, p. 436, letter no. 53.
15. Al-Sharif al-Radi, Nahj al-Balagha, p. 430, letter no. 53.
16. Al-Sharif al-Radi, Nahj al-Balagha, p. 432, letter no. 53.

Love and Kindness in Islamic and Christian Scriptures

"Whenever God the Glorified and Exalted intends to bless a community, He appoints for them a compassionate ruler and grants them a just vizier."[17]

The Prophet of Islam conveyed, "God the Glorified and Exalted said, 'Indeed, I am Allah; there is no deity except Me. I have created the kings, and their hearts are in My hands. So, whenever a community obeys Me, I incline the hearts of the kings towards them, and whenever a community transgresses against Me, I turn the hearts of the kings against them. Beware of indulging in cursing the kings. Repent to Me so that I make their hearts compassionate towards you.'"[18]

According to a hadith transmitted from the Commander of the Faithful, Imam ʿAli, "God's hand is above the head of the ruler, running over it with mercy. Whenever the ruler becomes oppressive, God will leave him to his own devices."[19]

A just ruler can win the hearts of the people, as Imam ʿAli emphasizes in another hadith: "The hearts of the people are the treasures of their rulers. They will find therein whatever they have entrusted, whether it be justice or injustice."[20]

In his letter of covenant to Malik al-Ashtar, Imam ʿAli asserts: "The most delightful achievement for rulers is the establishment of justice in their domains and the expression of affection from their subjects. However, the love of subjects is only evident when their hearts are pure."[21]

Rulers are advised to maintain a balanced approach of kindness and decisiveness in their governance, as excessive kindness may lead to abuse. For instance, Imam al-Sadiq advised al-Najashi, the ruler of Ahvaz at the time: "Know that your salvation and deliverance depend on safeguarding innocent lives, preventing harm to God's devoted, showing kindness to the people, and practicing tolerance and gentle treatment, while avoiding both weakness and harshness."[22]

In a letter addressed to one of his agents and officials, Imam ʿAli commented on his harsh treatment of some non-Muslim peasants: "Now, the farmers of your city have complained about your severity, hard-heartedness, humiliating behavior, and harshness. Reflecting on this, I realized that since they are non-believers, they cannot be either

---

17. Muhammad b. ʿAli Ibn Babawayh, al-Amali, p. 245.
18. Muhammad b. ʿAli Ibn Babawayh, al-Amali, p. 365.
19. Muhammad b. Yaʿqub al-Kulayni, al-Kafi, vol. 7, p. 410.
20. ʿAbd al-Wahid b. Muhammad al-Tamimi al-Amidi, Tasnif ghurar al-hikam wa-durar al-kilam, p. 346, hadith no. 7983.
21. Al-Sharif al-Radi, Nahj al-Balagha, p. 433, letter no. 53.
22. Muhammad Baqir al-Majlisi, Bihar al-anwar, vol. 72, p. 361.

closely integrated with or completely separated from us due to our agreement with them. Therefore, deal with them with a balance between strictness and gentleness, maintaining a manner that combines both distance and proximity, depending on Allah's will."[23]

While maintaining decisiveness and firmness, a judge must approach both parties of a claim with humility and kindness. In a letter to his appointed ruler in Egypt, Muhammad b. Abi Bakr, Imam 'Ali wrote: "When you judge between people, behave humbly with them, show leniency, greet them with open arms, and treat them equally so that the influential do not expect favoritism from you, and the weak do not lose hope in your justice."[24]

In a letter to another appointed ruler, Imam 'Ali wrote: "Mix a little harshness with leniency, but always lean towards leniency when it is more suitable. Embrace severity when necessary. Humble yourself before the subjects, greet them warmly, and maintain a gentle demeanor."[25]

---

23. Al-Sharif al-Radi, Nahj al-Balagha, p. 376, letter no. 19.
24. Al-Hasan b. 'Ali Ibn Shu'ba al-Harrani, Tuhaf al-'uqul, p. 177.
25. Al-Sharif al-Radi, Nahj al-Balagha, p. 420, letter no. 46.

Love and Kindness towards Enemies

In our lives, we may encounter individuals who offend us or act unjustly towards us, leading to disagreements or hostilities. Sometimes, these conflicts may escalate to physical confrontations or even military encounters. From an Islamic perspective, we have the right to seek justice for the wrongs done to us, but this does not give us license to respond with violence or withhold kindness and compassion from others.

Islamic teachings emphasize peaceful coexistence with all people, as long as they do not engage in aggression against us. In the Quran, God says, "Allah does not forbid you from those who do not fight you because of religion and do not expel you from your homes - from being righteous toward them and acting justly toward them. Indeed, Allah loves those who act justly" (Quran 60:8). This verse encourages treating others with righteousness and justice, regardless of their beliefs or actions towards us.

This means that if our adversaries do not declare a religious war against us, do not exert pressure on us, or do not expel us from our homes, Islamic teachings instruct us to treat them with justice and kindness.

Indeed, Islamic teachings offer explicit directives regarding love and kindness not only towards fellow believers but also towards all humanity, regardless of their religious inclinations. According to one hadith, "Those who refrain from sins and those with pure hearts should show kindness and compassion towards those who commit sins and transgress against God."[1]

In another hadith, the Prophet states, "Win over the people, treat them with kindness, and do not engage in conflict with them until you have invited them [to peace]."[2]

According to a hadith, a Bedouin Arab approached Prophet Muhammad, peace be upon him and his household, asking him to teach him an action that would lead him to Paradise. The Prophet replied, "You have asked a concise yet profoundly significant question. ... Be

---

1. Al-Sharif al-Radi, Nahj al-Balagha, p. 197, sermon no. 140.
2. Al-Muttaqi al-Hindi, Kanz al-'ummal, vol. 4, p. 437, hadith no. 11300.

kind to your unjust and unkind relatives. But if you find it difficult to do so, then feed the hungry and provide water to the thirsty."[3]

The fifth Shiite Imam, Muhammad al-Baqir, stated, "Truly, God the Glorified and Exalted is gentle and loves gentleness, and He rewards gentleness in a way that He does not reward violence."[4]

If the other party is in the wrong, then we should advise them gently and kindly. Imam al-Sajjad, the fourth Imam, remarked, "The right of the adversary who has a claim against you... If his claim against you is false, then you should act kindly towards him, showing nothing in his matter except kindness. By doing so, you do not displease your Lord. And there is no strength except in God."[5]

Imam al-Sajjad also says, "Regarding the right of one who has harmed your destiny through a word or action, if it was intentional, forgiveness is more fitting for you. This may lead them to abandon such behavior in the future and treat others with kindness and respect. … However, if the harm was unintentional, do not respond with injustice by intentionally seeking retribution, as this would be retaliating for an unintentional offense. Instead, exercise patience and respond with kindness as much as possible. And there is no strength except in God."[6]

There are many instances within the tradition of the Prophet and Shiite Imams, where they stayed patient towards offences and harms of their adversaries, and responded to their unjust behaviors with love and kindness. For instance, a man from the Levant reports that one day he saw a man in Medina who had a calm and gorgeous face with such an exquisiteness that he had never seen in a man before. The man was wearing a beautiful garment and was riding a mount. The man's heart was inclined towards him. He asked others who this man was, and they said this was al-Hasan the son of ʿAli b. Abi Talib. The man says that upon hearing his name, a burning anger filled his body. He approached Imam al-Hasan and asked "Are you ʿAli's son?" When he confirmed, the man cursed him and his father. When his curse finished, Imam al-Hasan smiled and greeted him, asking "O old man! I believe you are a stranger her. Perhaps you have confused me with someone else. If you want us to give something to you, we give it to you. If you are seeking guidance, we will guide you. If you need help in carrying a baggage, we will help you. If you are hungry, we will give you food. If you do not have

---

3. ʿAbd ʿAli b. Jumʿa al-ʿArusi al-Huwayzi, Tafsir nur al-thaqalayn, vol. 5, p. 583.
4. Muhammad b. Yaʿqub al-Kulayni, al-Kafi, vol. 2, p. 119.
5. Al-Hasan b. ʿAli Ibn Shuʿba al-Harrani, Tuhaf al-ʿuqul, p. 268.
6. Al-Hasan b. ʿAli Ibn Shuʿba al-Harrani, Tuhaf al-ʿuqul, p. 271.

clothes, we will give you garments. If you have any needs, we will fulfil them. If you are banished and shelterness, we will give you a shelter. If you are our guest, we will host you until you depart, as our home is open to all the needy."

Upon hearing these words, the man from the Levant was impressed by Imam al-Hasan's patience and began to cry. He then said, "I bear witness that you are God's successor on the earth and God knows better where to place His mission. Before I met you, you and your father were the most hatered creatures in my eyes, and now that I knew you and your father, you are the most beloved creatures to me." After this encounter, the Imam took the man from the Levant to his home. As long as he stayed in Medina, he was hosted by Imam al-Hasan. He become a friend and companion with the Imam. His view of the Prophet's Household transformed and he converted to Shiism."[7]

Islamic sources condemn severing ties with those who have wronged us, emphasizing instead the importance of reconciling with our enemies. For example, Imam ʿAli advises, "Extend your hand in friendship to your enemy and treat them kindly, even if they resist. This is what God, the Glorified and Exalted, has commanded [as stated in the Quran]: 'Repel [evil] with that which is better.'"[8]

Islam permits the oppressed to seek retribution against their oppressors, yet it also encourages forgiveness. In Surah al-Baqara, the Quran endorses the principle of legal retribution (*qisas*) for those murdered and retaliation in personal rights, while also urging individuals with such rights to pardon and forsake retribution. It states: "O you who have believed, prescribed for you is legal retribution for those murdered - the free for the free, the slave for the slave, and the female for the female. But whoever pardons his brother, then there should be a suitable payment to him and compensation with good conduct. This is a concession from your Lord and a mercy. But whoever transgresses after that will have a painful punishment" (Quran 2:178).

During the Battle of Siffin between Imam ʿAli, the legitimate caliph of the time, and Muʿawiya, who had unlawfully remained in power as the ruler of the Levant and rebelled against Imam ʿAli, Muʿawiya's army blocked access to water for Imam ʿAli's forces. Imam ʿAli's army endured a night and a day without water until he dispatched an army led by Malik al-Ashtar to secure access. After a fierce battle, Imam ʿAli's army finally gained control of the water source.[9] His companions, angered by the previous denial of water, vowed not to share it with Muʿawiya's army. However, Imam ʿAli intervened, instructing

---

7. Muhammad Baqir al-Majlisi, Bihar al-anwar, vol. 43, p. 344.
8. Muhammad b. ʿAli Ibn Babawayh, al-Khisal, vol. 2, p. 633.
9. Muhammad Baqir al-Majlisi, Bihar al-anwar, vol. 41, p. 145.

his companions to share the water with their adversaries, despite their past cruelty and injustice, saying, "They had been unjust and cruel; you should not be like that."[10]

Meanwhile, ʿAmr b. al-ʿAs, Muʿawiya's trusted advisor, felt uneasy. He voiced his concern to Muʿawiya, saying, "What if ʿAli and his followers obstruct our access to water, as we did yesterday?" Muʿawiya asked him, "What do you think about this?" ʿAmr b. al-ʿAs responded, "ʿAli is known for his generosity and compassion; I doubt he would resort to such actions against us."[11]

The Conquest of Mecca was the significant moment when Muslims, led by Prophet Muhammad himself, took control of the city from the polytheists who previously held power there. This event was triggered by the Quraysh polytheists' breach of the Hudaybiyya Peace Treaty, which had been established between Muslims and the polytheists. Following the conquest, nearly all the polytheists of the Arabian Peninsula embraced Islam in the years that followed. Notably, key figures among the Quraysh polytheists, such as Abu Sufyan, had already converted to Islam before the Muslims' entry into Mecca. However, despite the victory, some Muslims, like Saʿd, advocated for retaliation against the polytheists for their past transgressions against Muslims. They proclaimed, "Today is the day of shedding blood; today the sanctity [of the people of Mecca] will be violated." In contrast, Prophet Muhammad emphasized mercy, declaring, "Today is the day of mercy," and subsequently issued a public decree of general amnesty.[12]

Islamic teachings contain clear directives advocating kindness towards enemies. Islam emphasizes that God forgives only those who forgive others, as stated in the Quran: "Repel [evil] by that [deed] which is better; and thereupon the one whom between you and him is enmity [will become] as though he was a devoted friend" (Quran 41:34). Additionally, a hadith attributed to Prophet Muhammad instructs, "Forgive each other so that grudges between you disappear."[13]

The significance of treating enemies with kindness is underscored by the allocation of zakat charities to winning their hearts. This portion of zakat expenditure, termed "bringing hearts together," aims to foster goodwill and compassion among those who may be drawn to Islam through financial assistance (Quran 8:41; 9:60).[14]

---

10. ʿAli b. Muhammad Ibn al-Athir, al-Kamil fi al-tarikh, vol. 2, p. 365; Nasr b. Muzahim al-Minqari, Waqʿa Siffin, p. 162.
11. Mahdi Ahmadi, Sayf al-waʿizin wa-l-dhakirin, p. 94.
12. Ibn Abi al-Hadid, Sharh nahj al-balagha, vol. 17, p. 272.
13. Abolghasem Payandeh, Nahj al-fasaha, p. 385.
14. Al-Shaykh al-Hurr al-ʿAmili, Wasāil al-Shiʿa, vol. 9, pp. 212-213.

Love and Kindness in Islamic and Christian Scriptures

In Islamic tradition, one response to those who wrong us is to offer them financial assistance. According to a hadith, the Prophet, peace be upon him and his household, was asked, "Which charity is the best?" He responded, "Charity to a relative who holds grudges against you."[15]

Islam, from its inception, has presented itself to the world with the motto of peaceful coexistence. The Quran underscores this principle, stating, "peace [or settlement] is best" (Quran 4:128).

The Quran frequently uses the words "sulh" and "silm" (both meaning peace and reconciliation), along with their derivatives, in diverse contexts and meanings. For example, it urges believers to embrace peace and reconciliation wholeheartedly: "O you who have believed, enter into peace completely [and perfectly] and do not follow the footsteps of Satan. Indeed, he is to you a clear enemy" (Quran 2:208). According to the Quranic perspective, while some may reject peace, Muslims are instructed not to initiate hostilities when the enemy offers peace (Quran 4:94).

Furthermore, Islamic teachings advise offering gifts to those who hold resentments towards us, as grudges can go away through such gestures. For example, a hadith transmitted from Imam al-Sadiq states, "Give gifts to each other because gifts take away the grudges."[16]

Significance and Effects of Showing Kindness to Enemies

Significant emphasis is placed on the kind treatment of one's enemies within Islamic sources. Some of these teachings are outlined in the following sections.

Showing Kindness towards Enemies as a Sign of Rationality

Kind treatment of one's enemies is viewed as a sign of rationality within Islamic teachings. For example, Prophet Muhammad, peace be upon him and his household, stated, "The peak of rationality, after religious commitment, is friendship and kindness towards people, and doing good to all people, whether pious or wicked."[17]

Kindliness towards Enemies turning them into Allies

One effect of showing kindness towards one's enemies is that it may lead to their

---

15. Muhammad b. Ya'qub al-Kulayni, al-Kafi, vol. 4, p. 10.
16. Muhammad Baqir al-Majlisi, Bihar al-anwar, vol. 72, p. 44.
17. Muhammad Baqir al-Majlisi, Bihar al-anwar, vol. 71, p. 401.

transformation into friends and allies. The Quran advises: "Repel [evil] by that [deed] which is better; and thereupon the one whom between you and him is enmity [will become] as though he was a devoted friend" (Quran 41:34).

Kindliness towards Hostility leading to God's Affection

Islamic teachings stress that showing kindness towards one's enemies can draw God's affection and love towards the individual. The fifth Shiite Imam, Muhammad al-Baqir, said, "Indeed, God the Glorified and Exalted is kind and favors kindness, and He rewards kindness in a manner He does not reward harshness and severity."[18]

Kind Treatment towards Enemies resulting in Security

Showing kindness towards one's enemies can help diminish hostilities and promote security within society. The sixth Shiite Imam, Jaʿfar al-Sadiq, peace be upon him, stated, "Friendship is better than fear."[19] This hadith implies that kindliness can reduce fears and creates security.

Praying to God for Help in showing Kindness towards our Enemies

There is a significant emphasis in hadiths on the kind treatment of enemies, to the extent that some supplications mentioned in Islamic sources are dedicated to asking God for help in showing kindness towards our adversaries. For instance, in his supplications, Imam al-Sajjad, the fourth Shiite Imam, prays to God: "O God ... replace for me the animosity of those filled with hatred with love, the envy of the insolent with affection, ... the enmity of close ones with friendship, the disrespect from relatives with devotion, the abandonment from kin with assistance, the sycophantic attachment with genuine love, the rejection from peers with generous kindness, and the bitterness of fear from wrongdoers with the sweetness of security!"[20]

---

18. Muhammad b. Yaʿqub al-Kulayni, al-Kafi, vol. 2, p. 119.
19. Al-Hasan b. ʿAli Ibn Shuʿba al-Harrani, Tuhaf al-ʿuqul, p. 357.
20. Al-Sahifat al-Sajjadiyya, p. 94, supplication no. 20.

Love and Kindness towards Prisoners of War

Throughout history, prisoners of war were often taken as slaves and subjected to forced labor. However, from the Islamic perspective, both prisoners of war and slaves are entitled to certain rights that should be respected. In the Quran, God commands Muslims to treat prisoners of war and slaves with kindness, alongside other vulnerable groups: "and to parents do good, and to … those whom your right hands possess" (Quran 4:36).

Nabih b. Wahab, one of the companions of Prophet Muhammad, reports that during the aftermath of the Battle of Badr, the Prophet recommended to Muslims about kind treatment towards the prisoners of the war: "Advise each other to show kindness towards the prisoners."[1]

When the Commander of the Faithful, Imam ʿAli, was struck by a sword during his prayer by Ibn Muljam al-Muradi, leading to his martyrdom two days later, he instructed his eldest son, Imam al-Hasan, after Ibn Muljam's arrest: "My son, treat your prisoner with kindness, show mercy and compassion towards him." He then lost consciousness. Upon awakening, Imam al-Hasan offered him a bowl of milk. ʿAli drank from it and then said, "Give the rest to your prisoner."[2]

In a supplication to God, Imam al-Sajjad expresses: "A display of the dignity of noble individuals is their kindness towards prisoners of war."[3]

One principle that must be upheld regarding prisoners of war is respect for their emotions. Even in times of conflict, we are obligated to avoid causing unnecessary

---

1. Ibn Kathir, al-Bidaya wa-l-nihaya, vol. 3, p. 373.
2. Husayn b. Muhammad Taqi al-Nuri al-Tabarsi, Mustadrak al-wasáil wa-mustanbat al-masáil, vol. 11, p. 79, hadith no. 12467.
3. Muhammad Baqir al-Majlisi, Bihar al-anwar, vol. 91, p. 121.

emotional harm to the enemy. Ibn Ishaq reports an incident during the conquest of the famous fort of Khaybar, which belonged to the Jews of Medina. When Muslims captured two Jewish women, who were then being escorted by Bilal to the command center, they had to pass through the battlefield. Upon seeing the corpses of their family members, the women were deeply affected, and one of them began to cry sorrowfully. In response to this oversight, the Prophet reproached and criticized Bilal, saying, "Is there no mercy in your heart that you bring these women near the corpses of their family members?"

---

4. Muhammad Baqir al-Majlisi, Bihar al-anwar, vol. 21, p. 5.

Factors Contributing to and Obstacles in Attracting Others' Affection

We all desire to gain the affection of others, but how can we effectively win their hearts? Sometimes, certain behaviors or character traits can result in hostility or the loss of love from others. Both Islam and Christianity provide guidance on this matter, and adhering to their teachings can aid in attracting people's affection.

Factors Contributing to Gaining Others' Affection

From an Islamic viewpoint, there exist several factors that foster love in hearts, alongside obstacles that hinder it. These are mentioned within Islamic sources, as delineated in the sections that follow.[1]

Divine Inspiration

The Quran emphasizes that it is God who instills love and affection in people's hearts. For example, a Quranic verse states, "and He placed between you affection and mercy" (Quran 30:21). Furthermore, the Quran recounts Prophet Abraham's supplication to God to incline people's hearts towards his descendants in Mecca: "So make hearts among the people incline toward them" (Quran 14:37). Additionally, God communicates to Prophet Moses, "And I bestowed upon you love from Me that you would be brought up under My eye" (Quran 20:39).

---

1. In crafting this chapter, we utilized the research presented in the book Friendship in the Quran and Hadith by Mohammad Mohammadi Reyshahri.

Love and Kindness in Islamic and Christian Scriptures

▪ Seeking Help from God

In Islamic teachings, it is encouraged to pray to God for a tender and affectionate heart. In a supplication attributed to the fourth Shiite Imam al-Sajjad, he says, "O God! Instill love for me in the hearts of Your servants … Do not let me be among the ignorant. Love me and make me beloved. Make beloved to me the words and actions that You love, so that I may engage in them with joy."[2]

Imam al-Rida, the eighth Imam, recounts an encounter when the fourth Imam al-Sajjad visited the mausoleum of his grandfather, the revered Commander of the Faithful, Imam ʿAli. There, he implored to God: "O God! Grant my soul contentment with Your ordained destiny, satisfaction with Your decree, fervor in remembering You and praying to You, love for Your chosen friends, being loved in Your earth and Your heaven, and patience in the face of Your trials."[3]

One piece of advice given to Imam ʿAli, peace be upon him, by the Prophet was as follows: "O ʿAli! Whenever you want to enter a city or village, upon seeing it, supplicate to God: 'O God! Grant us its goodness and shield us from its evil. O God! Make us beloved to its inhabitants and make its righteous dwellers love us.'"[4]

▪ Faith

From the Islamic viewpoint, belief in God the Exalted fosters love from others. The Quran asserts, "Indeed, those who have believed and done righteous deeds – the Most Merciful will appoint for them affection" (Quran 19:96), indicating that faith in God and virtuous deeds lead to being loved by people.

One reason why faith engenders love is the shared origin of the spirit of faith. This spirit originates from a single source and then manifests in numerous beings, leading to intimacy and friendship among them. Imam al-Sadiq, the sixth Imam, states: "The spirit of faith is one, originating from One God, and then distributed among diverse bodies, thereby resulting in friendship and love among them."[5]

Another factor that draws love from others is religious devotion. Imam al-Sadiq asserts: "Three things engender love: religion, humility, and generosity."[6]

---

2. Muhammad Baqir al-Majlisi, Bihar al-anwar, vol. 92, p. 298.
3. Jaʿfar b. Qualawayh, Kamil al-ziyarat, p. 40, hadith no. 1.
4. Ahmad b. Muhammad b. Khalid al-Barqi, al-Mahasin, vol. 2, p. 374; Muhammad b. ʿAli Ibn Babawayh, Man la-yahduruh al-faqih, vol. 2, p. 298.
5. Muhammad Baqir al-Majlisi, Bihar al-anwar, vol. 69, p. 193.
6. Al-Hasan b. ʿAli Ibn Shuʿba al-Harrani, Tuhaf al-ʿuqul, p. 316.

Love and Kindness in Islamic and Christian Scriptures

■ Piety and Worship

Piety and sincere worship of and devotion to God attract love from others. The eleventh Shiite Imam, al-Hasan al-'Askari, peace be upon him, remarks, "Those with pious characters, generous nature, and patient attribute will have many friends and earn widespread praise. Through such praise, they will find support against their enemies."[7]

The Commander of the Faithful, Imam 'Ali, advised his companions, saying: "Those who prostrate before God between the adhan and iqama [two calls to prayers in Islam] and sincerely supplicate, saying, 'O Lord! I have prostrated humbly, submissively, and devotedly,' God the Exalted will decree, 'O My angels, I swear by My Glory and Majesty that I will instill love for him in the hearts of My faithful servants and awe for him in the hearts of hypocrites.'"[8]

■ Devotion and Sincerity

As mentioned previously, when a believer devotedly and sincerely directs themselves towards God, He will inspire love for them in the hearts of people. The Prophet said, "Detach yourselves from worldly concerns as much as possible. For those who turn to God, He will soften people's hearts, filling them with affection and mercy, and He will hasten all goodness for him."[9]

Furthermore, Imam al-Sadiq, peace be upon him, declares, "Every believer who turns to God in prayer with all his heart, God will turn towards him with His face, and He will engender love for him in the hearts of believers after His own love for him."[10]

■ Friendship for God's Sake

Love can manifest in both worldly and divine forms, yet its endurance depends on the continuity of its underlying factors. In this context, the Commander of the Faithful, Imam 'Ali, states, "Love for the pleasures of this world will come to an end as their causes come to an end."[11]

---

7. Muhammad Baqir al-Majlisi, Bihar al-anwar, vol. 75, p. 379.
8. Sayyid b. Tawus, Falah al-sail wa-najah al-masail, p. 152; Muhammad Baqir al-Majlisi, Bihar al-anwar, vol. 81, p. 152.
9. Muhammad Baqir al-Majlisi, Bihar al-anwar, vol. 74, p. 166.
10. Muhammad b. 'Ali Ibn Babawayh, Thawab al-a'mal wa-'iqab al-a'mal, p. 135.
11. 'Abd al-Wahid b. Muhammad al-Tamimi al-Amidi, Tasnif ghurar al-hikam wa-durar al-kilam, p. 137, hadith no. 2405.

Love and Kindness in Islamic and Christian Scriptures

▪ Harmony of Hearts

Certain hadiths suggest that souls or spirits are acquainted with one another, which is why when two individuals, though never having met, possess harmonious souls, they are drawn to each other and come to have mutual affection. Prophet Muhammad, peace be upon him and his household, states: "Souls are like assembled troops (*junud mujannada*); those acquainted with one another will become friends, while those unfamiliar will exhibit discord."[12]

The Commander of the Faithful, Imam ʿAli, affirmed, "Souls possess forms. Those sharing similar forms will become friends, as people are naturally inclined towards those who resemble them."[13]

In another hadith, Imam ʿAli says, "When souls are in harmony, they cultivate friendship and intimacy."[14]

Imam al-Sadiq states, "Souls are like assembled troops. When they encounter each other, they sense one another's smell akin to horses. Once they recognize each other, they form bonds of intimacy, while those that do not recognize each other may become hostile. For instance, when a believer enters a mosque among a crowd, and only one individual shares his belief, his soul will gravitate towards that believer, leading him to sit beside him."[15]

▪ Good Temperament

One crucial method emphasized in Islamic teachings to obtain love from others is through good temperament and kindness. The Commander of the Faithful, Imam ʿAli, stresses the significance of good temperament, stating: "Good temperament fosters love and strengthens friendships." Furthermore, he emphasizes, "Maintain good temperament, for it endears you to others."[16]

In this context, Prophet Muhammad asserts, "Good temperament fortifies friendships."[17]

A hadith narrated from Imam al-Sadiq states, "Good temperament draws friendships."[18]

---

12. Muhammad b. ʿAli Ibn Babawayh, Man la-yahduruh al-faqih, vol. 4, p. 380.
13. Muhammad Baqir al-Majlisi, Bihar al-anwar, vol. 78, p. 92.
14. ʿAbd al-Wahid b. Muhammad al-Tamimi al-Amidi, Tasnif ghurar al-hikam wa-durar al-kilam, p. 423, hadith no. 9714.
15. Attributed to the Sixth Imam al-Sadiq, Misbah al-Shariʿa, p. 156.
16. ʿAbd al-Wahid b. Muhammad al-Tamimi al-Amidi, Tasnif ghurar al-hikam wa-durar al-kilam, p. 255, hadiths no. 5373-5374.
17. Muhammad Baqir al-Majlisi, Bihar al-anwar, vol. 74, p. 148.
18. Muhammad b. Yaʿqub al-Kulayni, al-Kafi, vol. 1, p. 27.

Love and Kindness in Islamic and Christian Scriptures

Conversely, bad temperament breeds hostility. Imam ʿAli, peace be upon him, asserts, "One with a bad temperament will turn companions and friends into enemies."[19]

Moreover, exhibiting kindness and fostering good companionship are instrumental in attracting and creating love. The Commander of the Faithful, Imam ʿAli, affirms that good behavior results in love, stating: "Good companionship increases affection for a person in the hearts of others."[20]

He also emphasizes that good behavior sustains enduring friendships, saying, "Friendship endures through good and kind companionship."[21]

According to a hadith transmitted from Prophet Muhammad, "Whoever assumes a leadership role within my community and exhibits good character, God the Exalted will instill awe for them in the hearts of people. And whoever extends a hand for goodness towards the people will receive love from them."[22]

▪ Smiling and Cheerful Appearance

Smiling and maintaining a cheerful appearance when meeting others can greatly contribute to attracting their love. In this regard, the Commander of the Faithful, Imam ʿAli, stated, "The best way for people to win the hearts of their friends and to dispel hostility from the hearts of their enemies is through a cheerful countenance when meeting them, inquiring about them during their absence, and showing joy in their presence."[23]

Another hadith transmitted from Imam ʿAli asserts, "Maintaining a cheerful countenance, giving gifts, performing good deeds, and greeting people will attract their love and affection."[24]

According to Imam ʿAli, maintaining a cheerful demeanor is a helpful means for fostering friendships, as he says, "Cheerfulness is a cause leading to friendship."[25]

Another hadith states, "Cheerfulness is a way of attaining friendships."[26]

---

19. ʿAbd al-Wahid b. Muhammad al-Tamimi al-Amidi, Tasnif ghurar al-hikam wa-durar al-kilam, p. 265, hadith no. 5716.
20. ʿAbd al-Wahid b. Muhammad al-Tamimi al-Amidi, Tasnif ghurar al-hikam wa-durar al-kilam, p. 435, hadith no. 9951.
21. ʿAbd al-Wahid b. Muhammad al-Tamimi al-Amidi, Tasnif ghurar al-hikam wa-durar al-kilam, p. 435, hadith no. 9949.
22. Muhammad b. ʿAli al-Karajaki, Kanz al-fawaʾid, vol. 1, p. 135.
23. Al-Hasan b. ʿAli Ibn Shuʿba al-Harrani, Tuhaf al-ʿuqul, p. 218.
24. ʿAbd al-Wahid b. Muhammad al-Tamimi al-Amidi, Tasnif ghurar al-hikam wa-durar al-kilam, p. 434, hadith no. 9938.
25. ʿAbd al-Wahid b. Muhammad al-Tamimi al-Amidi, Tasnif ghurar al-hikam wa-durar al-kilam, p. 434, hadith no. 9927.
26. Al-Hasan b. ʿAli Ibn Shuʿba al-Harrani, Tuhaf al-ʿuqul, p. 202.

Love and Kindness in Islamic and Christian Scriptures

A hadith transmitted from the fifth Imam, Muhammad al-Baqir, declares: "A smiling face and cheerful countenance lead to the acquisition of love and friendship, drawing one closer to God the Glorified and Exalted, while a frowning face and sullen countenance lead to hatred and estrangement from God."[27]

Fudayl ibn Yasar, a companion of both the fifth and sixth Imams, narrates from either Imam al-Baqir or Imam al-Sadiq that "Performing acts of kindness towards others and maintaining a cheerful countenance will result in the acquisition of love and entry into Paradise, whereas stinginess and a sullen countenance will lead to remoteness from God and entry into Hell."[28]

Prophet Muhammad states, "Three things purify one's love and friendship with their Muslim brother, and one of them is to greet them with cheerfulness whenever encountering them."[29]

▪ Kind Speech

A gentle tongue is a highly effective tool for garnering the love of others. The Commander of the Faithful, Imam 'Ali, remarks in this regard, "One whose words are soft will inevitably attract love from others."[30]

Imam al-Sajjad, the fourth Imam, asserts that speaking gently leads to increase in wealth and love from others.

One means of winning the affection of others is through greetings. Prophet Muhammad advised his companions: "Shall I inform you of something that, if you do it, you will love one another? Spread greetings among yourselves frequently."[31]

The Commander of the Faithful, Imam 'Ali, asserts, "Greeting others will draw people's love."[32] He further emphasizes, "Shake hands with one another and exchange gifts, for handshakes foster love and gifts dissolve grudges."[33]

Luqman, the renowned wise man mentioned in the Quran, advises his son, "Let your words be pure and your countenance cheerful, thus becoming even more beloved among people than those who give them gifts."[34]

---

27. Al-Hasan b. 'Ali Ibn Shu'ba al-Harrani, Tuhaf al-'uqul, p. 296.
28. Muhammad b. Ya'qub al-Kulayni, al-Kafi, vol. 2, p. 103.
29. Muhammad b. Ya'qub al-Kulayni, al-Kafi, vol. 2, p. 643.
30. Al-Hasan b. 'Ali Ibn Shu'ba al-Harrani, Tuhaf al-'uqul, p. 91.
31. Abu al-Fadl 'Ali al-Tabarsi, Mishkat al-anwar fi ghurar al-akhbar, p. 123.
32. 'Abd al-Wahid b. Muhammad al-Tamimi al-Amidi, Tasnif ghurar al-hikam wa-durar al-kilam, p. 434, hadith no. 9938.
33. Nu'man b. Muhammad, Da'aim al-Islām, vol. 2, p. 326.
34. Ibn Hanbal, al-Zuhd, p. 65.

Love and Kindness in Islamic and Christian Scriptures

▪ Leniency

Within Islamic texts, fostering love is associated with leniency and kindness towards others. A hadith attributed to Imam ʿAli emphasizes this, stating, "Nothing can attract love like generosity, leniency, and a good temperament."[35]

In another hadith, Imam ʿAli advises, "Be gentle and kind, for those who embody gentleness will consistently receive love from those around them."[36]

Furthermore, Imam ʿAli emphasizes that leniency towards others sustains friendly relations: "Companionship and friendship endure through leniency and kindness."[37]

He also states, "Those with a lenient character will inevitably be loved."[38]

▪ Expression of Love and Friendship

To obtain others' love and friendship, we should openly express our affection. Expressing love is a powerful factor in attracting the love of others. The Commander of the Faithful, Imam ʿAli, emphasizes that expressing love and friendship fosters and strengthens relationships: "Friendship is formed through the expression of love."[39]

In another hadith, the Imam states, "Love is strengthened through the expression of affection."[40]

On the contrary, displaying hostile behavior and expressing hatred towards others will breed enmity. In this regard, Imam ʿAli states, "Those who cultivate intimacy with others will be loved by them, while those who express hostility towards others will be hated."[41]

▪ Restraint and Avoidance of Hostility

One factor leading to attraction of others' love is exercising restraint and self-control. In

---

35. ʿAbd al-Wahid b. Muhammad al-Tamimi al-Amidi, Tasnif ghurar al-hikam wa-durar al-kilam, p. 244, hadith no. 4991.
36. ʿAbd al-Wahid b. Muhammad al-Tamimi al-Amidi, Tasnif ghurar al-hikam wa-durar al-kilam, p. 250, hadith no. 5205.
37. ʿAbd al-Wahid b. Muhammad al-Tamimi al-Amidi, Tasnif ghurar al-hikam wa-durar al-kilam, p. 422, hadith no. 9673.
38. ʿAbd al-Wahid b. Muhammad al-Tamimi al-Amidi, Tasnif ghurar al-hikam wa-durar al-kilam, p. 417, hadith no. 9538.
39. ʿAbd al-Wahid b. Muhammad al-Tamimi al-Amidi, Tasnif ghurar al-hikam wa-durar al-kilam, p. 414, hadith no. 9448.
40. ʿAbd al-Wahid b. Muhammad al-Tamimi al-Amidi, Tasnif ghurar al-hikam wa-durar al-kilam, p. 414, hadith no. 9449.
41. ʿAbd al-Wahid b. Muhammad al-Tamimi al-Amidi, Tasnif ghurar al-hikam wa-durar al-kilam, p. 426, hadith no. 10582.

a lengthy hadith, Prophet Muhammad conveyed to Sham'un b. Lawi, "The rewards of self-restraint include ... making friends."[42]

Imam al-Sadiq, the sixth Shiite Imam, advises, "To ensure the purity and sincerity of your friendship with your religious brother, ... never exhibit hostility towards him."[43]

Imam 'Ali, peace be upon him, emphasizes that overlooking a friend's wrongdoings strengthens friendship: "Forgive the faults of your religious brothers so that your friendships with them endure."[44]

■ Forgiveness

The Quran teaches that responding to bad with good is a powerful practice. By choosing to respond to negativity with kindness, one can transform enemies into close friends. This principle is beautifully articulated in Quran 41:34: "The good deed and the bad deed are not equal. Repel [evil] with what is better; then the one whom between you and him is enmity [will become] as though he was a devoted friend."

In this regard, the Commander of the Faithful Imam 'Ali says, "Forgive the faults of your religious brothers so that your friendships with them endure."[45]

■ Exchanging Gifts

Offering gifts is another means of creating affection in relationships. Prophet Muhammad emphasized this when he said, "Gifts foster love and friendship, renew brotherhood, and erase grudges."[46]

He also encouraged, "Exchange gifts to foster love and exchange gifts to remove grudges."[47]

In another Hadith, the Prophet emphasized, "Exchange gifts, for they remove resentments from hearts and eradicate feelings of hostility and hatred."[48]

Imam 'Ali, the Commander of the Faithful, emphasizes that giving gifts fosters love, stating: "Gifts magnetize affection."[49]

---

42. Al-Hasan b. 'Ali Ibn Shu'ba al-Harrani, Tuhaf al-'uqul, p. 16.
43. Al-Hasan b. 'Ali Ibn Shu'ba al-Harrani, Tuhaf al-'uqul, p. 312.
44. 'Abd al-Wahid b. Muhammad al-Tamimi al-Amidi, Tasnif ghurar al-hikam wa-durar al-kilam, p. 422, hadith no. 9749.
45. 'Abd al-Wahid b. Muhammad al-Tamimi al-Amidi, Tasnif ghurar al-hikam wa-durar al-kilam, p. 422, hadith no. 9749.
46. Muhammad Baqir al-Majlisi, Bihar al-anwar, vol. 74, p. 166.
47. Muhammad b. Ya'qub al-Kulayni, al-Kafi, vol. 5, p. 144.
48. Muhammad b. Ya'qub al-Kulayni, al-Kafi, vol. 5, p. 143.
49. 'Abd al-Wahid b. Muhammad al-Tamimi al-Amidi, Tasnif ghurar al-hikam wa-durar al-kilam, p. 435, hadith no. 9960.

Love and Kindness in Islamic and Christian Scriptures

In this context, the eighth Imam, ʿAli b. Musa al-Rida, cites Prophet Muhammad as saying: "Gifts dissolve grudges from hearts."[50]

■ Generosity and Open-Handedness

Generosity and open-handedness are qualities that draw love from others. In Islamic traditions, Prophet Jesus is quoted as saying, "How can one fulfill the love of their companion if they do not share from what they possess?"[51]

The Commander of the Faithful, Imam ʿAli, underscores the key role of generosity in attracting love, expressing: "Generosity leads to acquisition of love,"[52] "Generosity cultivates love,"[53] and "The generous individual is loved and admired, even if none of their generosity reaches those who praise them, while the miserly person is the opposite of this."[54]

In this regard, Imam al-Rida asserts, "Hearts incline towards love for those who treat them kindly and towards hatred for those who treat them unkindly."[55]

Furthermore, a hadith transmitted from Imam al-Hasan al-ʿAskari states, "People show greater love towards those in whom they place more hope."[56]

According to hadiths, a key action that garners love from others is generosity and offering assistance. The Commander of the Faithful, Imam ʿAli, emphasizes that kindness towards others and acts of charity result in enduring love from them. He states, "Those who show kindness towards people will earn enduring love from them."[57]

In another hadith, Imam ʿAli asserts, "One who consistently shows benevolence will be loved by their fellow believers."[58]

Furthermore, Imam ʿAli highlights that kindness towards others will amplify love

---

50. Muhammad b. ʿAli Ibn Babawayh, ʿUyun akhbar al-Rida ʿalayh al-salam, vol. 2, p. 74.
51. Al-Hasan b. ʿAli Ibn Shuʿba al-Harrani, Tuhaf al-ʿuqul, p. 507.
52. ʿAbd al-Wahid b. Muhammad al-Tamimi al-Amidi, Tasnif ghurar al-hikam wa-durar al-kilam, p. 378, hadith no. 8523.
53. ʿAbd al-Wahid b. Muhammad al-Tamimi al-Amidi, Tasnif ghurar al-hikam wa-durar al-kilam, p. 378, hadith no. 8521.
54. ʿAbd al-Wahid b. Muhammad al-Tamimi al-Amidi, Tasnif ghurar al-hikam wa-durar al-kilam, p. 379, hadith no. 8587.
55. Muhammad b. ʿAli Ibn Babawayh, Man la-yahduruh al-faqih, vol. 4, p. 381.
56. Al-Husayn b. Muhammad b. al-Hasan b. Nasr al-Halawani, Nuzhat al-nazir wa-tanbih al-khatir, p. 145.
57. ʿAbd al-Wahid b. Muhammad al-Tamimi al-Amidi, Tasnif ghurar al-hikam wa-durar al-kilam, p. 386, hadith no. 8811.
58. ʿAbd al-Wahid b. Muhammad al-Tamimi al-Amidi, Tasnif ghurar al-hikam wa-durar al-kilam, p. 386, hadith no. 8812.

and affection from them, stating: "One who offers assistance without being requested will be esteemed and loved."[59]

According to hadiths, humans are bound to kindness, as Imam ʿAli, peace be upon him, stated, "Benevolence paves the way to love."[60]

The Imam also remarked, "Engaging in good deeds... attracts people's love."[61]

Regarding generous individuals, Imam ʿAli, peace be upon him, asserted, "The generous person not only receives blessings and rewards from God but also earns love and respect from people."[62]

A hadith transmitted from the ninth Imam, al-Jawad, peace be upon him, states: "Three character traits attract love, one of which is empathy with others during times of difficulty."[63]

▪ Lending Money

According to hadiths, lending money fosters love. Imam al-Sadiq, the sixth Imam, stated, "Three things foster love: religion, humility, and giving money."[64]

▪ Disinterest in People's Wealth

Showing disinterest in people's wealth can indeed win their hearts. Imam ʿAli, peace be upon him, advised, "Win people's love by showing indifference towards what they possess. In doing so, you will earn their love and friendship."[65]

▪ Empathy during Hardships

Empathy towards others and assisting them during times of hardship will lead to attraction of their love. Prophet Muhammad states, "Three things purify friendship: guiding the friend to their flaws, protecting them during their absence, and assisting them in adversity."[66]

---

59. ʿAbd al-Wahid b. Muhammad al-Tamimi al-Amidi, Tasnif ghurar al-hikam wa-durar al-kilam, p. 377, hadith no. 8511.
60. ʿAbd al-Wahid b. Muhammad al-Tamimi al-Amidi, Tasnif ghurar al-hikam wa-durar al-kilam, p. 109.
61. Husayn b. Muhammad Taqi al-Nuri al-Tabarsi, Mustadrak al-wasail wa-mustanbat al-masail, vol. 8, p. 454.
62. ʿAbd al-Wahid b. Muhammad al-Tamimi al-Amidi, Tasnif ghurar al-hikam wa-durar al-kilam, p. 124, hadith no. 2169.
63. ʿAli b. ʿIsa al-Irbili, Kashf al-ghimma fi maʿrifat al-aimma, vol. 2, p. 349.
64. Al-Hasan b. ʿAli Ibn Shuʿba al-Harrani, Tuhaf al-ʿuqul, p. 316.
65. ʿAbd al-Wahid b. Muhammad al-Tamimi al-Amidi, Tasnif ghurar al-hikam wa-durar al-kilam, p. 318, hadith no. 4506.
66. Masʿud b. ʿIsa al-Warram b. Abi Firas, Majmuʿat al-Warram, vol. 2, p. 121.

Love and Kindness in Islamic and Christian Scriptures

The Commander of the Faithful, Imam ʿAli, holds that fairness and empathy are key to sustaining friendship, while their absence may breed enmity. He articulates, "Religious brothers require three pillars in their relationship: mutual fairness, mutual compassion, and avoidance of envy. If they uphold these, their friendship endures; otherwise, they may drift apart and become enemies."[67]

Imam al-Jawad, the ninth Imam, peace be upon him, stated, "Love can be cultivated through three character traits: fairness in interactions, empathy in hardships, and possessing a pure and sincere heart."[68]

In Imam ʿAli's perspective, a hallmark of genuine love and friendship is its continuity during times of hardship and difficulty. He affirms, "True friendship reveals itself in times of hardship and adversity."[69]

■ Showing Goodwill

Another means to garner others' affection is through benevolence, kindness, and good intentions. It is not always necessary to spend money to win others' love; instead, we can achieve it through displaying goodwill. The Commander of the Faithful, Imam ʿAli, asserts, "Having good intentions fosters love."[70]

Another hadith transmitted from Imam ʿAli states: "The most effective means to attract divine mercy is to hold compassion for all people within your heart."[71]

The Imam also asserts, "One who harbors good intentions will receive abundant divine rewards, will lead a pleasant and fulfilling life, and will certainly be loved."[72]

■ Respect and Politeness

One factor that fosters and strengthens love and friendship is the practice of respect and politeness. The seventh Shiite Imam, Musa al-Kazim, peace be upon him, advises, "Do not let the respect between you and your fellow believer go away. Retain

---

67. Al-Hasan b. ʿAli Ibn Shuʿba al-Harrani, Tuhaf al-ʿuqul, p. 322.
68. Muhammad Baqir al-Majlisi, Bihar al-anwar, vol. 75, p. 82.
69. ʿAbd al-Wahid b. Muhammad al-Tamimi al-Amidi, Tasnif ghurar al-hikam wa-durar al-kilam, p. 424, hadith no. 9734.
70. ʿAbd al-Wahid b. Muhammad al-Tamimi al-Amidi, Tasnif ghurar al-hikam wa-durar al-kilam, p. 224, hadith no. 4547.
71. ʿAbd al-Wahid b. Muhammad al-Tamimi al-Amidi, Tasnif ghurar al-hikam wa-durar al-kilam, p. 450, hadith no. 10344.
72. ʿAbd al-Wahid b. Muhammad al-Tamimi al-Amidi, Tasnif ghurar al-hikam wa-durar al-kilam, p. 92, hadith no. 1604.

some of it, for its disappearance will erode modesty, whereas preserving respect will safeguard friendship."[73]

Moreover, the Commander of the Faithful, Imam ʿAli, states in this regard: "True and sincere friendship can only exist with those who are polite."[74]

One highly effective way to cultivate love from others is by showing respect when addressing them. Prophet Muhammad, peace be upon him and his household, said, "Three things purify one's love for his Muslim brother; among them is addressing him by the names he prefers and making room for him to sit in gatherings."[75]

Visits and Ties with Relatives

Visiting friends and maintaining ties with relatives can indeed foster love from others and promote the spread of kindness and affection. Prophet Muhammad stated, "Visits serve to strengthen friendships."[76]

He also said, "O relatives! Visit each other but do not become neighbors. Exchange gifts. For visits strengthen bonds, while becoming neighbors may lead to severance of ties."[77]

Imam ʿAli, peace be upon him, affirmed that having relationships with relatives fosters love: "Maintaining ties with relatives results in love and eradicates enmity."[78]

According to a hadith transmitted from the fifth Imam, Muhammad al-Baqir, "Maintaining ties with relatives purifies one's deeds... and endears one to their family."[79]

Gratitude

Gratitude and thankfulness are indeed significant in earning others' love. The sixth Imam, Jaʿfar al-Sadiq, peace be upon him, said, "Nothing can enhance love and friendship like gratitude."[80]

---

73. Al-Hasan b. ʿAli Ibn Shuʿba al-Harrani, Tuhaf al-ʿuqul, p. 370.
74. ʿAbd al-Wahid b. Muhammad al-Tamimi al-Amidi, Tasnif ghurar al-hikam wa-durar al-kilam, p. 434, hadith no. 9912.
75. Muhammad b. Yaʿqub al-Kulayni, al-Kafi, vol. 2, p. 634.
76. Muhammad Baqir al-Majlisi, Bihar al-anwar, vol. 71, p. 355.
77. Husayn b. Muhammad Taqi al-Nuri al-Tabarsi, Mustadrak al-wasáil wa-mustanbat al-masáil, vol. 13, p. 205.
78. ʿAbd al-Wahid b. Muhammad al-Tamimi al-Amidi, Tasnif ghurar al-hikam wa-durar al-kilam, p. 406, hadith no. 9309.
79. Muhammad b. Yaʿqub al-Kulayni, al-Kafi, vol. 2, p. 150.
80. Ibn Hammam al-Iskafi, al-Tamhis, p. 60.

Love and Kindness in Islamic and Christian Scriptures

■ Methodic Criticism

Methodic and compassionate criticism can also attract others' love. Prophet Muhammad stated, "Three things purify friendship: guiding the friend to their flaws, protecting them during their absence, and assisting them in adversity."[81]

In this context, Imam ʿAli emphasizes an exception: the individual being criticized should not be foolish or irrational. He advises, "Do not criticize a foolish person, as they may become hostile towards you. Criticize a rational person, as they will love you."[82]

Another hadith transmitted from the Imam states, "One who loves you will deter you from wrongdoing."[83]

■ Fairness

Imam ʿAli stated, "Fairness fosters intimacy between hearts."[84]

He also said, "Fairness leads to the endurance of love and friendship."[85]

A hadith transmitted from the ninth Imam al-Jawad states, "Three character traits attract love, one of which is empathy with others during times of difficulty."[86]

On the contrary, individuals who lack fairness are deprived of love and friendship. The Commander of the Faithful, Imam ʿAli, says, "One devoid of fairness will find himself without companions."[87]

One way to attract love is to uphold justice, as Imam ʿAli, peace be upon him, said, "People are naturally drawn towards those who act with righteousness."[88]

■ Loyalty

Another means of earning others' love is through loyalty. Imam ʿAli, peace be upon him, said, "Loyalty is a pathway to intimacy."[89]

---

81. Masʿud b. ʿIsa al-Warram b. Abi Firas, Majmuʿat al-Warram, vol. 2, p. 121.
82. ʿAbd al-Wahid b. Muhammad al-Tamimi al-Amidi, Tasnif ghurar al-hikam wa-durar al-kilam, p. 74, hadith no. 1131.
83. ʿAbd al-Wahid b. Muhammad al-Tamimi al-Amidi, Tasnif ghurar al-hikam wa-durar al-kilam, p. 415, hadith no. 9471.
84. ʿAbd al-Wahid b. Muhammad al-Tamimi al-Amidi, Tasnif ghurar al-hikam wa-durar al-kilam, p. 60, hadith no. 1173.
85. ʿAbd al-Wahid b. Muhammad al-Tamimi al-Amidi, Tasnif ghurar al-hikam wa-durar al-kilam, p. 394, hadith no. 9114.
86. ʿAli b. ʿIsa al-Irbili, Kashf al-ghimma fi maʿrifat al-aimma, vol. 2, p. 349.
87. ʿAbd al-Wahid b. Muhammad al-Tamimi al-Amidi, Tasnif ghurar al-hikam wa-durar al-kilam, p. 394, hadith no. 9121.
88. ʿAbd al-Wahid b. Muhammad al-Tamimi al-Amidi, Tasnif ghurar al-hikam wa-durar al-kilam, p. 628.
89. ʿAbd al-Wahid b. Muhammad al-Tamimi al-Amidi, Tasnif ghurar al-hikam wa-durar al-kilam, p. 395.

Love and Kindness in Islamic and Christian Scriptures

■ Commitment to Truth

One way to foster love is by upholding fairness and truth. The Commander of the Faithful, Imam ʿAli, says, "People are attracted to those who act upon the truth."[90]

■ Competence

One way to earn the love and trust of managers, employers, and rulers is by demonstrating competence. In this regard, Imam ʿAli says, "A person with good competence will be cherished by the ruler."[91]

■ Rationality and Virtue

Within Islamic teachings, another method of attracting love from others is by displaying rationality and virtue. In this context, Imam ʿAli, the Commander of the Faithful, says, "Rationality serves as a veil that hides imperfections, while virtue shines brightly. Therefore, let your virtue conceal any flaws in your character, and with your rationality, overcome your desires. Through this, you will earn friendship, and love will reveal itself to you."[92]

■ Posivitve Assumptions about Others

Within Islamic ethical teachings, harboring negative assumptions about others is condemned (see Quran 49:12), while having positive assumptions is praised. One way to attract love from others is by maintaining good assumptions about them. The Commander of the Faithful, Imam ʿAli, states, "Those who hold good assumptions about others will earn their love."[93]

■ Humility

Humility is indeed a commendable moral trait and a factor that fosters love and friendship from others. A hadith transmitted from Imam ʿAli states, "Three things cultivate love: good temperament, kindness, and humility."[94]

---

90. ʿAbd al-Wahid b. Muhammad al-Tamimi al-Amidi, Tasnif ghurar al-hikam wa-durar al-kilam, p. 69, hadith no. 963.
91. ʿAbd al-Wahid b. Muhammad al-Tamimi al-Amidi, Tasnif ghurar al-hikam wa-durar al-kilam, p. 478, hadith no. 10992.
92. Muhammad b. Yaʿqub al-Kulayni, al-Kafi, vol. 1, p. 20.
93. ʿAbd al-Wahid b. Muhammad al-Tamimi al-Amidi, Tasnif ghurar al-hikam wa-durar al-kilam, p. 253, hadith no. 5331.
94. ʿAbd al-Wahid b. Muhammad al-Tamimi al-Amidi, Tasnif ghurar al-hikam wa-durar al-kilam, p. 255, hadith no. 5372.

Love and Kindness in Islamic and Christian Scriptures

Imam al-Sadiq says, "Three things breed love: religion, humility, and generosity."[95]

In Islamic teachings, love is seen as the fruit of humility, as stated by the Commander of the Faithful, Imam ʿAli, who declared, "the fruit of humility is love and friendship."[96]

Conversely, a person who is arrogant will be deprived of others' love and friendship, as Imam ʿAli stated, "An arrogant individual has no friends."[97]

■ Truthfulness

In contrast to liars who seek love and respect through deceit and lies, Islamic teachings emphasize that genuine love and respect come from truthfulness and honesty. Imam ʿAli underscores this, stating, "A truthful person earns three things through honesty: the trust, love, and respect of others."[98]

■ Sincerity of the Heart

In a letter of covenant addressed to his companion Malik al-Ashtar, whom he appointed as the governor of Egypt, Imam ʿAli, the Commander of the Faithful, provided guidelines on governance. Among these, he emphasized, "The greatest joy for rulers... is fostering friendship among their subjects, a bond that can only arise with the sincerity of their hearts."[99]

■ Pure Heart

A hadith transmitted from the ninth Imam Muhammad al-Jawad states, "Three character traits attract love, one of which is possessing a pure and sincere heart."[100]

■ Silence

A defining trait of true believers is their inclination towards silence and restraint in speech, a quality that garners love from others. In a hadith attributed to the eighth Imam,

---

95. Al-Hasan b. ʿAli Ibn Shuʿba al-Harrani, Tuhaf al-ʿuqul, p. 316.
96. ʿAbd al-Wahid b. Muhammad al-Tamimi al-Amidi, Tasnif ghurar al-hikam wa-durar al-kilam, p. 149, hadith no. 5179.
97. ʿAbd al-Wahid b. Muhammad al-Tamimi al-Amidi, Tasnif ghurar al-hikam wa-durar al-kilam, p. 310, hadith no. 7162.
98. ʿAbd al-Wahid b. Muhammad al-Tamimi al-Amidi, Tasnif ghurar al-hikam wa-durar al-kilam, p. 219, hadith no. 4358.
99. Al-Sharif al-Radi, Nahj al-Balagha, p. 433, letter no. 53.
100. ʿAli b. ʿIsa al-Irbili, Kashf al-ghimma fi maʿrifat al-àimma, vol. 2, p. 349.

'Ali b. Musa al-Rida, it is stated, "Silence not only earns love from others but also directs towards all that is good."[101]

Avoidance of Evil

Human nature inherently leans towards beauty and avoids ugliness and evil. Thus, those who embrace beauty and detest evil naturally attract love from others. A hadith attributed to the sixth Imam, Ja'far al-Sadiq, conveys, "One whom God has made detest evil, God will bless with people's love and friendship. Such an individual will remain distant from hostility and estrangement. Neither they nor their family will be involved in any form of enmity."[102]

---

101. Muhammad b. 'Ali Ibn Babawayh, 'Uyun akhbar al-Rida 'alayh al-salam, vol. 1, p. 258.
102. Muhammad b. Ya'qub al-Kulayni, al-Kafi, vol. 8, p. 12.

Obstacles to Attraction of Love

Certain characteristics, traits, and behaviors act as barriers to attracting love from others. In Islamic sacred texts, specific entities and improper moral traits or actions are identified as obstacles that hinder one from being loved.

■ Satan

Satan and his deceptions can indeed obstruct the attraction of love among individuals. A hadith transmitted from the fifth Imam, Muhammad al-Baqir, states, "Satan sows discord among believers until one of them abandons their faith. When this occurs, Satan proudly declares victory. May God's mercy be upon those who reconcile two of our friends. O believers! Seek reconciliation and compassion towards one another."[1]

■ Quarrels

Anger, quarrels, and arguments are indeed behaviors that breed hatred and hostility. Prophet Muhammad stated, "When you love someone and consider him a friend, do not quarrel with him, do not compete with him, and do not harbor hostility towards him."[2]

The Commander of the Faithful, Imam ʿAli, advised, "Avoid egotism, bad temperaments, and impatience, for with these traits, no one will be your friend, and people will always steer clear of you."[3]

Another hadith transmitted from Imam ʿAli states, "If one displays violent behavior, no one will remain around them as friends."[4]

According to another Hadith, "Love cannot coexist with frequent quarrels."[5]

---

1. Muhammad Baqir al-Majlisi, Bihar al-anwar, vol. 2, p. 345.
2. Abolghasem Payandeh, Nahj al-fasaha, p. 180.
3. Muhammad b. ʿAli Ibn Babawayh, al-Khisal, vol. 1, p. 147.
4. ʿAbd al-Wahid b. Muhammad al-Tamimi al-Amidi, Tasnif ghurar al-hikam wa-durar al-kilam, p. 264, hadith no. 5714.
5. ʿAbd al-Wahid b. Muhammad al-Tamimi al-Amidi, Tasnif ghurar al-hikam wa-durar al-kilam, p. 311, hadith no. 7194.

Love and Kindness in Islamic and Christian Scriptures

This is so significant that Imam al-Sadiq even remarked, "If a person says 'fie!' to their fellow believer, they will be expelled from their circle of friendship."[6]

Boasting

People often dislike it when someone boasts about their achievements, possessions, or abilities in a self-satisfied manner. If one seeks to attract the love of others, they should refrain from boasting. Imam al-Sadiq says, "If you desire sincere friendship from your fellow believers, then do not mock them, do not argue with them, do not boast to them, and do not harbor hostility towards them."[7]

Imam 'Ali remarks in this regard, "If one displays arrogance towards his fellow believers, no one will be his devoted friend."[8]

Imam al-Sadiq also describes egotism and self-conceit as factors leading to hostility, stating: "Three things result in hatred and enmity: hypocrisy, oppression, and egotism."[9]

Grudges and Evil Intentions

Evil intentions, grudges, and inner impurities indeed hinder others' love and respect. Imam 'Ali, peace be upon him, said, "Indeed, you are brothers in God's religion. Nothing divides you except inner malice and evil intentions. Consequently, you refrain from visiting each other, showing benevolence, giving, and fostering mutual friendship and love."[10]

Hypocrisy

Another factor leading to hostility and preventing love and friendship is hypocrisy. Imam al-Sadiq states: "Three things result in hatred and enmity: hypocrisy, oppression, and egotism."[11]

A hadith transmitted from the Commander of the Faithful, Imam 'Ali, says: "The companionship of a friend does not endure with deceptions and trickeries."[12]

---

6. Muhammad b. Ya'qub al-Kulayni, al-Kafi, vol. 2, p. 361.
7. Al-Hasan b. 'Ali Ibn Shu'ba al-Harrani, Tuhaf al-'uqul, p. 312.
8. 'Abd al-Wahid b. Muhammad al-Tamimi al-Amidi, Tasnif ghurar al-hikam wa-durar al-kilam, p. 419, hadith no. 9605.
9. Al-Hasan b. 'Ali Ibn Shu'ba al-Harrani, Tuhaf al-'uqul, p. 316.
10. Al-Sharif al-Radi, Nahj al-Balagha, p. 168, sermon 168.
11. Al-Hasan b. 'Ali Ibn Shu'ba al-Harrani, Tuhaf al-'uqul, p. 316.
12. 'Abd al-Wahid b. Muhammad al-Tamimi al-Amidi, Tasnif ghurar al-hikam wa-durar al-kilam, p. 316.

Love and Kindness in Islamic and Christian Scriptures

■ Greed

A factor that leads to the attraction of love from others is displaying disinterest in others' possessions and having no greed towards their money and power. In Islamic sources, it is reported that a man asked the Prophet, "O Apostle of God! Teach me something that, if I do it, God will love me, and the inhabitants of the earth will also love me." The Prophet replied, "Have interest in what God possesses so that God loves you, and have disinterest in what people possess so that people love you."[13]

Imam ʿAli said in a Hadith, "Win people's love and friendship by showing disinterest in what they possess. This way, you will earn their friendship."[14]

Moreover, he says, "Adorn yourself with disinterest in what people possess, so that you become shielded from their grudges and earn their friendship and love."[15]

■ Envy

In Islamic sources, there are hadiths emphasizing that an envious person is despised by others, while a person who harbors no envy will gain their affection and friendship. The Commander of the Faithful, Imam ʿAli, said in this regard, "One who abandons envy will earn people's love."[16]

In contrast, envy destroys love and friendship. Another hadith transmitted from Imam ʿAli states, "An envious individual will find themselves without friends."[17]

The Imam also asserts, "When a friend harbors envy towards another friend, it indicates the sickness of their friendship."[18]

■ Malicious Nature

Islamic sources suggest that one reason for the absence of love and friendship within religious communities is having a malicious nature. Imam ʿAli, for instance, says, "Indeed, you are brothers in God's religion. Nothing divides you except inner malice

---

13. Muhammad b. ʿAli Ibn Babawayh, al-Khisal, vol. 1, p. 61.
14. ʿAbd al-Wahid b. Muhammad al-Tamimi al-Amidi, Tasnif ghurar al-hikam wa-durar al-kilam, p. 437, hdith no. 10025.
15. ʿAbd al-Wahid b. Muhammad al-Tamimi al-Amidi, Tasnif ghurar al-hikam wa-durar al-kilam, p. 398, hdith no. 9251.
16. Al-Hasan b. ʿAli Ibn Shuʿba al-Harrani, Tuhaf al-ʿuqul, pp. 89, 99.
17. ʿAbd al-Wahid b. Muhammad al-Tamimi al-Amidi, Tasnif ghurar al-hikam wa-durar al-kilam, p. 301, hdith no. 6848.
18. Al-Sharif al-Radi, Nahj al-Balagha, p. 507, hadith no. 214.

and evil intentions. Consequently, you refrain from visiting each other, showing benevolence, giving, and fostering mutual friendship and love."[19]

Sadness and Downheartedness

Within Islamic lifestyle, cheerfulness is a factor that fosters love, while sadness and downheartedness are factors that hinder it. In this regard, Imam ʿAli said, "Distress tarnishes one's character and drives friends away," and also stated, "Downheartedness corrodes friendships and brotherhoods."[20]

In another hadith, the Imam said, "There are no friends for a downhearted person."[21]

A hadith transmitted from Imam al-Sadiq states, "Do not place your trust in friendship with a downhearted, cheerless person… for when you invest all your trust in such a person, they will disappoint you, and when you form the strongest bond with them, they will sever it."[22]

Consumption of Intoxicating Drinks and Gambling

The Quran states that consumption of intoxicating drinks and gambling foster animosity within communities: "O you who have faith! Indeed wine, gambling, idols, and the divining arrows are abominations of Satan's doing, so avoid them, so that you may be felicitous. Indeed Satan seeks to cast enmity and hatred among you through wine and gambling, and to hinder you from the remembrance of Allah and from prayer. Will you, then, relinquish?"

Mockery

One factor contributing to the spread of hatred in communities is mockery and teasing others. The Quran advises believers: "O you who have faith! Let not any people ridicule another people: it may be that they are better than they are; nor let women [ridicule] women: it may be that they are better than they are. And do not defame one another, nor insult one another by [calling] nicknames" (Quran 49:11).

A hadith transmitted from Imam al-Sadiq states: "One who ridicules and mocks others should not expect genuine, sincere friendships."[23]

---

19. Al-Sharif al-Radi, Nahj al-Balagha, p. 168, sermon 113..
20. ʿAbd al-Wahid b. Muhammad al-Tamimi al-Amidi, Tasnif ghurar al-hikam wa-durar al-kilam, p. 59, hdith no. 1151.
21. Al-Hasan b. ʿAli Ibn Shuʿba al-Harrani, Tuhaf al-ʿuqul, p. 215.
22. Al-Hasan b. ʿAli Ibn Shuʿba al-Harrani, Tuhaf al-ʿuqul, p. 316.
23. Muhammad Baqir al-Majlisi, Bihar al-anwar, vol. 69, p. 190.

Love and Kindness in Islamic and Christian Scriptures

In another hadith, the Imam said, "If you desire sincere friendship from your fellow believers, then do not mock them, do not argue with them, do not boast to them, and do not harbor hostility towards them."[24]

False accusations against others, whether in jest or in seriousness, also contribute to the spread of animosity and hatred.

▪ Reproaching and Fault-Finding

Another factor that contributes to the spread of hatred and animosity within society is the attitude of fault-finding. The Commander of the Faithful, Imam ʿAli, said, "Do not reproach others excessively, as this fosters grudges and fuels hatred. Too much of this indeed instantiates impoliteness."[25]

Imam ʿAli also remarked, "Excessive blaming and reproach sow grudges in hearts and drive friends away."[26]

All people may have faults and flaws, but fault-finding is a disrespectful behavior that results in hatred and enmity. Prophet Muhammad, peace be upon him and his household, says, "When you make friends with someone, do not inquire about him from others, for you may come across one of his enemies who tells you a fault in him that he does not indeed possess, and this could lead to your separation."[27]

A hadith from the Commander of the Faithful, Imam ʿAli, says, "One who seeks out hidden flaws in others, God will deprive him of genuine love and friendship."[28]

In another hadith, Imam ʿAli states, "One who probes into the affairs of his friend will see their friendship come to an end."[29]

▪ Failing to Inquire after a Friend

One negligence that can lead to the severance of friendship relations is failing to inquire after one's friend or show care and concern about their condition. A hadith

---

24. Al-Hasan b. ʿAli Ibn Shuʿba al-Harrani, Tuhaf al-ʿuqul, p. 312; Muhammad Baqir al-Majlisi, Bihar al-anwar, vol. 75, p. 291.
25. Muhammad b. ʿAli al-Karajaki, Kanz al-fawaʾid, vol. 1, p. 93.
26. ʿAbd al-Wahid b. Muhammad al-Tamimi al-Amidi, Tasnif ghurar al-hikam wa-durar al-kilam, p. 479, hdith no. 11006.
27. Abolghasem Payandeh, Nahj al-fasaha, p. 180.
28. ʿAbd al-Wahid b. Muhammad al-Tamimi al-Amidi, Tasnif ghurar al-hikam wa-durar al-kilam, p. 421, hdith no. 9656.
29. ʿAbd al-Wahid b. Muhammad al-Tamimi al-Amidi, Tasnif ghurar al-hikam wa-durar al-kilam, p. 422, hdith no. 9680.

narrated from Imam ʿAli states: "One who does not care about his friend will lose his companion."[30]

According to a collection of poems attributed to the Commander of the Faithful, Imam ʿAli, "Failing to care about the friend leads to separation."[31]

■ Blameworthy Types of Love

While love is generally regarded as positive, both Islamic and Christian ethical teachings caution against certain types of love deemed improper or blameworthy. In the Quran, God says, "Yet it may be that you dislike something which is good for you, and it may be that you love something which is bad for you, and Allah knows, and you do not know" (Quran 2:216).

---

30. ʿAbd al-Wahid b. Muhammad al-Tamimi al-Amidi, Tasnif ghurar al-hikam wa-durar al-kilam, p. 422, hdith no. 9892.
31. Muhammad b. Muhammad al-Mufid, al-Irshad fi maʿrifa hujaj Allah ʿala al-ʿibad, vol. 1, p. 303.

Instances of Blameworthy Love

■ **Improper Love**

Sometimes, love is improperly directed where it should not be, and the other party may misuse or misinterpret such sincere devotion. In hadiths, it is emphasized that one should not scatter their love everywhere and for every individual. The Commander of the Faithful, Imam ʿAli, states, "Do not bestow your love where you do not find a fitting place for it."[1]

A hadith transmitted from Imam al-Sadiq states, "One who places his love in an improper position has subjected himself to separation."[2]

■ **Love and Friendship with God's Enemies**

While Quranic verses emphasize kind treatment of both civil and armed enemies, they strongly prohibit forming friendships with God's enemies to the extent that they become one's guardians. Love and kindness should not lead to surrender to the enemy or allow them dominance over believers. God says in the Quran, "O you who have faith! Do not take My enemy and your enemy for friends, [secretly] offering them affection, if you have set" (Quran 60:1). Another verse states, "You will not find a people believing in Allah and the Last Day endearing those who oppose Allah and His Apostle even though they were their own parents, or children, or brothers, or kinsfolk" (Quran 58:22). Another verse of the Quran emphasizes: "Allah does not forbid you from dealing with kindness and justice with those [polytheists] who did not make war against you on account of religion and did not expel you from your homes. Indeed Allah loves the just. Allah forbids you only in regard to those who made war against you on account of religion and expelled you from your homes and supported [the polytheists of Makkah] in your expulsion, that you make friends with them, and whoever makes friends with them—it is they who are the wrongdoers" (Quran 60:8-9).

---

1. Al-Laythi al-Wasiti, ʿUyun al-hikam wa-l-mawaʿiz, p. 522.
2. Ahmad b. Muhammad b. Khalid al-Barqi, al-Mahasin, vol. 1, p. 266.

Love and Kindness in Islamic and Christian Scriptures

The Commander of the Faithful, Imam ʿAli, says in this regard: "Avoid love and friendship with God's enemies or devoting sincere love for anyone other than God's friends, since one who loves a group of individuals will be resurrected along with them on the Day of Resurrection."[3]

■ Worldly Allures

Islamic sacred texts caution against excessive attachment to worldly temptations, as highlighted in the Quran: "The love of [worldly] allures, including women and children, accumulated piles of gold and silver, horses of mark, livestock, and farms has been made to seem decorous to mankind. Those are the wares of the life of this world, but the goodness of one's ultimate destination lies near Allah" (Quran 3:14).

This point is further echoed in certain hadiths within Islamic sources, such as: "God revealed to Prophet David to warn and advise his companions against becoming attracted to worldly temptations, as those who indulge in such desires will be veiled from God."[4]

Zuleikha, Potiphar's wife, fell in love with Prophet Joseph when he was young, but this was a blameworthy, lustful, and forbidden love, as the Quran says, "Some of the townswomen said, 'The chieftain's wife has solicited her slave boy! He has captivated her love. Indeed, we see her to be in manifest error'" (Quran 12:30).

The sixth Imam Jaʿfar al-Sadiq, peace be upon him, stated, "One who becomes ensnared by forbidden (lustful) love becomes a partner with Satan."[5]

■ Love of This World

Numerous Quranic verses and hadiths transmitted from the Prophet and Shiite Imams have strongly prohibited attachment to worldly desires and wealth. In the Quran, God reproaches those who harbor excessive love for worldly possessions: "and love wealth with much fondness" (Quran 89:20). Another Quranic verse says, "No! Indeed, you love this transitory life" (Quran 75:20), and another states, "Indeed, man is ungrateful to his Lord, and indeed, he is [himself] witness to that! And indeed, he is an avid lover of wealth" (Quran 100:6-8).

The fourth Shiite Imam al-Sajjad also asserts that love for worldly belongings is the root of all evils: "Love for this world is the origin of all wrongdoings."[6]

---

3. ʿAbd al-Wahid b. Muhammad al-Tamimi al-Amidi, Tasnif ghurar al-hikam wa-durar al-kilam, p. 204, hdith no. 4015.
4. Muhammad Baqir al-Majlisi, Bihar al-anwar, vol. 1, p. 154.
5. Muhammad Baqir al-Majlisi, Bihar al-anwar, vol. 76, p. 21.
6. Muhammad b. Yaʿqub al-Kulayni, al-Kafi, vol. 2, p. 131.

Love and Kindness in Islamic and Christian Scriptures

It should be noted, however, that what is criticized and reproached here is the excessive love and attachment to wealth solely for worldly gains. Conversely, accumulating wealth for personal comfort, maintaining reputation, and achieving success in the afterlife is indeed encouraged in hadiths. For instance, a hadith transmitted from Imam al-Sadiq states: "There is no blessing in someone who does not strive to gather wealth through legitimate means to preserve their reputation, settle debts, and maintain ties with relatives."[7]

▪ Love with Expectations

Love and friendship should be sincere and without expectations. If one loves someone else, expecting to gain an advantage or benefit from them, that will not be genuine love. A hadith transmitted from the Commander of the Faithful, Imam ʿAli, states, "Every friendship formed with expectations will dissolve in disappointment."[8]

Those who form friendships or love others solely for the sake of gaining benefits will find that their relationships endure only as long as those benefits persist, and then their love fades away. In another hadith, Imam ʿAli says, "One who loves you for something will turn away from you once they attain it."[9]

▪ Love and Friendship towards the Wicked

It is indeed true that many Quranic verses and hadiths stress the significance of showing kindness even to enemies, yet this kindness is contingent upon not empowering them or enabling their wrongdoings. Imam ʿAli says, "Showing mercy to those who lack mercy will hinder [other instances] of mercy."[10]

In a letter to his son Imam al-Hasan, Imam ʿAli said, "Bear yourself towards your brother in such a way that if he disregards kinship you keep to it; when he turns away be kind to him and draw near to him… But take care that this should not be done inappropriately, and that you should not behave so with an undeserving person."[11]

▪ Love of Corrupt Scholars

Another case where love is forbidden is affection towards corrupt scholars. Prophet

---

7. Muhammad b. ʿAli Ibn Babawayh, Man la-yahduruh al-faqih, vol. 3, p. 166.
8. Masʿud b. ʿIsa al-Warram b. Abi Firas, Majmuʿat al-Warram, vol. 1, p. 72.
9. ʿAbd al-Wahid b. Muhammad al-Tamimi al-Amidi, Tasnif ghurar al-hikam wa-durar al-kilam, p. 418, hdith no. 9555.
10. ʿAbd al-Wahid b. Muhammad al-Tamimi al-Amidi, Tasnif ghurar al-hikam wa-durar al-kilam, p. 343, hdith no. 7856.
11. Al-Sharif al-Radi, Nahj al-Balagha, p. 403, letter no. 31.

Love and Kindness in Islamic and Christian Scriptures

Muhammad, peace be upon him and his household, cautioned one of his companions, 'Abd Allah b. Mas'ud, saying: "O Ibn Mas'ud! Non-righteous scholars and jurists are treacherous and malicious. Beware, for they are among the most wicked creatures of God. The same applies to their followers, those who visit them, those who learn from them, those who harbor affection for them, those who keep their company, and those who seek their counsel. All of them are among the most wicked creatures of God, whom God will cast into the fires of Hell."[12]

▪ Wicked Friends

The Quran reports that wrongdoers will regret on the Day of Resurrection having associated with non-righteous, wicked friends: "It will be a day when the wrongdoer will bite his hands, saying, 'I wish I had followed the Apostle's way! Woe to me! I wish I had not taken so-and-so as a friend!'" (Quran 25:28).

▪ Love for False Deities

The Quran condemns those who harbor love and affection for false deities like idols: "Among the people are those who set up equals with Allah, loving them as they should love Allah... and they shall not leave the Fire" (Quran 2:165, 167).

Another Quranic verse states: "He said, 'You have taken idols [for worship] besides Allah for the sake of [mutual] affection amongst yourselves in the life of the world" (Quran 29:25).

▪ Love not for God's Sake

Mufaddal b. 'Umar, a companion of the sixth Imam Ja'far al-Sadiq, peace be upon him, asked the Imam about false love. The Imam replied: "They are hearts devoid of God's remembrance, to whom God has granted the taste of loving things other than Himself."[13]

Consequences of Blameworthy Love

According to Islamic sacred texts, those who are attached to worldly possessions and wealth may face punishment from God, but if they relinquish such attachments, they will receive boundless divine rewards. Here are some of the consequences outlined for forbidden and blameworthy kinds of love:

---

12. Al-Hasan b. Fadl al-Tabarsi, Makarim al-akhlaq, p. 450.
13. Muhammad b. 'Ali Ibn Babawayh, 'Ilal al-sharai', vol. 1, p. 140.

Love and Kindness in Islamic and Christian Scriptures

▪ Failure to See Truths

Those who are ensnared by false forms of love lose their ability to perceive truths. Imam 'Ali, peace be upon him, said, "One who becomes infatuated with something becomes blind [to truths]."[14]

▪ Sickness of Heart

One who becomes attached to worldly values finds their heart afflicted, as Imam 'Ali, peace be upon him, stated, "One who becomes infatuated with something... his heart becomes sick, and thus, he sees with unsound vision and hears with deaf ears."[15]

▪ Loss of Rationality

Those who become infatuated will lose their rationality and reasoning abilities, as Imam 'Ali, peace be upon him, said, "One who becomes infatuated with something... desires will shred his intellect, and the world will suffocate his heart."[16]

▪ Enslavement to Worlly Attractions

One who becomes enamored with worldly pursuits will become enslaved to their allure, as Imam 'Ali, Peace be upon him, cautioned: "One who becomes infatuated with something... his own desires will subjugate them, making him a slave to these desires, and he will become a slave to anyone who possesses something from the wealth of this world."[17]

▪ Obedience to the Beloved

A lover follows the beloved wherever they go and becomes entirely obedient to them. Imam 'Ali said, "One who becomes infatuated with something... wherever that thing goes, he will go, and whenever it turns, he will turn."[18]

▪ Unresponsiveness to Advice

Those who are attached to worldly love often become unresponsive to advice, as Imam 'Ali, peace be upon him, said, "One who becomes infatuated with something... nothing will deter him from sinning against God, and he will remain impervious to any counsel from advisors."[19]

---

14. Al-Sharif al-Radi, Nahj al-Balagha, p. 160, sermon 109.
15. Al-Sharif al-Radi, Nahj al-Balagha, p. 160, sermon 109.
16. Al-Sharif al-Radi, Nahj al-Balagha, p. 160, sermon 109.
17. Al-Sharif al-Radi, Nahj al-Balagha, p. 160, sermon 109.
18. Al-Sharif al-Radi, Nahj al-Balagha, p. 160, sermon 109.
19. Al-Sharif al-Radi, Nahj al-Balagha, p. 160, sermon 109.

Love and Kindness in Christian Scriptures

Love and Kindness in Islamic and Christian Scriptures

Love in Christian Scriptures

The Christian religion places special emphasis on the concepts of love and kindness. The Bible frequently underscores the importance of showing love and kindness towards others. In this chapter, we delve into the theme of love as depicted in the Bible.

Importance and Etiquettes of Kindness

Within the Christian ethical system, showing love and mercy to others is of particular importance. Both the Old and New Testaments contain numerous recommendations emphasizing the necessity of showing kindness to others. In the Second Epistle to Timothy, he is advised to "pursue righteousness, faith, love, and peace" (2 Timothy 2:22).

In the Book of Proverbs, Solomon characterizes love and kindness as praiseworthy conducts, stating: "What a person desires is unfailing love" (Proverbs 19:22).

Sacrifice is a significant ritual in the Old Testament, but in the Book of Hosea, love is depicted as being even more valuable than sacrifice, as Hosea asserts: "What can I do with you, Ephraim? What can I do with you, Judah? Your love is like the morning mist, like the early dew that disappears. ..For I desire mercy, not sacrifice, and acknowledgment of God rather than burnt offerings" (Hos 6:4-6).

Moreover, Micah states: "He has shown you, O mortal, what is good. And what does the LORD require of you? To act justly and to love mercy and to walk humbly with your God" (Micah 6:8).

While most people place a high value on wealth, gold, and silver, Solomon believes that being loved is more valuable than wealth. As he says in the Book of Proverbs, "A good name is more desirable than great riches; to be esteemed is better than silver or gold" (Proverbs 22:1).

In addition, the First Epistle to the Corinthians asserts that "If I give all I possess to the poor and give over my body to hardship that I may boast, but do not have love, I gain nothing" (I Corinthians 13:3).

It is also emphasized that "Better a small serving of vegetables with love than a fattened calf with hatred" (Proverbs 15:17).

God is a God of love, and those who claim to know God without showing love and kindness have not truly known Him: "Whoever does not love does not know God, because God is love" (I John 4:8).

From the perspective of both Old and New Testaments, love is even more valuable than faith, as the First Epistle to Corinthians states: "And now these three remain: faith, hope and love. But the greatest of these is love" (I Corinthians 13:13).

Love and Kindness in Islamic and Christian Scriptures

Furthermore, faith is more valuable when accompanied by love, as the Epistle to the Galatians asserts: "For in Christ Jesus neither circumcision nor uncircumcision has any value. The only thing that counts is faith expressing itself through love" (Gal 5:6).

The Bible emphasizes that without love, miraculous or extraordinary acts are of no value, as the First Epistle to the Corinthians states: "If I speak in the tongues of men or of angels, but do not have love, I am only a resounding gong or a clanging cymbal. If I have the gift of prophecy and can fathom all mysteries and all knowledge, and if I have a faith that can move mountains, but do not have love, I am nothing" (I Corinthians 13:1-2).

The New Testament views love as an exemplification of the law of the Old Testament, as the Epistle to the Romans emphasizes: "Let no debt remain outstanding, except the continuing debt to love one another, for whoever loves others has fulfilled the law" (Rom 13:8). It also asserts: "love is the fulfillment of the law" (Romans 13:10).

Even the New Testament describes love as the fulfilment of the divine law: "For the entire law is fulfilled in keeping this one command: 'Love your neighbor as yourself'" (Galatians 5:14).

Impacts of Showing Love and Kindness

From the perspective of Christian scriptures, showing love and kindness towards others can have valuable impacts, including the following:

Love as Assurance on the Day of Judgment

We need assurance on the Day of Judgment, and love is what provides assurance. In his First Epistle, John writes: "God is love. Whoever lives in love lives in God, and God in them. This is how love is made complete among us so that we will have confidence on the Day of Judgment" (I John 4:16-17).

Love resulting in Forgiveness of Sins

One impact of love is that one's sins will be forgiven and covered by God. A story is narrated in the New Testament as follows:

When one of the Pharisees invited Jesus to have dinner with him, he went to the Pharisee's house and reclined at the table. A woman in that town who lived a sinful life learned that Jesus was eating at the Pharisee's house, so she came there with an alabaster jar of perfume. As she stood behind him at his feet weeping, she began to wet his feet with her tears. Then she wiped them with her hair, kissed them and poured perfume on them. When the Pharisee who had invited him saw this, he said to himself, "If this man were a prophet, he would know who is touching him and what kind of woman she is—that she is a sinner." Jesus answered him, "Simon, I have something to tell you." "Tell me, teacher," he said. (Luke 7:36-40)

Then he turned toward the woman and said to Simon, "Do you see this woman? I came into your house. You did not give me any water for my feet, but she wet my feet with her tears and wiped them with her hair. You did not give me a kiss, but this woman, from the time I entered, has not stopped kissing my feet. You did not put oil on my head, but she has poured perfume on my feet. Therefore, I tell you, her many sins have been forgiven—as her great love has shown. But whoever has been forgiven little loves little." Then Jesus said to her, "Your sins are forgiven." (Luke 7:36-48)

All people make mistakes, but the mistakes of those who show love and kindness will remain unseen. In the Book of Proverbs, Solomon states: "love covers over all wrongs" (Proverbs 10:12); "Through love and faithfulness sin is atoned for" (Proverbs 16:6). Further, Solomon emphasizes: "Whoever would foster love covers over an offense" (Proverbs 17:9). Similarly, Peter asserts: "Above all, love each other deeply, because love covers over a multitude of sins" (I Pet 4:8).

Love leading to Esteem

The Old Testament states that showing love and kindness results in one's esteem, as Solomon says: "Whoever pursues righteousness and love finds life, prosperity and honor" (Proverbs 21:21).

Love and Perfection

From the perspective of the New Testament, love is constructive, as the First Epistle to Corinthians emphasizes: "knowledge puffs up while love builds up" (I Corinthians 8:1).

Moreover, love results in perfection: "And over all these virtues put on love, which binds them all together in perfect unity" (Colossians 3:14).

Love and Salvation

The foundation of Christian theology of salvation is built upon divine grace. The Bible depicts grace as God's gift bestowed upon individuals in accordance with their love towards others, as David says in the Book of Psalms: "Have mercy on me, O God, according to your unfailing love" (Psalms 51:1) and John asserts in his First Epistle: "We know that we have passed from death to life, because we love each other. Anyone who does not love remains in death" (I John 3:14).

Love and Kindness in Islamic and Christian Scriptures

According to Paul, women were recognized as affected by sin through Adam's transgression, and for salvation, they should endure the pains of childbirth, embrace faith, and cultivate love: "But women will be saved through childbearing—if they continue in faith, love and holiness with propriety" (I Timothy 2:15).

In the Second Epistle to the Thessalonians, failure to embrace love for the truth is considered to impede salvation, leading to wretchedness and damnation: "They perish because they refused to love the truth and so be saved" (2 Thessalonians 2:10).

Prayer for Love

Love is so valuable that we should beseech God to help us earn it. In the Old Testament, God is asked to show love to Abraham: "LORD, God of my master Abraham, make me successful today, and show kindness to my master Abraham" (Genesis 24:12).

Paul tells Philippians: "And this is my prayer: that your love may abound more and more in knowledge and depth of insight" (Philippians 1:9).

Jude prays for others: "Mercy, peace and love be yours in abundance" (Jude 1:2).

Etiquettes of Love

The Bible establishes etiquettes and laws for showing love to others, which those who seek to practice kindness and love must adhere to. These include the following:

Sincere Love

Though a flattering hypocrite may appear to exhibit love and kindness on the surface, it does not constitute genuine love. The Epistle to the Romans emphasizes: "Love must be sincere. Hate what is evil" (Romans 12:9).

Practical Love

From the perspective of the New Testament, love is not merely expressed through verbal flattery; it should also be reflected in our actions towards others, as John advises: "Dear children, let us not love with words or speech but with actions and in truth" (I John 3:18).

Further, the Epistle to Corinthians recommends: "Therefore show these men the proof of your love and the reason for our pride in you, so that the churches can see it" (II Corinthians 8:24).

Paul characterizes self-sacrifice and selflessness as requirements of true love, writing: "and walk in the way of love, just as Christ loved us and gave himself up for us as a fragrant offering and sacrifice to God" (Ephesians 5:2).

Love and Kindness in Islamic and Christian Scriptures

■ Patient Love

Love should be accompanied by patience and tolerance, as the New Testament states: "Love is patient, love is kind" (I Corinthians 13:4).

Moreover, genuine love entails magnanimity and tolerance, as the First Epistle to Corinthians asserts: "It always protects, always trusts, always hopes, always perseveres" (I Corinthians 13:7).

■ Moral Love

Both Old and New Testaments underscore a close tie between love and morally acceptable conduct, as Paul writes in his Epistle to Corinthians: "Love is patient, love is kind. It does not envy, it does not boast, it is not proud. It does not dishonor others, it is not self-seeking, it is not easily angered, it keeps no record of wrongs. Love does not delight in evil but rejoices with the truth. It always protects, always trusts, always hopes, always perseveres" (I Corinthians 13:4-7).

■ Courageous Love

Love knows no fear, and those who demonstrate love and kindness have nothing to fear, as John proclaims: "There is no fear in love. But perfect love drives out fear, because fear has to do with punishment. The one who fears is not made perfect in love" (I John 4:18).

■ Persistent Love

The New Testament states that one day all divine blessings and bounties will cease, but love never ends, as Paul writes: "Love never fails. But where there are prophecies, they will cease; where there are tongues, they will be stilled; where there is knowledge, it will pass away" (I Corinthians 13:8); "And now these three remain: faith, hope and love. But the greatest of these is love" (I Corinthians 13:13).

Love towards People

The Christian scriptures advocate for Christians to demonstrate kindness towards others and to share love with them. Within Christian ethical teachings, numerous commands emphasize showing love towards others. Some of these commands include:

The Old Testament advises: "And you are to love those who are foreigners, for you yourselves were foreigners in Egypt" (Deuteronomy 10:19).

In his First Epistle, Peter underscores the necessity of showing love to everyone, stating: "Finally, all of you, be like-minded, be sympathetic, love one another, be compassionate and humble" (I Peter 3:8).

Paul also insists upon this recommendation in his epistles, writing: "Let no debt remain outstanding, except the continuing debt to love one another" (Romans 13:8).

Moreover, he prays for the Thessalonian Church: "May the Lord make your love increase and overflow for each other and for everyone else, just as ours does for you" (1 Thessalonians 3:12).

The Old Testament recommends people to be kind and forgiving towards each other, as Zechariah asserts: "This is what the LORD Almighty said: 'Administer true justice; show mercy and compassion to one another'" (Zechariah 7:9).

Significance and Impacts of Love towards Believers

There are numerous instructions and commands within Christian scriptures regarding the significance and love of believers. Some of these are outlined in what follows.

Loving Believers as Loving God

John holds that showing love towards believers is so significant that it is deemed equal to loving God: "This is how we know that we love the children of God: by loving God" (I John 5:2). Moreover, he asserts: "Whoever claims to love God yet hates a brother or sister is a liar. For whoever does not love their brother and sister, whom they have seen, cannot love God, whom they have not seen. And he has given us this command: Anyone who loves God must also love their brother and sister" (I John 4:20-21).

Love and Kindness in Islamic and Christian Scriptures

■ Loving Believers as Compliance with the Divine Law

Paul asserts that showing love towards believes fulfils the law of the Old Testament: "Let no debt remain outstanding, except the continuing debt to love one another, for whoever loves others has fulfilled the law" (Romans 13:8).

■ Loving Believers as Sign of Faith

The greater love believers have towards one another, the greater their faith in God. The Epistle to Thessalonians reads: "your faith is growing more and more, and the love all of you have for one another is increasing" (II Thessalonians 1:3).

Jesus the Christ emphasizes that believers' love towards one another indicates that they true follow him: "By this everyone will know that you are my disciples, if you love one another" (John 13:35).

■ Loving Believers and Hosting God in the Heart

Those who demonstrate love and kindness towards believers will open their hearts to God, allowing Him to dwell within them, as John proclaims: "if we love one another, God lives in us and his love is made complete in us" (I John 4:12).

Moreover, John writes: "Anyone who loves their brother and sister lives in the light, and there is nothing in them to make them stumble. But anyone who hates a brother or sister is in the darkness and walks around in the darkness. They do not know where they are going, because the darkness has blinded them" (I John 2:10-11).

John also describes love towards believers as a measure for genuine faith: "Anyone who claims to be in the light but hates a brother or sister is still in the darkness" (I John 2:9).

■ Loving Believers and Being Born of God

Showing love towards believers can lead to a degree of perfection, where one attains the status of being God's child, as John advises: "Dear friends, let us love one another, for love comes from God. Everyone who loves has been born of God and knows God" (I John 4:7).

In contrast, those who refuse to show love towards their fellow believers align themselves with the devil, as John emphasizes: "This is how we know who the children of God are and who the children of the devil are: Anyone who does not do what is right is not God's child, nor is anyone who does not love their brother and sister" (I John 3:10).

Love and Kindness in Islamic and Christian Scriptures

▪ Loving Believers and Delight of Prophets

When believers show genuine love to each other, this results in the delight of their spiritual and divine guides, prophets. Paul writes: "then make my joy complete by being like-minded, having the same love, being one in spirit and of one mind" (Philippians 2:2).

▪ Loving Believers and Forgiveness of Sins

When believers show love and kindness towards each other, their sins will be covered and forgiven, as Paul states: "Above all, love each other deeply, because love covers over a multitude of sins" (I Peter 4:8).

▪ Loving Believers and Divine Reward

The Bible emphasizes that showing love towards believers will be rewarded by God, whereas hatred towards believers leads to sin: "Do not hate a fellow Israelite in your heart. Rebuke your neighbor frankly so you will not share in their guilt" (Leviticus 19:17).

▪ Loving Believers and Salvation

In Christian sources, showing love to fellow believers is deemed to lead to salvation, while animosity towards believers is described as a factor leading to damnation. As John says, "We know that we have passed from death to life, because we love each other. Anyone who does not love remains in death. Anyone who hates a brother or sister is a murderer, and you know that no murderer has eternal life residing in him" (I John 3:14-15).

▪ Prayer for Love of Believers

In the Two Testaments, there are prayers where God is asked to bestow upon us love for fellow believers. For instance, in his Epistle to the Ephesians, Paul prays to God: "Peace to the brothers and sisters, and love with faith" (Ephesians 6:23).

Moreover, he wrote to the Philippians: "And this is my prayer: that your love may abound more and more in knowledge and depth of insight" (Philippians 1:9).

He also prays for the Thessalonian Church as follows: "May the Lord make your love increase and overflow for each other…, just as ours does for you" (I Thessalonians 3:12).

Love for Those of Other Faiths in Christian Scriptures

In the Old Testament, it is recommended to show love and kindness towards non-Israelite ethnicities living among the Israelites: "The foreigner residing among you must be treated as your native-born. Love them as yourself, for you were foreigners in Egypt" (Leviticus 19:34).

Samaritans constituted a group of Israelites with stark religious differences from the Jews and were indeed hated by the Jews. Jesus Christ uses an analogy to highlight the importance of showing love towards those of other faiths for a Jewish scholar:

A man was going down from Jerusalem to Jericho, when he was attacked by robbers. They stripped him of his clothes, beat him and went away, leaving him half dead. A priest happened to be going down the same road, and when he saw the man, he passed by on the other side. So too, a Levite, when he came to the place and saw him, passed by on the other side. But a Samaritan, as he traveled, came where the man was; and when he saw him, he took pity on him. He went to him and bandaged his wounds, pouring on oil and wine. Then he put the man on his own donkey, brought him to an inn and took care of him. The next day he took out two denarii and gave them to the innkeeper. 'Look after him,' he said, 'and when I return, I will reimburse you for any extra expense you may have.' "Which of these three do you think was a neighbor to the man who fell into the hands of robbers?" The expert in the law replied, "The one who had mercy on him." Jesus told him, "Go and do likewise." (Luke 10:30-37)

Within the Old Testament, no man had the right to marry a non-Israelite woman, and no woman had the right to marry a non-Israelite man (Ezra 9:12). Even upon return from Babylonian imprisonment, Ezra learned that numerous Israelite men had married non-Israelite women and had many children with them. He ordered that they all had to divorce their non-Israelite wives and set their children free. If they disobeyed the order, all their property would be confiscated (Ezra 10:1-44). However, in the New Testament, the ban was lifted. In the Epistle to the Corinthians, it asserts:

To the rest I say this (I, not the Lord): If any brother has a wife who is not a believer and she is willing to live with him, he must not divorce her. And if a woman has a husband who is not a believer and he is willing to live with her, she must not divorce him. For the unbelieving husband has been sanctified through his wife, and the unbelieving wife has been sanctified through her believing husband. Otherwise your children would be unclean, but as it is, they are holy. But if the unbeliever leaves, let it be so. The brother or the sister is not bound in such circumstances; God has called us to live in peace. How do you know, wife, whether you will save your husband? Or, how do you know, husband, whether you will save your wife? (I Corinthians 7:12-16)

Love of Spouse

In Christian scriptures, there is great emphasis on love of one's spouse. In his Epistle to the Colossians, Paul asserts: "Husbands, love your wives and do not be harsh with them" (Col 3:19), and the Epistle to Ephesians advises: "Husbands, love your wives, just as Christ loved the church and gave himself up for her" (Ephesians 5:25).

According to the New Testament, one obligation wives and husbands have toward one another is to show love and kindness to each other. Paul writes: "Likewise, teach the older women to be reverent in the way they live, not to be slanderers or addicted to much wine, but to teach what is good. Then they can urge the younger women to love their husbands and children, to be self-controlled and pure, to be busy at home, to be kind, and to be subject to their husbands, so that no one will malign the word of God" (Titus 2:3-5).

Further, Paul advises the Ephesian Church: "Husbands, love your wives, just as Christ loved the church and gave himself up for her… In this same way, husbands ought to love their wives as their own bodies. He who loves his wife loves himself. After all, no one ever hated their own body, but they feed and care for their body, just as Christ does the church— for we are members of his body… each one of you also must love his wife as he loves himself" (Ephesians 5:25-33).

In the Book of Proverbs, Solomon highlights the advantages of a woman's kindness towards her husband: "Under three things the earth trembles. … a contemptible woman who gets married" (Proverbs 30: 21-23).

In addition, Paul more emphatically advises the Colossian Church: "Husbands, love your wives and do not be harsh with them" (Col 3:19).

In the Old Testament, Solomon addresses his beloved, telling her: "Come, let's drink deeply of love till morning; let's enjoy ourselves with love!" (Proverbs 7:18); "Let him kiss me with the kisses of his mouth—for your love is more delightful than wine" (Song 1:2).

While divorce is deemed legitimate in the Old Testament, it is disliked by God. Malachi quotes God as saying: "'The man who hates and divorces his wife,' 'does violence to the one he should protect,' says the LORD Almighty. So be on your guard, and do not be unfaithful" (Malachi 2:16).

Love and Kindness in Islamic and Christian Scriptures

A number of Pharisees approached Jesus to test him: "They asked, 'Is it lawful for a man to divorce his wife for any and every reason?' … Jesus replied, "Moses permitted you to divorce your wives because your hearts were hard. But it was not this way from the beginning. I tell you that anyone who divorces his wife, except for sexual immorality, and marries another woman commits adultery'" (Matthew 19:3-9).

◉ Significance and Impacts of Love for Spouse

The Christian texts place strong value on showing love and kindness towards one's spouse.

▪ Unity of Man and Woman

Christian scriptures strongly emphasize the significance of showing love and kindness towards one's spouse. In principle, both the Old and New Testaments treat man and woman not as separate individuals, but rather as one body. This is why woman was created from part of man's bones, with Adam saying after her creation: "'This is now bone of my bones and flesh of my flesh; she shall be called 'woman,' for she was taken out of man'" (Genesis 2:23).

The Book of Genesis asserts: "That is why a man leaves his father and mother and is united to his wife, and they become one flesh" (Genesis 2:24).

Further, the Book of Mark emphasizes: "For this reason a man will leave his father and mother and be united to his wife, and the two will become one flesh.' So they are no longer two, but one flesh" (Mark 10:7-8).

▪ Love of Spouse akin to Love of One's Own Body

The New Testament underscores the importance of love between spouses:

Wives, submit yourselves to your own husbands as you do to the Lord. For the husband is the head of the wife as Christ is the head of the church, his body, of which he is the Savior. Now as the church submits to Christ, so also wives should submit to their husbands in everything. Husbands, love your wives, just as Christ loved the church and gave himself up for her to make her holy, cleansing her by the washing with water through the word, and to present her to himself as a radiant church, without stain or wrinkle or any other blemish, but holy and blameless. In this same way, husbands ought to love their wives as their own bodies. He who loves his wife loves himself. After all, no one ever hated their own body, but they feed and care for their body, just as Christ does the church— for we are members of his body. "For this reason a man will leave his father and mother and be united to his wife, and the two will become one flesh. This is a profound mystery—but I am talking about Christ and the church. However, each one of you also must love his wife as he loves himself, and the wife must respect her husband. (Ephesians 5:22-33)

■ Spousal Love alleviating the Problems

Love of one's spouse can mitigate problems and difficulties in life, just as "Jacob was in love with Rachel… So Jacob served seven years to get Rachel, but they seemed like only a few days to him because of his love for her" (Genesis 29:18-20).

Love of Children

All people need to be loved, but love for children is particularly necessary. In an epistle to his student Titus, Paul writes: "Then they can urge the younger women to love their husbands and children" (Titus 2:4).

Jesus Christ also loved children:

People were bringing little children to Jesus for him to place his hands on them, but the disciples rebuked them. When Jesus saw this, he was indignant. He said to them, "Let the little children come to me, and do not hinder them, for the kingdom of God belongs to such as these. Truly I tell you, anyone who will not receive the kingdom of God like a little child will never enter it." And he took the children in his arms, placed his hands on them and blessed them. (Mark 10:13-16)

It is recommended to show love to children by kissing them. Jesus Christ "took the children in his arms, placed his hands on them and blessed them" (Mark 10:16).

It is narrated that Jesus "took a little child whom he placed among them. Taking the child in his arms, he said to them" (Mark 9:36).

Within the Biblical tradition, whenever parents intended to display their love to their children, they kissed them. One example is Laban, the father of Jacob's wife, who kissed and blessed his grandchildren and daughters when Jacob departed towards Palestine (Gen 31:55).

Solomon emphasizes that one means to show love to children is through measured punishment and admonishment: "Whoever spares the rod hates their children, but the one who loves their children is careful to discipline them" (Proverbs 13:24); "Whoever loves discipline loves knowledge, but whoever hates correction is stupid" (Proverbs 12:1).

Love and Kindness towards Parents

The Bible underscores the importance of parents, commanding children to respect and display kindness towards them. Joseph hugged his parents when he met them after a long period of separation, and as per the Old Testament, he wept while he had his arms around them (Genesis 46:29).

One obligation children have towards their parents is to fulfill their wishes. For instance, in the Book of Genesis, it has stated that as Jacob's death neared, "he called for his son Joseph and said to him, 'If I have found favor in your eyes, put your hand under my thigh and promise that you will show me kindness and faithfulness. Do not bury me in Egypt'" (Genesis 47:29). Joseph honored his father's request, carrying his body to Canaan and burying him there.

Love for Relatives

The Bible emphasizes the significance of showing love and kindness towards one's relatives as among the good deeds. David asserts: "How good and pleasant it is when God's people live together in unity!" (Psalms 133:1).

This kind of love towards relatives does not hinder the love of God. Jesus Christ teaches that one's spiritual family is more significant than one's blood-related family, emphasizing that one should prioritize their spiritual relatives over their physical ones. He states: "Do not suppose that I have come to bring peace to the earth. I did not come to bring peace, but a sword. For I have come to turn a man against his father, a daughter against her mother, a daughter-in-law against her mother-in-law—a man's enemies will be the members of his own household. Anyone who loves their father or mother more than me is not worthy of me; anyone who loves their son or daughter more than me is not worthy of me" (Matthew 10:34-37)

He also asserts: "'Truly I tell you,' Jesus replied, 'no one who has left home or brothers or sisters or mother or father or children or fields for me and the gospel will fail to receive a hundred times as much in this present age: homes, brothers, sisters, mothers, children and fields—along with persecutions—and in the age to come eternal life. But many who are first will be last, and the last first'" (Mark 10:29-31).

Elsewhere, Jesus Christ says: "If anyone comes to me and does not hate father and mother, wife and children, brothers and sisters—yes, even their own life—such a person cannot be my disciple" (Luke 14:26).

One obligation relatives have towards each other is to ask about each other's condition and greet them. In his epistles, Paul greets his relatives: "Greet Andronicus and Junia, my fellow Jews who have been in prison with me" (Romans 16:7); "Greet Herodion, my fellow Jew. Greet those in the household of Narcissus who are in the Lord" (Romans 16:11).

Furthermore, he conveys his relatives' regards to others, writing to the Church of the Romans: "My co-worker sends his greetings to you, as do Lucius, Jason, and Sosipater, my fellow Jews" (Romans 16:21).

In Christian texts, it is recommended to forgive and condone the sins and mistakes of one's fellow believers. The Old Testament advises: "Do not hate a fellow Israelite in your heart" (Leviticus 19:17).

Love and Kindness towards Teachers and Students

In the New Testament, believers are encouraged to show love and kindness towards teachers who have taught them guidance. Paul says that he always prays for Philemon: "because I hear about your love for all his holy people" (Philemon 1:5).

Moreover, he prays the Colossian Church for love of the holy people: "because we have heard of your faith in Christ Jesus and of the love you have for all God's people" (Colossians 1:4).

Showing love to one's students stems from pure faith and a righteous conscience. Paul writes to his pupil Timothy, asking him to stay in Ephesus and teach, adding: "The goal of this command is love, which comes from a pure heart and a good conscience and a sincere faith" (1 Timothy 1:5).

God never forgets when one shows love and kindness to religious scholars. Paul writes to the Hebrews, appreciating their love for the holy people: "God is not unjust; he will not forget your work and the love you have shown him as you have helped his people and continue to help them" (Hebrews 6:10).

In the New Testament, believers are encouraged to show eagerness to visit religious scholars. Paul writes to the Thessalonian Church: "But Timothy has just now come to us from you and has brought good news about your faith and love. He has told us that you always have pleasant memories of us and that you long to see us, just as we also long to see you" (1 Thessalonians 3:6).

One obligation people have towards religious scholars and clergy is to show respect for them. Paul admonishes the Thessalonian Church: "Now we ask you, brothers and sisters, to acknowledge those who work hard among you, who care for you in the Lord and who admonish you. Hold them in the highest regard in love because of their work. Live in peace with each other" (1 Thessalonians 5:12-13).

Moreover, it is stated that "The elders who direct the affairs of the church well are worthy of double honor, especially those whose work is preaching and teaching" (I Timothy 5:17).

Love and Kindness in Islamic and Christian Scriptures

A teacher is obliged to show kindness and love towards their students. Paul sent his student Timothy to preach and advised him: "Set an example for the believers in speech, in conduct, in love, in faith, and in purity" (1 Timothy 4:12).

Further, he states: "But you, man of God, … pursue righteousness, godliness, faith, love, endurance and gentleness" (I Timothy 6:11).

In another piece of advice, he warns Timothy: "Don't have anything to do with foolish and stupid arguments, because you know they produce quarrels. And the Lord's servant must not be quarrelsome but must be kind to everyone, able to teach, not resentful. Opponents must be gently instructed, in the hope that God will grant them repentance leading them to a knowledge of the truth" (II Timothy 2:23-25). He adds: "And the Lord's servant must not be quarrelsome but must be kind to everyone, able to teach, not resentful" (II Timothy 2:24).

Peter instructs religious clergy to offer guidance to the people out of a desire to serve, not coercion: "Be shepherds of God's flock that is under your care, watching over them—not because you must, but because you are willing, as God wants you to be; not pursuing dishonest gain, but eager to serve" (1 Peter 5:2).

In the Old Testament, religious clergy are permitted to use punishment out of kindness to guide believers. In the Psalms, David asserts: "Let a righteous man strike me—that is a kindness; let him rebuke me—that is oil on my head. My head will not refuse it" (Psalms 141:5).

Love and Kindness towards Friends

In both Testaments, there is a strong emphasis on showing love and kindness towards one's friends. For instance, in the Old Testament, an exemplary case of friendship is depicted in the bond between Jonathan, son of Saul, and David. Jonathan saved David's life several times and protected him from Saul's attempts to kill him. The two forged a deep friendship. When David learned of Jonathan's death, he mourned deeply for his friend and composed the following lament: "I grieve for you, Jonathan my brother; you were very dear to me. Your love for me was wonderful, more wonderful than that of women" (2 Samuel 1:26).

In both the Old and New Testaments, there are instructions on how to demonstrate love towards a friend. One such recommendation is to exhibit kindness and mercy in all circumstances. In the Book of Proverbs, Solomon states: "A friend loves at all times, and a brother is born for a time of adversity" (Proverbs 17:17).

He also says: "One who has unreliable friends soon comes to ruin, but there is a friend who sticks closer than a brother" (Proverbs 18:24).

Solomon suggests it is preferable to endure the rebukes of a friend than to accept the flattery of an enemy: "Wounds from a friend can be trusted, but an enemy multiplies kisses" (Proverbs 27:6).

Solomon counsels his followers to conceal their friend's flaws and mistakes, never divulging them to others. He asserts: "Whoever would foster love covers over an offense, but whoever repeats the matter separates close friends" (Proverbs 17:9).

In the Old Testament, one tradition was the making of a pledge of friendship between friends. For instance, it is written: "And Jonathan made a covenant with David because he loved him as himself" (1 Samuel 18:3). It then continues:

But if my father intends to harm you, may the LORD deal with Jonathan, be it ever so severely, if I do not let you know and send you away in peace. May the LORD be with you as he has been with my father. But show me unfailing kindness like the LORD's

Love and Kindness in Islamic and Christian Scriptures

kindness as long as I live, so that I may not be killed, and do not ever cut off your kindness from my family—not even when the LORD has cut off every one of David's enemies from the face of the earth." So Jonathan made a covenant with the house of David, saying, "May the LORD call David's enemies to account." And Jonathan had David reaffirm his oath out of love for him. (1 Samuel 20:13-17)

John believes that the pinnacle of friendship is to sacrifice one's life for a friend. He states: "Greater love has no one than this: to lay down one's life for one's friends" (John 15:13).

Solomon suggests that consultation or advice is crucial to friendship: "Perfume and incense bring joy to the heart, and the pleasantness of a friend springs from their heartfelt advice" (Proverbs 27:9).

While one should be kind to friends, one should never fully trust them. Micah advises: "Do not trust a neighbor; put no confidence in a friend. Even with the woman who lies in your embrace, guard the words of your lips" (Micah 7:5).

A friend that one fully trusts may betray. David also laments this: "Even my close friend, someone I trusted, one who shared my bread, has turned against me" (Psalms 41:9).

Love and Kindness towards Charitable Individuals

In the Old Testament, consequences are mentioned for failing to show love and kindness towards charitable individuals. In the Book of Judges, Gideon, chosen as a judge of God, exemplifies this. He demonstrated charity and kindness to the Israelites, making numerous sacrifices for them. However, after his death, the Israelites forgot his benevolence and treated his family unjustly, leading to God's rebuke. The Book of Judges states: "They did not remember the LORD their God, who had rescued them from the hands of all their enemies on every side. They also failed to show any loyalty to the family of Jerub-Baal (that is, Gideon) in spite of all the good things he had done for them" (Judges 8:35).

Moreover, the Book of Chronicles recounts that during Joash's reign, Jehoiada served as the high priest and revitalized the temple. After Jehoiada's death, idol worship resurged. When Zechariah, the son of Jehoiada, warned against idolatry, the people stoned him. Joash forgot the kindness Jehoiada had shown him, leading to Zechariah's death. As Zechariah died, he uttered, "May the Lord see this and call you to account." Consequently, God later avenged Zechariah's blood from them (2 Chronicles 24:1-27).

Love and Kindness to Neighbors

The Bible frequently emphasizes loving our neighbor as ourselves: "Love your neighbor as yourself. I am the LORD" (Leviticus 19:18).

It also asserts: "Love your neighbor as yourself" (Mat 19:19, Mat 22:39, Mark 12:31, Luk 10:27, Rom 13:9, Gal 5:14).

There is no distinction whether the neighbor is one's friend, fellow citizen, or a stranger from another land, as the Old Testament states: "The foreigner residing among you must be treated as your native-born. Love them as yourself, for you were foreigners in Egypt. I am the LORD your God" (Leviticus 19:34).

The Old Testament advises love and kindness towards neighbors: "Do not seek revenge or bear a grudge against anyone among your people, but love your neighbor as yourself. I am the LORD" (Leviticus 19:18).

Jesus Christ says: "You have heard that it was said, 'Love your neighbor and hate your enemy'" (Matthew 5:43).

Further, in another part of the New Testament, as narrated by Matthew, Jesus Christ is quoted as saying: "Love your neighbor as yourself" (Matthew 19:19).

The Bible suggests: "Do not seek revenge or bear a grudge against anyone among your people, but love your neighbor as yourself. I am the LORD" (Leviticus 19:18).

Love of neighbor is a significant religious instruction. One day a group of Pharisees approached Jesus Christ. As Matthew says, "One of them, an expert in the law, tested him with this question: 'Teacher, which is the greatest commandment in the Law?' Jesus replied: 'Love the Lord your God with all your heart and with all your soul and with all your mind.' This is the first and greatest commandment. And the second is like it: 'Love your neighbor as yourself'" (Matthew 22:35-39).

In the Old Testament, sacrifices and offerings held great significance. However, Mark highlights the supremacy of love for one's neighbor over these rituals, stating, "And to love your neighbor as yourself is more important than all burnt offerings and sacrifices" (Mark 12:33).

From the biblical standpoint, the essence of all religious laws is summed up in love for one's neighbor: "For the entire law is fulfilled in keeping this one command: 'Love your neighbor as yourself'" (Galatians 5:14).

Love and Kindness in Islamic and Christian Scriptures

Moreover, in the Epistle to the Romans, Paul emphasizes: "Let no debt remain outstanding, except the continuing debt to love one another, for whoever loves others has fulfilled the law. The commandments, 'You shall not commit adultery,' 'You shall not murder,' 'You shall not steal,' 'You shall not covet,' and whatever other command there may be, are summed up in this one command: 'Love your neighbor as yourself'" (Romans 13:8-9).

James also refers to love for neighbors as the royal law: "If you really keep the royal law found in Scripture, 'Love your neighbor as yourself,' you are doing right" (James 2:8).

The Book of Proverbs asserts that failing to show kindness towards neighbors is the action of the wicked: "The wicked crave evil; their neighbors get no mercy from them" (Proverbs 21:10).

The New Testament also commands: "Love does no harm to a neighbor. Therefore love is the fulfillment of the law" (Romans 13:10).

It also advises us to please our neighbors: "Each of us should please our neighbors for their good, to build them up" (Romans 15:2).

Significance and Effects of Love towards Neighbors

Christian sacred texts emphasize the importance and impact of showing love and kindness towards neighbors.

Kindness towards Neighbors as a Good Deed

Showing kindness to one's neighbors has many positive effects and consequences. The New Testament highlights love and mercy for neighbors as virtuous deeds. James, a disciple of Jesus Christ, states: "If you really keep the royal law found in Scripture, 'Love your neighbor as yourself,' you are doing right" (James 2:8).

Kindness towards Neighbors leading to Eternal Life

Showing kindness to neighbors can help one inherit eternal life. According to a story in the New Testament, Jesus Christ had a dialogue with his companions: "On one occasion an expert in the law stood up to test Jesus. 'Teacher,' he asked, 'what must I do to inherit eternal life?' 'What is written in the Law?' he replied. 'How do you read it?' He answered, 'Love the Lord your God with all your heart and with all your soul and with all your strength and with all your mind'; and, 'Love your neighbor as yourself.' 'You have answered correctly,' Jesus replied. 'Do this and you will live'" (Luke 10:25-28).

Unkindness towards Neighbors as a Sign of Wickedness

Solomon states that failing to show kindness towards neighbors is a sign of wickedness: "The wicked crave evil; their neighbors get no mercy from them" (Proverbs 21:10).

Love and Kindness towards Guests

Hospitality is a moral conduct emphasized in both Testaments. The Epistle to Romans advises: "Share with the Lord's people who are in need. Practice hospitality" (Romans 12:13).

Hospitality should be offered without any complaints about the guests. Peter advises Christians to host each other with passion: "Offer hospitality to one another without grumbling" (1 Peter 4:9).

Sometimes, to further honor guests, hosts would kiss their feet and wash them with perfumes. For instance, when Jesus Christ was a guest in the house of a Pharisee, a woman washed Jesus's feet with perfume. When the Pharisee harbored doubts regarding Jesus in his heart, Jesus told him: ""Do you see this woman? I came into your house. You did not give me any water for my feet, but she wet my feet with her tears and wiped them with her hair. You did not give me a kiss, but this woman, from the time I entered, has not stopped kissing my feet. You did not put oil on my head, but she has poured perfume on my feet" (Luke 7:44-46).

This narrative suggests that Jesus expected the host to wash and kiss his feet. As illustrated at the Last Supper, a woman took a precious perfume made of hyacinth, about a liter, and anointed Jesus's feet with it. She then dried his feet with her hair, filling the house with fragrance. However, Judas Iscariot, a disciple of Jesus who would later betray him, objected, saying: "Why wasn't this perfume sold and the money given to the poor? It was worth a year's wages." Jesus replied, "Leave her alone. It was intended that she should save this perfume for the day of my burial. You will always have the poor among you, but you will not always have me" (John 12:3-8).

According to the Book of Matthew, that woman not only anointed Christ's feet but also his head with the perfume (Matthew 26:7). In the Old Testament, it was common to anoint a guest's head (Psalms 23:5).

Significance and Effects of Showing Kindness to Guests

In both the Old and the New Testaments, hospitality is considered highly valuable, which encompasses the following aspects.

Love and Kindness in Islamic and Christian Scriptures

■ A Sign of Serving the Church

In the Old Testament, hospitality is a characteristic often associated with religious clergy. In the Epistle to Timothy, the characteristics of a religious servant are outlined as follows: "Now the overseer is to be above reproach, faithful to his wife, temperate, self-controlled, respectable, hospitable, able to teach" (1 Timothy 3:2).

■ Hospitality towards Guests as Serving Angels

Paul, in his Epistle to the Hebrews, advises not to neglect hospitality and warm reception of guests. He warns them that without this, they may miss the chance to receive and serve angels: "Do not forget to show hospitality to strangers, for by so doing some people have shown hospitality to angels without knowing it" (Hebrews 13:2).

Kindness towards the Poor and Indigent

In both the Old and New Testaments, there is a profound emphasis on demonstrating love and mercy towards the impoverished. This section will delve into these directives, highlighting that a central practice of kindness towards this group is providing financial assistance. For instance, Deuteronomy 15:7 admonishes, "If anyone is poor among your fellow Israelites in any of the towns of the land the LORD your God is giving you, do not be hardhearted or tightfisted toward them."

John's counsel to Christians is clear: "If anyone has material possessions and sees a brother or sister in need but has no pity on them, how can the love of God be in that person?" (1 John 3:17).

According to the New Testament, assisting impoverished believers is seen as lending to God. In the Book of Proverbs, Solomon draws a parallel between aiding the poor and lending money to God, stating, "Whoever is kind to the poor lends to the LORD, and he will reward them for what they have done" (Proverbs 19:17).

Solomon asserts that generosity attracts affection and favor from others. A benevolent individual naturally draws people towards them, as Solomon expresses by stating, "Many curry favor with a ruler, and everyone is the friend of one who gives gifts" (Proverbs 19:6).

Showing Love and Kindness to Orphans

Caring for orphans is considered a sacred duty. In Hosea 14:3, it is acknowledged that in God, the fatherless find compassion. Hosea addresses God, saying, "In you the fatherless find compassion."

Orphans and widows, being among the most vulnerable members of society, are often faced with to oppression and injustice. In the Old Testament, God commands that their rights be protected and that what has been taken from them by oppressors be restored. As stated in Deuteronomy 10:18, "He defends the cause of the fatherless and the widow, and loves the foreigner residing among you, providing them with food and clothing."

Showing Love and Kindness to Patients

Indeed, Both the Old and New Testaments contain instructions on showing kindness towards the sick. For example, the New Testament encourages empathy with those who are ill, stating, "If one part suffers, every part suffers with it" (1 Corinthians 12:26).

■■■

Reciprocal Kindness between Rulers and Citizens

Solomon emphasizes that demonstrating kindness to citizens is crucial for the stability and longevity of a king's reign: "Love and faithfulness keep a king safe; through love his throne is made secure" (Proverbs 20:28).

According to the teachings of the Old Testament, following Solomon's death and his son Rehoboam's rise to power, the Israelites, who had suffered Solomon's stringent policies, pleaded with Rehoboam, urging him to govern with more leniency: "Then King Rehoboam consulted the elders who had served his father Solomon during his lifetime. 'How would you advise me to answer these people?' he asked. They replied, 'If you will be kind to these people and please them and give them a favorable answer, they will always be your servants'" (II Chr 10:6-7).

Kindness to Enemies and Opponents

Christian sacred texts emphasize kindness even towards enemies, whether they be armed military adversaries or individuals with whom we have strained social relationships. The Bible presents a nuanced perspective, recognizing the necessity of both peace and war. As Solomon states in Ecclesiastes 3:8, "There is a time for love and a time for hate, a time for war and a time for peace."

In the Psalms, David petitions God to deal with his enemies. He implores, "In your unfailing love, silence my enemies; destroy all my foes" (Psalm 143:12).

Jesus Christ strongly underscores the necessity of showing kindness to those who have wronged us. In Luke, He is quoted as saying:

If you love those who love you, what credit is that to you? Even sinners love those who love them. And if you do good to those who are good to you, what credit is that to you? Even sinners do that. And if you lend to those from whom you expect repayment, what credit is that to you? Even sinners lend to sinners, expecting to be repaid in full. But love your enemies, do good to them, and lend to them without expecting to get anything back. Then your reward will be great, and you will be children of the Most High, because he is kind to the ungrateful and wicked. (Luke 6:32-35)

In the Book of Matthew, Jesus reportedly stated: "that you may be children of your Father in heaven. He causes his sun to rise on the evil and the good, and sends rain on the righteous and the unrighteous. If you love those who love you, what reward will you get? Are not even the tax collectors doing that? And if you greet only your own people, what are you doing more than others? Do not even pagans do that?" (Mat 5:45-47).

In the Acts of the Apostles, a fierce conflict erupted within the Corinthian Church between Paul's opponents and proponents. This discord deeply disheartened Paul, but through subsequent measures, he garnered significant support within the church. Consequently, he wrote a letter to his advocates in the Corinthian Church, urging them to show kindness to their opponents: "If anyone has caused grief, he has not so much grieved me as he has grieved all of you to some extent—not to put it too severely. The punishment inflicted on him by the majority is sufficient. Now instead, you ought to forgive and comfort him, so that he will not be overwhelmed by excessive sorrow. I urge you, therefore, to reaffirm your love for him" (2 Corinthians 2:5-8).

Moreover, in his letter to the Romans, Paul advises, "If it is possible, as far as it depends on you, live at peace with everyone" (Romans 12:18).

One commendable practice in dealing with enemies is to offer positive prayers for those who have wronged us. For instance, when Solomon rose to power, he dedicated a thousand burnt offerings to God on an altar made of bronze. That same night, God appeared to Solomon and said, "Ask for whatever you want me to give you." Solomon responded, "Give me wisdom and knowledge." God then said to Solomon, "Since this is your heart's desire and you have not asked for wealth, possessions or honor, nor for the death of your enemies, and since you have not asked for a long life but for wisdom and knowledge to govern my people over whom I have made you king" (2 Chronicles 1:7-11).

Jesus Christ also teaches that offering prayers is a way to deal with one's enemies. The Book of Matthew states, "You have heard that it was said, 'Love your neighbor and hate your enemy.' But I tell you, love your enemies and pray for those who persecute you" (Matthew 5:43-44).

In the Book of Luke, he commands: "Bless those who curse you, pray for those who mistreat you" (Luke 6:28).

Further, Jesus Christ orders us to be kind to those who have wronged us: "But to you who are listening I say: Love your enemies, do good to those who hate you" (Luke 6:27).

Paul advises his companions: "When we are slandered, we answer kindly" (1 Corinthians 4:13).

Paul the Apostle writes: "Make every effort to live in peace with everyone" (Hebrews 12:14); "Do not repay anyone evil for evil. Be careful to do what is right in the eyes of everyone. If it is possible, as far as it depends on you, live at peace with everyone" (Romans 12:17-18); and "Let us therefore make every effort to do what leads to peace and to mutual edification" (Romans 14:19).

James also advises: "But the wisdom that comes from heaven is first of all pure; then peace-loving, considerate, submissive, full of mercy and good fruit, impartial and sincere. Peacemakers who sow in peace reap a harvest of righteousness" (James 3:17-18).

Those who show kindness to their enemies will achieve higher degrees of spirituality: "But love your enemies, do good to them, and lend to them without expecting to get anything back. Then your reward will be great, and you will be children of the Most High, because he is kind to the ungrateful and wicked" (Luke 6:35).

Kindness to Prisoners of War

In both the New and Old Testaments, there are directives regarding kindness to prisoners of war, captives, and slaves. This chapter reviews the most important teachings within the Testaments about kindness to captives and slaves.

The Old Testament categorizes servants and slaves into two groups. First, those from the Israelite race who had to sell themselves due to poverty. The Old Testament commands that these individuals and their children be treated as day laborers. The Book of Leviticus states: "If any of your fellow Israelites become poor and sell themselves to you, do not make them work as slaves. They are to be treated as hired workers or temporary residents among you; they are to work for you until the Year of Jubilee. Then they and their children are to be released, and they will go back to their own clans and to the property of their ancestors" (Leviticus 25:39-41).

During Paul's time, a slave named Onesimus escaped from his Christian owner, Philemon, and ended up in Rome, where he was imprisoned. It was there in prison that he met Paul. Paul then sends Onesimus back to Philemon, urging Philemon to forgive him and to treat him not just as a slave, but as a brother (Philemon 1:12-19).

Factors Contributing to and Obstacles in Attracting Others' Affection

⦿ Factors contributing to Gaining Others' Love

In Christian sources, various factors are introduced as contributors to attracting the love of others. This chapter examines the most significant of these factors.

▪ Love inspired by God

From a Biblical perspective, God, as the creator of all, has the ability to inspire love or hatred in people's hearts. In the Epistle to the Ephesians, it is emphasized that even before the creation of the world, God selected certain individuals to be recipients of His love: "For he chose us in him before the creation of the world to be holy and blameless in his sight. In love" (Ephesians 1:4).

Moreover, the Old Testament asserts: "Then the LORD raised up against Solomon an adversary, Hadad the Edomite, from the royal line of Edom" (1 Kings 11:14). Also, it states: "And God raised up against Solomon another adversary, Rezon son of Eliada, who had fled from his master, Hadadezer king of Zobah" (1 Kings 11:23).

In the Epistle to the Galatians, Paul describes love as the fruit of the Holy Spirit: "For the flesh desires what is contrary to the Spirit, and the Spirit what is contrary to the flesh. They are in conflict with each other, so that you are not to do whatever you want… But the fruit of the Spirit is love, joy, peace, forbearance, kindness, goodness, faithfulness, gentleness, and self-control" (Galatians 5:17-26).

▪ Trust and Loyalty breeding Love

One factor that brings love is trust and loyalty, as David says in the Psalms: "Many are the woes of the wicked, but the LORD's unfailing love surrounds the one who trusts in him" (Psalm 32:10).

Love and Kindness in Islamic and Christian Scriptures

David believes that love and loyalty are mutually entailing characteristics: "Love and faithfulness meet together" (Psalm 85:10).

Solomon observes: "Many claim to have unfailing love, but a faithful person who can find?" (Proverbs 20:6).

Proper Criticism garnering Love

According to the Old Testament, well-intentioned criticism can cultivate love. In the Book of Proverbs, Solomon says: "Whoever rebukes a person will in the end gain favor rather than one who has a flattering tongue" (Proverbs 28:23). Additionally, he warns that "the one who hates correction will die" (Proverbs 15:10).

Within the value system of both Testaments, manifest rebuke is considered more valuable than hidden love. Solomon states: "Better is open rebuke than hidden love" (Proverbs 27:5).

Good Intention

Another factor contributing to attracting love from others is good intention, which the Book of Proverbs says builds love: "But those who plan what is good find love and faithfulness" (Proverbs 14:22).

Obstacles in Attracting Others' Love

From the perspective of Christian sources, certain factors can hinder love and kindness. The following subsections will review some of these.

Devil as Hindering Love

According to both the Old and New Testaments, the devil sows seeds of hatred in people's hearts. When Jesus Christ alluded to the analogy of weeds in the wheat field, his disciples asked him in private to explain the analogy to them. He stated: "The field is the world, and the good seed stands for the people of the kingdom. The weeds are the people of the evil one, and the enemy who sows them is the devil. The harvest is the end of the age, and the harvesters are angels" (Matthew 13:38-39).

Violence and Dispute

Another obstacle on the path of love, from a Christian perspective, is violence, as Solomon asserts: "The bloodthirsty hate a person of integrity and seek to kill the upright" (Proverbs 29:10). He also says: "Whoever loves a quarrel loves sin" (Proverbs 17:19).

Blameworthy Love and Kindness

In both the Old and New Testaments, love is strongly emphasized, yet not all forms of love are deemed virtuous. Both testaments identify scenarios where displaying love and kindness may be deemed blameworthy. The following subsections will explore these instances.

■ Love of Disbelievers

While the Bible commands us to show love, it also advises caution against forming alliances or close friendships between believers and non-believers. In the Old Testament, Jehu the seer, son of Hanani, visited King Jehoshaphat and warned him, saying: "Should you help the wicked and love those who hate the LORD? Because of this, the wrath of the LORD is on you" (2 Chronicles 19:2).

David also expresses his aversion towards non-believers, supplicating to God: "Do I not hate those who hate you, LORD, and abhor those who are in rebellion against you? I have nothing but hatred for them; I count them my enemies" (Psalm 139:21-22).

The New Testament also emphasizes the significance of refraining from yielding to the domination of non-believers. Paul writes to the Corinthians: "Do not be yoked together with unbelievers. For what do righteousness and wickedness have in common? Or what fellowship can light have with darkness?" (2 Corinthians 6:14).

■ Love of Evildoers

The Old Testament asserts that love of animals is a sign of piety, but love of the wicked is forbidden. Solomon states, "The righteous care for the needs of their animals, but the kindest acts of the wicked are cruel" (Proverbs 12:10).

■ Mercy towards Enemies

Numerous verses of the Bible warn against showing mercy towards enemies:
- "In your unfailing love, silence my enemies; destroy all my foes" (Psalm 143:12).

Love and Kindness in Islamic and Christian Scriptures

- "When the LORD your God brings you into the land you are entering to possess and drives out before you many nations... then you must destroy them totally. Make no treaty with them, and show them no mercy" (Deuteronomy 7:1-2).
- "Show no pity: life for life, eye for eye, tooth for tooth, hand for hand, foot for foot" (Deuteronomy 19:21).
- Yahweh says: "I will smash them one against the other, parents and children alike... I will allow no pity or mercy or compassion to keep me from destroying them" (Jeremiah 13:14).
- He also says: "Therefore as surely as I live, declares the Sovereign LORD, because you have defiled my sanctuary with all your vile images and detestable practices, I myself will shave you; I will not look on you with pity or spare you" (Ezekiel 5:11).
- "I will not look on you with pity; I will not spare you. I will surely repay you for your conduct and for the detestable practices among you. Then you will know that I am the LORD" (Ezekiel 7:4).
- "He answered me, 'The sin of the people of Israel and Judah is exceedingly great... So I will not look on them with pity or spare them, but I will bring down on their own heads what they have done'" (Ezekiel 9:9-10).
- "For I will no longer have pity on the people of the land," declares the LORD. "I will give everyone into the hands of their neighbors and their king. They will devastate the land, and I will not rescue anyone from their hands" (Zechariah 11:6).

■ Love of (Illegitimate) Women and Prostitutes

While the two Testaments emphasize love for certain women, such as wives, mothers, and relatives, they discourage love for prostitutes and illegitimate relationships. For instance, the Old Testament prohibited marriage with non-Israelite women, yet Solomon, as depicted in the Bible, disregarded this divine directive and married numerous non-Israelite women, resulting in rebuke (1 Kings 11:2).

Moreover, the New Testament condemns homosexuality. Paul writes: "Because of this, God gave them over to shameful lusts. Even their women exchanged natural sexual relations for unnatural ones. In the same way the men also abandoned natural relations with women and were inflamed with lust for one another. Men committed shameful acts with other men, and received in themselves the due penalty for their error" (Romans 1:26-27).

Love and Kindness in Islamic and Christian Scriptures

■ Love of this World

Love of this world and worldly affairs is also rebuked in the Bible. One cannot simultaneously love this world and love God, as John writes: "Do not love the world or anything in the world. If anyone loves the world, love for the Father is not in them" (1 John 2:15). James, Jesus's disciple, emphasizes: "You adulterous people, don't you know that friendship with the world means enmity against God? Therefore, anyone who chooses to be a friend of the world becomes an enemy of God" (James 4:4).

Moreover, another blameworthy love, as depicted in the two Testaments, is love of money and wealth. Jesus Christ states: "No one can serve two masters. Either you will hate the one and love the other, or you will be devoted to the one and despise the other. You cannot serve both God and money" (Luke 16:13). Paul advises his disciple Timothy: "Those who want to get rich fall into temptation and a trap and into many foolish and harmful desires that plunge people into ruin and destruction. For the love of money is a root of all kinds of evil. Some people, eager for money, have wandered from the faith and pierced themselves with many griefs" (1 Timothy 6:9-10).

References

The Quran, English translation by Ali Quli Qarai.

The Bible, New International Version.

Ahmadi Mianaji, Ali. 1411 AH. *Al-Asir fi al-Islam*. Qom: Islamic Publishing Office affiliated with the Society of Seminary Teachers of Qom.

Ahmadi Mianaji, Ali. 1419 AH. *Makatib al-rasul*. Qom: Dar al-Hadith.

Ahmadi, Mahdi. 1389 Sh. *Sayf al-wa'izin wa-dhakirin*. Qom: Nasayeh.

Al-Amirkani, James Anas. 1890. *Nizam al-ta'lim fi 'ilm al-lahut al-qawim*. Beirut: Matba'at al-Amirkan.

'Amili, Ja'far Murtada. 1426 AH. *Al-Sahih min sirat al-nabi al-a'zam*. Qom: Dar al-Hadith.

'Arusi al-Huwayzi, 'Abd 'Ali b. Jum'a al-. 1412 AH. *Tafsir nur al-thaqalayn*. Edited by Seyed Hashem Rasouli Mahallati. Qom: Esmailian Institute.

Astarabadi, Ahmad b. Taj al-Din. n.d. *Athar Ahmadi: tarikh-i zindigani-yi payambar-i khuda va aimmih-yi athar*. N.p.

Attributed to Imam al-Rida. 1406 AH. *Fiqh al-Rida, al-fiqh al-mansub ila al-Imam al-Rida 'alayh al-salam*. Qom: Nashr al-Mu'tamar al-'Alami li-l-Imam al-Rida.

Augustine of Hopp. 1392 Sh. *Shahr-i khuda (City of God)*. Translated by Hossein Tofighi. Qom: University of Religions and Denominations.

Ayer, Joseph Cullen. 1926. *A Source Book for Ancient Church History, from the Apostolic Age to the Close of the Conciliar Period*. New York: Scribner's.

Bahrani, Sayyid Hashim. 1411 AH. *Hilyat al-abrar fi ahwal Muhammad wa-alih al-athar*. Edited by Sheikh Gholamreza Boroujerdi. Qom: Mu'assasat al-Ma'arif al-Islamiyya.

Baladhuri, Ahmad b. Yahya. n.d. *Ansab al-ashraf*. Edited by Mohammad Bagher Mahmoudi. Beirut: Dar al-Ma'arif.

Barqi, Ahmad b. Muhammad. 1341 AH. *Al-Mahasin*. Edited by Seyed Mahdi Rajai. Qom: Ahl al-Bayt World Assembly.

Bayhaqi, Ahmad b. al-Husayn. n.d. *Al-Sunan al-kubra*. Beirut: Dar al-Fikr.

Borujerdi, Hossein. 1422 AH. *Jami' ahadith al-Shi'a*. Qom: al-Wasif Institute.

Brantl, George. 1381 Sh. *Ayin-i Catholic (Catholicism)*. Translated into Persian by Hassan Ghanbari. Qom: Center of Studies and Research on Religions and Denominations.

Chervin, Ronda. 1973. *Church of Love*. Los Angeles, California: Ligouri.

Daylami, al-Hasan b. Abi al-Hasan al-. 1398 AH. *Irshad al-qulub*. Beirut: al-A'lami Institute.

Daylami, al-Hasan b. Muhammad. 1414 AH. *A'lam al-din fi sifat al-mu'minin*. Qom: Al al-Bayt Institute.

Dhahabi, Muhammad b. Ahmad al-. 1407 AH. *Tarikh al-Islam wa-wafiyyat al-mashahir wa-l-a'lam*. Beirut: Dar al-Kitab al-'Arabi.

Ehsanbakhsh, Sadegh. 1374 Sh. *Athar al-sadiqin*. Rasht: Friday Prayer Headquarters.

Elwell, Walter A. 1997. "Prophet, Prophetess, Prophecy." In *Evangelical Dictionary of Theology*. Ada, Michigan: Baker Academic.

Farahidi, Khalil b. Ahmad al-. 1383 Sh. *Kitab al-ʿayn*. Qom: Osveh.

Fattal al-Nishaburi, Muhammad b. al-Hasan al-. 1406 AH. *Rawdat al-waʿizin*. Edited by Hossein Alami. Beirut: al-Aʿlami Institute.

Fayd al-Kashani, Mulla Muhsin al-. 1383 AH. *Mahajjat al-baydà fi tahdhib al-ihyà*. Qom: Society of the Seminary Teachers of Qom.

Florovsky, George. 2003. "The Function of Tradition in the Ancient Church." In Daniel B. Clendenin (Ed.), *Eastern Orthodox Christianity: A Western Perspective* (2nd edition). Ada, Michigan: Baker Academic.

Furat al-Kufi, Abu al-Qasim. 1401 AH. *Tafsir Furat al-Kufi*. Edited by Mohammad Kazem Mahmoudi. Tehran: Ministry of Culture and Islamic Guidance.

Gharawi Husayni Astarabadi, ʿAli. 1409 AH. *Tàwil al-ayat al-zahira fi fadàil al-ʿitrat al-tahira*. Edited by Hossein Ostadvali. Qom: Islamic Publishing Institute.

Gilani, Mulla ʿAbd al-Razzaq. 1366 Sh. *Misbah al-shariʿa wa-miftah al-haqiqa* (Attributed to Imam al-Sadiq, peace be upon him). Tehran: Maktabat al-Saduq.

Gordon, Tracy. 2009. "Survey: Two-thirds of Protestant pastors consider Islam 'dangerous.'" Religion News Service. April 24, 2024. https://religionnews.com/2009/12/19/survey-two-thirds-of-protestant-pastors-consider-islam-dangerous/

Haghani Fazl, Mohammad. 1392 Sh. *Khatanapaziri-yi kitab-i muqaddas*. Qom: University of Religions and Denominations.

Hakim al-Nishaburi, Muhammad b. ʿAbd Allah al-. 1411 AH. *Al-Mustadrak ʿala al-sahihayn*. Edited by Mostafa ʿAbd al-Qadir ʿAta. Beirut: Dar al-Kutub al-ʿIlmiyya.

Halabi, Abu al-Faraj Nur al-Din ʿAli b. Ibrahim al-. n.d. *Sira Halabiyya, wa-huwa al-kitab al-musamma insan al-ʿuyun fi sirat al-amin al-maʿmun*. Beirut: Dar al-Kutub al-ʿIlmiyya.

Halwani, al-Husayn b. Muhammad al-. 1408 AH. *Nuzhat al-nazir wa-tanbih al-khatir*. Qom: al-Imam al-Mahdi Institute.

Hanson, Bradley. 1997. *Introduction to Christian Theology*. Minneapolis, Minnesota: Fortress Press.

Harent, Stéphane. 1911. "Original Sin." *The Catholic Encyclopedia*. Vol. 11. New York: Robert Appleton Company. <http://www.newadvent.org/cathen/11312a.htm>.

Harvey, Philip. 2003. *New Catholic Encyclopedia*. 2nd ed., vol. 12. Detroit: Thomson/Gale; Washington, D.C.: Catholic University of America.

Hilli al-Asadi, Ahmad b. Muhammad al-. n.d. *ʿUddat al-daʿi wa-nijat al-saʿi*. Edited by Ahmad Movahedi. Qom: Maktaba Vejdani.

Hilli Sayyid b. Tawus, ʿAli b. Musa al-. 1414 AH. *Iqbal al-aʿmal*. Edited by Javad Ghayoomi. Qom: Islamic Propagation Office.

Hilli Sayyid b. Tawus, ʿAli b. Musa al-. 1419 AH. *Falah al-sàil wa-najah al-masàil*. Qom: Islamic Propagation Office.

Hilli, al-Hasan b. Yusuf al-. 1413 AH. *Kashf al-murad fi sharh tajrid al-iʿtiqad*. Qom: Islamic Publishing Institute.

Hilli, Warram b. Abi Firas al-. n.d. *Tanbih al-khawatir wa-nuzhat al-nawazir: majmuʿa Warram*. Beirut: Dar al-Taʿaruf wa-Dar Saʿb.

Himyari al-Qummi, ʿAbd Allah b. Jaʿfar al-. 1413 AH. *Qurb al-isnad*. Qom: Al-Bayt Institute.

Himyari, ʿAbd al-Malik b. Hisham al-. 1355 AH. *Sira Ibn Hisham, al-Sirat al-Nabawiyya*. Edited by Mustafa al-Saqqa and Ibrahim al-Anbari. Qom: Maktabat al-Mustafa.

Husayni al-ʿAmili, Sayyid Muhammad b. al-Hasan al-. 1414 AH. *Mawaʿiz al-ʿadadiyya*. Edited by Mirza Ali Meshkini Ardabili. Qom: Dar Nashr al-Hadi.

Husayni al-Rawandi, Fadl Allah b. ʿAli al-. 1370 AH. *Nawadir al-Rawandi*. Najaf: al-Matbaʿat al-Haydariyya.

Ibn Abi al-Hadid al-Muʿtazili, ʿAbd al-Hamid b. Muhammad. 1387 AH. *Sharh nahj al-balagha*. Edited by Muhammad Abu al-Fadl Ibrahim. Beirut: Dar Ihyá al-Turath al-ʿArabi.

Ibn Abi Jumhur, Muhammad b. ʿAli. 1430 AH. *ʿAwali al-liʾali al-ʿaziziyya fi al-ahadith al-diniyya*. Edited by Mojtaba Araghi. Qom: Matbaʿa Sayyid al-Shuhadaʾ ʿAlayh al-Salam.

Ibn Ashʿath al-Kufi, Muhammad b. Muhammad. n.d. *Al-Jaʿfariyyat (al-Ashʿathiyyat)*. Tehran: Maktaba Ninawi.

Ibn Athir, ʿIzz al-Din ʿAli b. Muhammad. 1408 AH. *Al-Kamil fi al-tarikh*. Edited by Ali Shiri. Beirut: Dar Ihyá al-Turath al-ʿArabi.

Ibn Babawayh al-Qummi, Muhammad b. ʿAli. 1361 Sh. *Maʿani al-akhbar*. Edited by Ali Akbar Ghaffari. Qom: Islamic Publishing Institute.

Ibn Babawayh al-Qummi, Muhammad b. ʿAli. 1398 AH. *Al-Tawhid*. Edited by Hashem Hosseini Tehrani. Qom: Islamic Publishing Institute.

Ibn Babawayh al-Qummi, Muhammad b. ʿAli. 1400 AH. *Amali al-Saduq*. Beirut: Al-Aʿlami Institute.

Ibn Babawayh al-Qummi, Muhammad b. ʿAli. 1408 AH. *ʿIlal al-sharaʾiʿ*. Beirut: Dar Ihyá al-Turath al-ʿArabi.

Ibn Babawayh al-Qummi, Muhammad b. ʿAli. 1410 AH. *Al-Khisal*. Edited by Ali Akbar Ghaffari. Beirut: al-Aʿlami Institute.

Ibn Babawayh al-Qummi, Muhammad b. ʿAli. 1410 AH. *Musadaqat al-ikhwan*. Qom: al-Imam al-Mahdi Institute.

Ibn Babawayh al-Qummi, Muhammad b. ʿAli. n.d. *Man la-yahduruh al-faqih*. Edited by Ali Akbar Ghaffari. Qom: Islamic Publishing Institute.

Ibn Babawayh al-Qummi, Muhammad b. ʿAli. n.d. *Thawab al-aʿmal wa-ʿiqab al-aʿmal*. Edited by Ali Akbar Ghaffari. Tehran: Maktabat al-Saduq.

Ibn Babawayh al-Qummi, Muhammad b. ʿAli. n.d. *ʿUyun akhbar al-Rida ʿalayh al-salam*. Edited by Seyed Mahdi Hosseini Lajevardi. Tehran: Jahan.

Ibn Hanbal al-Shaybani, Ahmad b. Muhammad. 1414 AH. *Musnad Ahmad*. Edited by Abdullah Muhammad al-Darwish. Beirut: Dar al-Fikr.

Ibn Hayyun al-Tamimi al-Maghribi, Nuʿman b. Muhammad. 1389 AH. *Daʿaim al-Islam wa-dhikr al-halal wa-l-haram wa-l-qadaya wa-l-ahkam*. Edited by Asif ibn Ali Asghar Faydi. Egypt: Dar al-Maʿarif.

Ibn Hilal al-Thaqafi, Ibrahim b. Muhammad. 1395 AH. *Al-Gharat*. Edited by Seyed Jalal al-Din Muhaddith Urmawi. Tehran: Society for the National Heritage of Iran.

Love and Kindness in Islamic and Christian Scriptures

Ibn Idris al-Hilli, Muhammad b. Ahmad. 1414 AH. *Mustatrafat al-saràir*. Qom: Islamic Publishing Institute.

Ibn Kathir, Abu al-Fadà Ismaʿil b. ʿUmar. n.d. *Al-Bidaya wa-l-nihaya*. Beirut: Maktabat al-Maʿarif.

Ibn Kathir, Ismaʿil. 1410 AH. *Al-Bidaya wa-l-nihaya*. Beirut: Maktabat al-Maʿarif.

Ibn Manzur al-Misri, Muhammad b. Mukarram. 1410 AH. *Lisan al-ʿArab*. Beirut: Dar Sadir.

Ibn Qulawayh, Jaʿfar b. Muhammad. 1356 AH. *Kamil al-ziyarat*. Edited by Abdolhossein Amini Tabrizi. Najaf: al-Matbaʿat al-Murtadawiyya.

Ibn Saʿd, al-Katib al-Waqidi. n.d. *Tabaqat al-kubra*. Beirut: Dar Sadir.

Ibn Sayyid al-Nas, Muhammad b. Muhammad. n.d. *ʿUyun al-athar fi funun al-maghazi wa-l-shamàil wa-siyar*. N.p.

Ibn Shuʿba al-Harrani, al-Hasan b. ʿAli. 1404 AH. *Tuhaf al-ʿuqul*. Edited by Ali Akbar Ghaffari. Qom: Islamic Publishing Institute.

Imam Zayn al-ʿAbidin ʿAli b. al-Husayn. 1376 Sh. *Sahifa Sajjadiyya*. Qom: Daftar Nashr al-Hadi.

Imam Zayn al-ʿAbidin ʿAli b. al-Husayn. n.d. *Al-Sahifat al-Sajjadiyyat al-kamila*. Edited by Ali Ansarian. Damascus: al-Mustashariyyat al-Thiqafiyya.

Inbody, Tyron. 2005. *The Faith of the Christian Church: An Introduction to Theology*. Grand Rapids, MI: Wm. B. Eerdmans Publishing.

Irbili, Bahà al-Din ʿAli b. ʿIsa al-. 1401 AH. *Kashf al-ghumma fi maʿrifat al-àimma*. Edited by Seyed Hashem Rasuli Mahallati. Beirut: Dar al-Kitab al-Islami.

Isfahani, Ahmad b. ʿAbd Allah al-. 1410 AH. *Tarikh Asbahan*. Edited by Hassan Kasravi. Beirut: Dar al-Kutub al-ʿIlmiyya.

Jabaʿi al-ʿAmili (al-Shahid al-Thani), Zayn al-Din b. ʿAli. 1409 AH. *Munyat al-murid fi adab al-mufid wa-l-mustafid*. Edited by Reza Mokhtari. Qom: Islamic Propagation Office.

Jabaʿi al-ʿAmili (al-Shahid al-Thani), Zayn al-Din. 1388 Sh. *Al-Rawdat al-bahiyya fi sharh al-lumʿat al-Dimashqiyya*. Edited by Hassan Gharooei Tabrizi. Qom: Dar al-Tafsir.

Javadi Amoli, Abdollah. 1393 Sh. *Mafatih al-hayat*. Qom: Esra.

Johann, R. 1967. "Love." In *New Catholic Encyclopedia*. New York: McGraw-Hill.

Jurka, Gene. (2001). "Love." In *Encyclopedia of Ethics*. London: Routledge.

Juwayni, Ibrahim b. Muhammad al-. 1398 AH. *Faràid al-simtayn fi fadàil al-Murtada wa-l-Batul wa-l-sibtayn wa-l-àimma min dhurriyyatihim ʿalayhim al-salam*. Edited by Mohammad Bagher Mahmoudi. Beirut: al-Mahmudi Institute.

Karajaki al-Tirablusi, Muhammad b. ʿAli al-. 1410 AH. *Kanz al-fawàid*. Edited by Abdullah Nama. Qom: Dar al-Dhakhàir.

Khatib al-Baghdadi, Ahmad b. ʿAli al-. 1422 AH. *Tarikh Baghdad*. Edited by Bashar Awad Maruf. Beirut: Dar al-Gharb al-Islami.

Khatib al-Baghdadi, Ahmad b. ʿAli al-. n.d. *Tarikh Baghdad aw madinat al-salam*. Medina: al-Maktabat al-Salafiyya.

Khazzaz al-Qummi, ʿAli b. Muhammad al-. 1401 AH. *Kifayat al-athar fi al-nass ʿala al-àimmat al-ithnaʿashar*. Edited by Seyed Abdollatif Hosseini Koohkamarei. Qom: Bidar.

Khwarazmi, Muwaffaq b. Ahmad al-. 1414 AH. *Al-Manaqib*. Edited by Malik Mahmoudi. Qom: Islamic Publishing Institute.

Khwarazmi, Muwaffaq b. Ahmad al-. n.d. *Maqtal al-Husayn 'alayh al-salam*. Edited by Muhammad Samawi. Qom: Maktabat al-Mufid.

Kufi al-Ahwazi, al-Husayn b. Sa'id al-. 1402 AH. *Al-Zuhd*. Edited by Gholamreza Erfanian. Qom: Hosseinian.

Kulayni, Muhammad b. Ya'qub al-. 1389 AH. *Al-Kafi*. Edited by Ali Akbar Ghaffari. Tehran: Dar al-Kutub al-Islamiyya.

Laythi al-Wasiti, 'Ali b. Muhammad al-. 1376 Sh. *'Uyun al-hikam wa-l-mawa'iz*. Qom: Dar al-Hadith.

Liddell, H. G. and Scott, Robert. 2010. *An Intermediate Greek-English Lexicon: Founded upon the Seventh Edition of Liddell and Scott's Greek-English Lexicon*. Collegeville, Minnesota: Benedictine Classics.

Liddell, Henry George and Scott, Robert. 1901. *A Lexicon Abridged from Liddell and Scott's Greek-English Lexicon*. Oxford: Clarendon Press.

Majlisi, Muhammad Baqir al-. 1403 AH. *Bihar al-anwar*. Beirut: al-Wafa Institute.

Mazandarani, Ibn Sahrashub al-. n.d. *Manaqib Al Abi Talib*. Qom: al-Matba'at al-'Ilmiyya.

McGrath, Alister. 1384 Sh. *Darsnamih-yi ilahiyat-i Masihi (Christian Theology: An Introduction)*. Qom: Center for Studies and Research on Religions and Denominations.

McGrath, Alister. 1385 Sh. *Daramadi bar ilahiyat-i Masihi (Christian Theology: An Introduction)*. Tehran: Ketab-e Roshan Publications.

Meftah, Ahmad Reza, Hassan Ghanbari, and Hossein Soleimani (Trans.). 1393 Sh. *Ta'alim-i kilisayi Catholic (Catechism of the Catholic Church)*. Qom: University of Religions and Denominations.

Minqari, Nasr b. Muzahim al-. 1382 AH. *Waq'a Siffin*. Edited by Abd al-Salam Muhammad Harun. Qom: Ayatollah Mar'ashi Najafi Library.

Miqrizi, Taqi al-Din al-. 1420 AH. *Imta' al-asma' bi-ma li-l-Nabi min al-ahwal wa-l-amwal wa-l-hafada wa-l-mata'*. Beirut: Dar al-Kutub al-'Ilmiyya.

Mohammadi Reyshahri, Mohammad. 1386 Sh. *Hikmat-namih-yi payambar-i a'zam*. Qom: Dar al-Hadith.

Mohammadi Reyshahri, Mohammad. 1416 AH. *Mizan al-hikma*. Qom: Dar al-Hadith.

Moseley, Alexander. 1385 Sh. "Falsafih-yi 'ishq" [Philosophy of love]. *Madrisih quarterly* 2, no. 3.

Mubarrad, Muhammad b. Yazid al-. 1497 AH. *Al-Kamil fi al-lugha wa-l-adab*. Beirut: Dar al-Kutub al-'Ilmiyya.

Mufid, Muhammad b. Muhammad al-. 1404 AH. *Al-Amali li-l-Mufid*. Edited by Hossein Ostad Vali and Ali Akbar Ghaffari. Qom: Islamic Publishing Institute.

Mufid, Muhammad b. Muhammad al-. 1413 AH. *Al-Irshad fi ma'rifa hujaj Allah 'ala al-'ibad*. Qom: Al al-Bayt Institute.

Mufid, Muhammad b. Muhammad al-. 1414 AH. *Al-Ikhtisas*. Edited by Ali Akbar Ghaffari. Qom: Islamic Publishing Institute.

Muttaqi al-Hindi, 'Alà al-Din 'Ali b. Hisam al-Din al-. 1397 AH. *Kanz al-'ummal fi sunan al-aqwal wa-l-af'āl*. Edited by Safwa al-Saqqa. Beirut: Maktabat al-Turath al-Islami.

Muzaffar, Muhammad Rida. 1392 Sh. *Usul al-fiqh*. Qom: Islamic Publishing Office affiliated with the Society of the Seminary Teachers of Qom.

Najafi, Muhammad Hasan al-. 1365 AH. *Jawahir al-kalam fi sharh sharài' al-Islam*. Tehran: Dar al-Kutub al-Islamiyya.

Najashi, Abu al-'Abbas Ahmad b. 'Ali al-. 1408 AH. *Rijal al-Najashi, fihris asmà musannifi al-Shi'a*. Beirut: Dar al-Adwà.

Namazi Shahroudi, Ali. 1419 AH. *Mustadrak safinat al-bihar*. N.p.

Naraqi, Muhammad Mahdi. 1383 Sh. *Jami' al-sa'adat*. Qom: Esmailian Press Institute.

Neufeld, Karl Heinz. 2004. "Tradition." In *Encyclopedia of Christian Theology*. London: Routledge.

Nisài, Ahmad b. Shu'ayb b. 'Ali al-Khurasani al-. 1411 AH. *Sunan al-kubra*. Beirut: Dar al-Kutub al-'Ilmiyya.

Nuri al-Tabarsi, Mirza Husayn b. Muhammad Taqi al-. 1408 AH. *Mustadrak al-wasàil wa-mustanbat al-masàil*. Qom: Al al-Bayt Institute.

Payandeh, Abolghassem. 1382 Sh. *Nahj al-fasaha*. Tehran: Donya-ye Danesh.

Peters, Francis E. 1384 Sh. *Yahudiyat, Masihiyat va Islam (Judaism, Christianity, and Islam)*. Translated by Hossein Tofighi. Qom: Center of Studies and Research on Religions and Denominations.

Qadi Abu Yusuf, Ya'qub b. Ibrahim b. Habib b. Sa'd b. Habta al-Ansari. n.d. *Al-Kharaj*. Edited by Taha 'Abd al-Ràuf Sa'd and Sa'd Hasan Muhammad. Cairo: al-Maktabat al-Azhariyya li-l-Turath.

Qadi, Muhammad b. Sulayman al-Kufi al-. 1412 AH. *Manaqib al-Imam Amir al-Mu'minin 'alayh al-salam*. Edited by Mohammad Bagher Mahmoudi. Qom: Majma' Ihyà al-Thaqafat al-Islamiyya.

Qummi Ibn Razi, Ja'far b. Ahmad al-. 1413 AH. *Jami' al-ahadith*. Edited by Seyed Mohammad Hosseini Neishabouri. Mashhad: Publication Institute affiliated with Astan Quds Razavi.

Qummi, 'Ali b. Ibrahim al-. 1404 AH. *Tafsir al-Qummi*. Edited by Seyed Tayeb Mousavi Jazaeri. Qom: Dar al-Kitab Institute.

Qummi, Shaykh 'Abbas al-. 1414 AH. *Safinat al-bihar*. Qom: Osveh.

Qummi, Shaykh 'Abbas al-. n.d. *Al-Anwar al-bahiyya fi tawarikh al-hujaj al-ilahiyya*. N.p.

Qummi, Shaykh 'Abbas al-. n.d. *Mafatih al-jinan*. Qom: Matba'at al-Hadi.

Qunduzi al-Hanafi, Sulayman b. Ibrahim al-. 1416 AH. *Yanabi' al-mawadda li-dhawi al-qurba*. Edited by Ali Jamal Ashraf al-Hosseini. Tehran: Dar al-Uswa.

Qutb al-Din al-Rawandi, Abu al-Husayn Sa'id b. 'Abd Allah. 1409 AH. *Al-Kharàij wa-l-jaràih*. Qom: al-Imam al-Mahdi Institute.

Qutb al-Din al-Rawandi, Sa'id b. Hibat Allah. 1407 AH. *Al-Da'awat*. Qom: Imam Mahdi School Press.

Raghib al-Isfahani, Abu al-Qasim al-Husayn al-. 1999. *Mufradat fi gharib al-Qur'an*. Beirut: Dar al-Ma'rifa.

Ramm, Bernard. n.d. *'Ilm-i tafsir-i kitab-i muqaddas dar mazhab-i Protestan (Protestant Biblical Interpretation)*. Translated by Arman Roshdi. Tehran: Jama'at-e Rabbani.

Sabzawari, Abu Sa'id al-Hasan b. al-Husayn al-Shi'i al-. 1375 Sh. *Masabih al-qulub*. Edited by Mohammad Sepehri. Tehran: Bonyan Publications.

Saffar al-Qummi, Abu Jaʿfar Muhammad b. al-Hasan Ibn al-Farrukh al-. 1404 AH. *Basāir al-darajat*. Qom: Ayatollah Marʿashi Library.

Salihi al-Shami, Muhammad b. Yusuf al-. 1414 AH. *Subul al-huda wa-l-rashad fi sira khayr al-ʿibad*. Beirut: Dar al-Kutub al-ʿIlmiyya.

Samarqandi al-ʿAyyashi, Muhammad b. Masʿud al-. 1380 AH. *Tafsir al-ʿAyyashi*. Edited by Seyed Hashem Rasouli Mahallati. Tehran: al-Maktabat al-ʿIlmiyya.

Several authors. 1405 AH. *Al-Usul al-sitta ʿashar*. Qom: Dar al-Shabistari.

Shams al-Shami, Muhammad b. Yusuf al-. 1414 AH. *Subul al-huda wa-l-rashad fi sira khayr al-ʿibad*. Beirut: Dar al-Kutub al-ʿIlmiyya.

Sharif al-Murtada al-. 1405 AH. *Rasāil al-Murtada*. Edited by Seyed Ahmad Hosseini. N.p.

Sharif al-Radi, Abu al-Hasan Muhammad b. al-Husayn al-. 1369 Sh. *Nahj al-Balagha*. Edited by Seyed Mohammad Kazem Mohammadi and Mohammad Dashti. Qom: Imam ʿAli Publications.

Sharif al-Radi, Muhammad b. al-Husayn al-. 1378 AH. *Tanbih al-ghafilin wa-tadhkirat al-ʿarifin*. Tehran: Payam-e Hagh.

Shaykh al-Hurr al-ʿAmili, Muhammad b. al-Hasan al-. 1409 AH. *Wasāil al-Shiʿa*. Qom: Al al-Bayt Institute.

Shaykh al-Tusi, Muhammad b. al-Hasan al-. 1414 AH. *Al-Amali*. Edited by al-Biʿtha Institute. Qom: Dar al-Thaqafa.

Shuʿayri al-Sabzawari, Muhammad b. Muhammad al-. 1414 AH. *Jamiʿ al-akhbar aw maʿarij al-yaqin fi usul al-din*. Edited by ʿAlā Al Jaʿfar. Qom: Al al-Bayt Institute.

Shushtari, al-Qadi Nur Allah al-. 1411 AH. *Ihqaq al-haqq wa-izhaq al-batil*. Edited by Sayyid Shahab al-Din al-Marʿashi. Qom: Ayatollah Marʿashi Library.

Sijistani al-Azdi, Abu Dawud Sulayman b. Ashʿath al-. n.d. *Sunan Abi Dawud*. Edited by Muhammad Muhyi al-Din ʿAbd al-Hamid. Beirut: Dar Ihyā al-Turath al-ʿArabi.

Solomon, Robert. 1386 Sh. "Fazilat-i ʿishq (erotic)." Translated into Persian by Arash Naraghi. *Kitab-i naqd*, no. 43: 320-56.

Stott, John. n.d. *Mabani-yi Masihiyat (Basic Christianity)*. Translated into Persian by Robert Aserian. Tehran: Hayat-e Abadi.

Sutton, Philip W. and Stephen Vertigans. 2005. *Resurgent Islam: A Sociological Approach*. Cambriedge, UK: Polity Press.

Suyuti, ʿAbd al-Rahman b. Abi Bakr al-. n.d. *Al-Jamiʿ al-saghir fi ahadith al-bashir al-nadhir*. Beirut: Dar al-Fikr.

Suyuti, Jalal al-Din al-. 1424 AH. *Al-Durr al-manthur*. Edited by Abdullah ibn Abd al-Muhsin al-Turki. Cairo: Markaz Hijr li-l-Buhuth wa-l-Dirasat al-ʿArabiyya wa-l-Islamiyya.

Tabarani, Abu al-Qasim Sulayman b. Ahmad al-Lakhmi al-. 1404 AH. *Al-Muʿjam al-kabir*. Edited by Hamdi ʿAbd al-Majid al-Salafi. Beirut: Dar Ihyā al-Turath al-ʿArabi.

Tabari, Abu Jaʿfar Muhammad b. Muhammad b. ʿAli. 1383 AH. *Bisharat al-Mustafa li-Shiʿa al-Murtada*. Najaf: al-Matbaʿat al-Haydariyya.

Tabari, Muhammad b. Jarir al-. n.d. *Tarikh al-Tabari, tarikh al-umam wa-l-muluk*. Beirut: al-Aʿlami Institute.

Tabarsi, Abu al-Fadl ʿAli al-. 1385 AH. *Mishkat al-anwar fi ghurar al-akhbar*. Tehran: Dar al-Kutub al-Islamiyya.

Tabarsi, Abu Mansur Ahmad b. ʿAli b. Abi Talib al-. 1341 AH. *Al-Ihtijaj ʿala ahl al-lijaj*. Edited by Ebrahim Bahadori and Mohammad Hadi Beh. Tehran: Dar al-Uswa.

Tabarsi, al-Hasan b. Fadl al-. 1414 AH. *Makarim al-akhlaq*. Edited by Ala Al Jafar. Qom: Islamic Publishing Institute.

Tabarsi, Fadl b. al-Hasan al-. 1399 AH. *Iʿlam al-wara bi-aʿlam al-huda*. Edited by Ali Akbar Ghaffari. Beirut: Dar al-Maʿrifa.

Tabarsi, Fadl b. al-Hasan al-. 1408 AH. *Tafsir majmaʿ al-bayan*. Edited by Seyed Hashem Rasuli Mahallati and Seyed Fazlollah Yazdi Tabatabai. Beirut: Dar al-Maʿrifa.

Tabatabai, Sayyid Muhammad Husayn. 1417 AH. *Al-Mizan fi tafsir al-Qurʾan*. Qom: Society of the Seminary Teachers of Qom.

Tamimi al-Amidi, ʿAbd al-Wahid b. Muhammad al-. 1360 Sh. *Ghurar al-hikam wa-durar al-kilam*. Edited by Sayyid Jalal al-Din Muhaddith al-Urmawi. Tehran: University of Tehran.

"The Chicago Statement on Biblical Inerrancy." Retrieved from http://www.bible-researcher.com/chicag1.html

Tirmidhi, Muhammad b. ʿIsa al-. 1419 AH. *Sahih al-Tirmidhi*. Edited by Ahmad Muhammad Shakir. Cairo: Dar al-Hadith.

Turayhi, Fakhr al-Din al-. 1362 Sh. *Majmaʿ al-bahrayn*. Edited by Ahmad Hosseini. Tehran: Mortazavi.

Tusi, Abu Jaʿfar Muhammad b. al-Hasan al-. 1411 AH. *Misbah al-mutahajjid*. Edited by Ali Asghar Morvarid. Beirut: Muʾassasa Fiqh al-Shiʿa.

Tusi, Muhammad b. al-Hasan al-. 1387 AH. *Al-Mabsut fi fiqh al-imamiyya*. Edited by Muhammad ʿAli al-Kashfi. Tehran: al-Maktabat al-Murtadawiyya.

Tusi, Muhammad b. al-Hasan al-. 1401 AH. *Tahdhib al-ahkam fi sharh al-muqniʿa*. Beirut: Dar al-Taʿaruf.

Tusi, Muhammad b. al-Hasan al-. 1411 AH. *Al-Ghayba*. Qom: Muʾassasat al-Maʿarif al-Islamiyya.

Tuysirkani, Muhammad Nabi b. Ahmad. n.d. *Liʾali al-akhbar*. Qom: Maktabat al-ʿAllama.

Waqidi, Muhammad b. ʿUmar al-. 1966. *Al-Maghazi*. London: Marsden Jones.

Weaver, Mary Jo. 1381 Sh. *Daramadi bih Masihiyat (Introduction to Christianity)*. Qom: Center of Studies and Research on Religions and Denominations.

Yahya b. al-Husayn. n.d. *Durar al-ahadith al-nabawiyya bi-l-asanid al-Yahyawiyya*. Edited by Yahya ʿAbd al-Karim al-Fudayl. Beirut: al-Aʿlami Institute.

Yaʿqubi, Ahmad b. Ishaq al-. n.d. *Tarikh al-Yaʿqubi*. Qom: Institute for Publication of Ahl al-Bayt's Culture.

Zamani, Mostafa (trans.). 1374 Sh. *Al-Diwan al-mansub ila al-Imam ʿAli ʿalayh al-salam*. Tehran: Nasayeh Publications.

Zuhayli, Wahba b. Mustafa al-. 1401 AH. *Athar al-harb fi al-fiqh al-Islami*. Damascus: Dar al-Fikr.

www.ingramcontent.com/pod-product-compliance
Lightning Source LLC
Chambersburg PA
CBHW080323080526
44585CB00021B/2454